SENSES

Guest editors:
Regina Bendix
Donald Brenneis

Colofon

ETNOFOOR appears twice a year.

Editorial Board: Yolanda van Ede, Rob van Ginkel, Francio Guadeloupe, Suzanne Kuik, Birgit Meyer, Martijn Oosterbaan, Mattijs van de Port, Rachel Spronk, Irene Stengs, Alex Strating, Thijl Sunier, Milena Veenis, Marleen de Witte.

Guest Editors: Regina Bendix, Donald Brenneis

Address: Anthropological-Sociological Centre, Spinhuis, Oudezijds Achterburgwal 185, 1012 DK Amsterdam. Telephone: (+31 20) 525.2614 Fax: (+31 20) 525.3010.

Submissions: Articles should be sent to the editorial address. For style of referencing please refer to the standard of the *American Anthropologist*. Books for review, please add: c/o Yolanda van Ede.

Subscription Price: €20,00 annually (students and unemployed: €15,00; institutes: €40,00; single editions: €12,00). Postgiro 4753313, Irene Stengs, ETNOFOOR, Amsterdam, the Netherlands.

Advertisements: entire page: €80,00, half a page €50,00, a quarter of a page: €30.

Cover Design: Jos Hendrix

Printing: LIT Verlag

ISSN: 09215158

At the margins is where the adventurous mind wants to dwell. This is where received modes of thinking and writing dissolve, and new ones emerge. At the margins we often remain puzzled, confused, lost, and eager to re-make sense of our life worlds and those of others. And from the margins, all good work that has been done in anthropology stays within view.

For that reason, ETNOFOOR has been, and wishes to remain, a marginal anthropological journal. The journal will continue to operate at the interface of academic anthropology and the world out there, with all its ever-changing issues to be studied, debates to be debated, disciplines and arts to be explored.

ETNOFOOR appears twice a year, each issue dedicated to a special theme. Whoever likes to contribute is welcome!

© LIT Verlag, Fresnostraße 2, 48159 Münster.

ISBN 3-8258-9108-9

Contents

Introduction: Ear to Ear, Nose to Nose, Skin to Skin The Senses in Comparative Ethnographic Perspective *Regina Bendix*	3
Sensing Nature Encountering the World in Hunting *Garry Marvin*	15
Seeing in Motion and the Touching Eye Walking over Scotland's Mountains *Katrín Lund*	27
Race, Place and Taste Making Identities through sensory Experience *Emily Walmsley*	43
The Smell of Green-ness Cultural Synaesthesia in the Western Desert (Australia) *Dianne Young*	61
Acute Pain Infliction as Therapy *Elisabeth Hsu*	78
Japanese Fragrance Descriptives and Gender Constructions Preliminary Steps towards an Anthropology of Olfaction *Brian Moeran*	97
Signs and Sight in Southern Uganda Representing Perception in Ordinary Conversation *Ben Orlove & Merit Kabugo*	124
Afterword Sense, Sentiment, and Sociality *Donald Brenneis*	142

Editorial

Already for a long time the editorial board of Etnofoor had plans to publish an issue on the Anthropology of the Senses. Recently, there is a growing number of researchers working in this field. They show what anthropologists can contribute to a better understanding of the cultural dimensions of sensory experiences. During the latest conference of the European Association of Social Anthropologists in Vienna, September 2004, Regina Bendix and Donald Brenneis convened a workshop on the topic. They got in touch with members of the editorial board of Etnofoor and so we are happy to publish the results of this workshop and to introduce Bendix and Brenneis as our guest editors for the latest issue of Etnofoor entitled 'Senses'.

Introduction: Ear to Ear, Nose to Nose, Skin to Skin—The Senses in Comparative Ethnographic Perspective

Regina Bendix, Universität Göttingen

> ABSTRACT   Interest in understanding the cultural dimensions of sensory perception has been rising since the 1980s. As in early explorations of the senses, combinations of scholarly and poetic approaches appear to resonate most strongly. The challenge for anthropologists is twofold: 1) Attention to the senses should not develop into a new subdiscipline but rather become a focus integrated into the overall ethnographic project. 2) Ethnographic sensibility for sensory dimensions within cultural practices still require further development.

Researchers seeking to move the senses to center stage often resort to customary and plurivalent phrases and puns. The concluding biography of David Howes' latest edited collection of essays on what he terms 'sensual culture' carries the heading 'Fifty Ways to Come to your Senses' (Howes 2005:404-406)—with Paul Simon's popular hit from 1975 echoing in the back. A recent review in the *American Anthropologist* is entitled 'Knocking Some Sense into Anthropology'. Its author accuses anthropology to have been 'despite its rhetoric of holism ... surprisingly tone deaf' (Shannon 2004:395). Veronica Strang titles her article on a comparative study of human experience with and of water 'Common Senses' (2005)—seeking to make a move toward universalism and out of relativism. Michael Herzfeld wonders how much by way of case studies will be needed to 'resensetize' anthropology (2001:242). Not one but several German studies on hearing and listening in ethnographic and historical perspective are teasingly entitled *Ganz Ohr*—'all ears' (Koch 2005; Zuhören e.V. 2002; Stadelmann and Hengartner 1994). This is an understandable reflex. The senses are located between the physical and the cognitive; hence, drawing conscious attention to the workings of our tacitly operating senses requires translation. More often than not, vocabulary to express just what it is a particular sense 'senses' is lacking or else vocabularies associated with one sense are metaphorically applied to another, demonstrating the necessarily intricate interplay underlying the full sensorium: a bitter voice, a sharp tongue, a soft gaze, a loud color.

Ethnography can contribute to an understanding of the sensorium's role in human experience as well as its culturally divergent deployment and valuation. Equally important, ethnographers can examine and expand their own practice, so as to consider their own body and senses more fully as a part of their ethnographic toolkit (Stoller 1997; Sklar 1994). The papers gathered here pursue both of these goals, acknowledging fully that the potential of anthropological research goes beyond the present social and aesthetic rediscovery of the accomplishments, beauty and miracle of the senses. Television documentaries based on widely translated publications for the general public (for example Ackermann 1991) are one sign of this new revelling in the senses, as is the celebration of cooking and tasting in countless performance venues or the attention to the body in a diversifying mass spa culture. High caliber exhibition cum conference endeavors such as the multi-year production on the senses by Germany's *Kunst- und Ausstellungshalle der Bundesrepublik Deutschland* in Bonn in the 1990s spoke to this interest in intriguing ways (Brandes 1994, 1995, 1996, 1998; Brandes and Neumann 1995, 1996). In these volumes, much as in a growing if still marginal German *cultural studies*, sense-based aesthetic theories of the late 18th century are rediscovered (for example Böhme 2001) and inspire efforts in different fields to retrace discourses on the number and hierarchy of the senses over time (for example Naumann-Beyer 2001; Wagener 2000; Wagener 2003). In English-language anthropology of the senses, quite similarly, an openness is evident to bring together ethnographic-anthropological work with impulses from literature and literary theory, cultural history, geography and philosophy (for example Howes 1991, 2005).

That there is an audience for such mixtures of aesthetic, poetic, philosophical, historical, and anthropological spotlights on the senses is in and of itself worthy of interpretive attention. Simultaneously, much as with the predilection for puns cited initially, there is another recognition here: to understand the senses within culture, anthropology can profit from alternate perspectives, poetic retellings or philosophical underpinnings. For anthropologists, though, there are farther reaching opportunities here as well. As Veit Erlmann states from his perch as ethnomusicologist: 'It is possible to conceptualize new ways of knowing a culture and of gaining a deepened understanding of how the members of a society know each other' (2004:3). Not just the ethnographer's ear, which James Clifford famously wondered about in the midst of initiating the writing culture movement (1986:12), but the full spectrum of (ultimately more than) five senses are awaiting better integration in ethnographic methodology.

This introduction will not recapitulate all of the avenues taken in recent years within an emergent anthropology of the senses, as there are a number of authors and publishing endeavors who have done so very recently and as several papers included here offer perspectives on aspects of this literature.[1] In his goal to critically summarize work carried out thus far, Michael Herzfeld's chapter on the senses in his *Anthropology: Theoretical Practice in Society* (Herzfeld 2001:240-253) is particularly germaine to the stance represented in this thematic issue of *Etnofoor*. Herzfeld is intrigued if somewhat hesitant with the perspectives opened up: sensory knowledge, closely tied to aesthetic categories, is for him in danger of becoming yet another subfield of anthropology. The proliferation of subthemes or subdisciplines does, however, often divert from the holistic grasp that has been, historically, the field's foundation and that, in times of quite wild interdisciplinary foraging, can constitute a strength. What is needed then is a means of integrating the sensual in the overall ethnographic and analytic projects. Much as neurophysiologists speak of multisensory integration or sensory fusion with regard to the operating of the senses as a whole, it is crucial for anthropology to not lose sight – while unavoidably addressing specific senses individually – of the fusion of the senses in cultural terms and the recovery and insertion of this dimension in anthropology and ethnography at large.

Locating the senses within the discipline(s)

'A heightened interest in the role of the senses in society is sweeping the social sciences, supplanting older paradigms and challenging conventional theories of representation'. With this bold statement, Berg Publishers announces the journal *The Senses and Society* to appear for the first time in 2006, edited by Michael Bull, Paul Gilroy, David Howes and Douglas Kahn. Berg has also initiated a new book series entitled *Sensory Formations* which thus far, aside from series editor David Howes' collection *Empire of the Senses* (2005), has already published a reader on auditory culture (Bull and Back 2004); further readers on touch, taste, smell, vision, and 'the sixth sense' are to follow. The interest in the working of the senses has, however, a quite steady presence in the history of anthropology and the social sciences and humanities more generally, though works explicitly focused on the senses are perhaps more rare.

Elaborations on the 'disappearance of the senses' from a philosophically oriented anthropology drew wider attention already in the 1980s (Kamper and Wulf 1984) and other developments in anthropology contributed as well. The emergence of the body as a site of ethnographic attention, in conjunction with the emergence of feminist critiques of anthropological practice throughout the last third of the 20th century contributed to an interest in an embodied, holistic ethnographic practice and in case studies providing inroads toward an understanding of the culturally constructed and yet physically experienced body and gender (for example Martin 1987).[2] A further, more general and hence more implicit impetus to turn toward the senses can be attributed to the theoretical and empirical focus on experience (Turner and Bruner 1986). Adding to the formal and structural understandings of events the ways in which they were experienced, researchers turned toward a more dramatic, performance-based look at cultural productions. The performance-orientation naturally tended toward understanding what techniques brought forth experience (for example Bauman 1984) and thus the sensory, corporeal effects of performance and their cultural relevance remained somewhat hidden. Nonetheless, performance and experience perspectives are part of the holistic groundwork within which anthropological interest in the senses could take hold.

Interest was also generated through the work of a number of cultural historians who have found avenues to reimagine past lifeworlds in sensory terms. Alain Corbin, building on Lucien Febvre's call for a history of human sensibility or sensitive faculty from the 1930s and 40s (Febvre 1953), sought to bring an anthropology of sensory perception into cultural historical work (1991:197-211).[3] In part stimulated by work from anthropologist David Howes, Corbin suggested a number of methodological options to achieve this goal. He called for establishing an inventory of the sensory impressions inducible for a given time (1991:199) and suggested a series of historical source materials such as writings that set down norms systematically (advice books on raising children, on hygiene, and so forth) and, more importantly, diaries. Such works would be potentially useful for uncovering what was, in a given time and place, registered as "pleasant and unpleasant, attractive and repulsive, desirable and rejected, tolerated and intolerable" and how these sensations mutually constituted each other (ibid.:202). In his *Les cloches de la terre* (1995), Corbin modeled methodological and interpretive approaches for imagining the sensory dimensions of 19th century French village life. Richard Cullin Rath's exploration of *How early America Sounded* (2003) goes back in time still further and adds dimensions of ethnic difference in perception as well as pointing to scholarly blindspots with regard to their own sensory preferences in vocabulary and hence interpretation. Though working with written source materials, such works offer interesting possibilities for where anthropologists might turn in their work on the sensorium in culture.

Canadian anthropologist David Howes, strongly influenced by Marshall McLuhan (whose ideas are cited as a major stimulus by many scholars researching the senses) as well as by religious studies specialist Constance Classen, has published on the senses since 1980, offering a more overarching conceptualization for 'sensorial anthropology' in 1991.[4] In this piece, he draws attention to classic areas of anthropological research – such as child rearing practices or the relation of sensory enculturation and sociability – that might lead to new, culturally specific insights based on taking in account sensory hierarchies and relationships. In his book length study *Sensual Relations* (2003), Howes seeks to demonstrate this through, among other elements, a restudy of the Trobriand Kula as analyzed by Bronislaw Malinowski.

Howes is easily the most active anthropologist in arguing for a subdiscipline in sensory anthropology. Others have come to the topic as part of ethnographic endeavors differently focused. Not surprisingly, among those ethnomusicologists have contributed some of the most stimulating work, starting with Steven Feld's study of the nature, role and symbolism of Kaluli soundscape and audition (1982). That a particular habitat, in this case rainforest, can place the senses in different if not necessarily hierarchical relations to one another, is an added insight of this work which is reconfirmed in other work by ethnomusicologists, such as Roseman's study on music and healing among the Temiar in Malaysia (1991). Soundscapes and manipulation of the environment through sound occurs also, albeit naturally very differently, in highly modern or post-industrial places, such as the urban sites studied by Michael Bull (2000). The technological possibilities of recording devices and their role in shaping or crafting auditory pleasure have been further examined by Feld himself (Feld and Brenneis 2005) as well as others interested in issues beyond musical practices, such as the aesthetics and politics of listening (for example Bendix 2000, Hirschkind 2001).

The acute linkage between memory and the senses which French novelist Marcel Proust has archetypically inscribed in the opening madelaine episode in *A la recherche du temps perdu* is evident, for instance, in Nadia Seremetakis' work where olfaction and taste are recognized as crucial sites of individual and cultural memory (1994). The relationship between memory and experiences of pain has, if not centrally, been addressed in Susan Slyomovics' study of Moroccon victims of torture (2005). Paul Stoller was made aware of the diverse cultural coding and power of the senses, here in particular taste, through his research among the Songhay. He has repeatedly called for an integration of a sensory perspective both in research content *and* methodology (1989, 1997), an issue I will turn to in the next section.

In his assessment of the anthropology of the senses, Herzfeld sought to draw attention to research areas that could be augmented most powerfully by a sensory perspective. Ritual is one of them, violence and pain another, such as in the use of sensory technologies to distort political violence. Further possibilities can easily be thought of, such as for instance the sensory dimension of the human relationship to the environment in 'peaceful times' (in habitual patterns of making use of or growing natural resources as well as simple co-existance with 'nature') and – most acutely obvious in the present time with its seeming preponderance of violent to catastrophic weather manifestations and natural catastrophes such as earthquakes – during times of danger and harm. Similarly, the commodification of sensory pleasure in post-industrial societies, albeit building on an historical trajectory, warrants further exploration.

Acknowledging and exploring the sensory dimensions in anthropological research is a programme to which younger scholars such as Rane Willerslev with his work on the disposition of hunters (2004)[5] or Cristina Grasseni's work with pastoralists (2003)[6] have begun contributing as well.

Methodological Terrain

Herzfeld attributes the relative dearth of anthropological work on the senses to the fact that anthropology, like all academic disciplines, is primarily a verbal activity (2001:240). One might specify this further to say that a great deal of scholarly knowledge is processed and communicated textually: there is a big difference between the oral exchange in a seminar which engages the sensorium rather differently than producing and reading the textual, printed monograph. Furthermore, ethnography was strongly patterned by the Enlightenment's emphasis on the truth-value of visual perception, an ideology that has been reflected particularly effectively in critical histories of travel (Pratt 1992; Urry 1990). More recently, this tendency has been examined under the label of "ocularcentrism" which in turn is seen as closely linked to the textual or logocentric paradigm.

Sensory semiosis as a constitutive ingredient of cultural experience thus often fell outside the purview of anthropological knowledge production. The diagnosis can be summarized as follows: logocentrism, generated in conjunction with ocularcentrism has contributed to a certain amount of neglect of culturally shaped sensory knowledge. One might add that primary ethnographic techniques of speech recording, visual documentation and the constant rendering of the ethnographer's experience into field diaries, that is, more text, have assisted the sensory deprivation of the ethnographic record. The senses do pose methodological problems for cultural research. This also led to their marginalization in ethnographic practice. The challenges in this endeavor are manifold. Yet paramount for a holistic, ethnographic project is achieving an awareness of sensorial components and competence in observed cultural practice coupled with a reflexive deployment and awareness of sense perception in the ethnographer's own work. Simultaneously, the miracle of physiological, cognitive, individual and cultural teamwork that sense perception ultimately represents is not to overwhelm the ethnographic task and become its sole focus. The senses operate habitually; in their self-understood workings they contribute in greater and lesser degrees to cultural experience and agency. There is some justification for the current flurry of interest in casting a deeper ethnographic probe into the interplay of culture and the sensorium. Yet the goal to which the papers assembled here hope to contribute is rendering the sensorial dimensions a habitual component of ethnographic work, that is, expanding the profession's gaze to include an ethnographic ear, touch, taste, smell, feel, balance and so forth – open to culturally divergent sensorial categories and differentiations. The present endeavor is decidely not an effort at 'writing against ocularcentrism' which reverberates in some of the literature discovering the full sensorium. And, in contrast to David Howes' stance, attention to the senses' workings is here not perceived as a revolution toppling the linguistic turn, the textual revolution or discourse analysis (Howes 2005:1, 2003:22-28). Rather, Michael Herzfeld's concern is shared here. An ethnography and anthropology of the senses need not turn into yet another sub-specialization. Instead, the sensory project could support an 'anthropology that is attuned, at once [...] to both empirical and phenomenological concerns' (Herzfeld 2001:251, 253).

Just how ethnographers are to acquire sensory reflexivity and, concomitantly, sensory effectiveness in participant observation has thus far hardly been discussed, nor has there been much experimentation or explication as to how sensory ethnography is to find its way back on the printed page. Deirdre Sklar, a dance ethnologist, has advocated an ethnographic empathy relying on registering the body's participation in fieldwork already in 1994, going considerably further in her reporting than did Paul Stoller in his advocating of letting the scholar's body rediscover 'the seamless fit of the intelligible and the sensible (Stoller 1997:xi). More recently, Sklar has sought to explicate how somatic impressions reverberate in the ethnographic writing process, choosing herself to experiment with creative ethnographic writing:

> But it is also possible to bid words to continue to participate in the pool of somatic understandings that constitute them as embodied schemata. Then the process of thinking with words becomes a process of evoking their somatic reverberations. The critical distinction is not between embodied knowledge and verbal knowledge, or, the old bugaboo, body and mind, but between conventions of knowing, or modes of apprehending. In somatic, and often spiritual knowing, words are not asked to stand apart from and explain, but to participate in and evoke, one stream in a larger and deeper somatoconceptual process (Sklar 2005:13).

David Howes, though without a concrete program of the sort that Sklar suggests, also sees translation into writing as still the most effective means to convey culturally specific sensory relations, though he also puts stock in potential future technologies that might convey sensory experiences electronically (2003:58).

Yet it is not only the translation from the ethnographic experience to the written analysis or, in Sklar's case, evocation that hampers a sensory holism in the field. Nor can the burden be placed solely at the feet of a logo- and ocularcentrically overdetermined ethnographic project. A good deal of the sensory paucity may also be attributable to the technologies we bring to the field. Pencil and paper, typewriter and other, newer technologies employed by the ethnographer also have stood in the way of allowing him or her to recognize her own body as a primary instrument of research. One of my favorite instances of this almost unsolvable conundrum can be found in ethnolinguist Dennis Tedlock's work. He reports how he stumbled onto a story telling session. He lacked his customary paper and pencil or any other recording equipment and as he sat there and felt the power of performed speech he was torn: By not writing while experiencing he was unencumbered and felt closer than ever to understanding the aesthetic thrill those around him experienced. And yet he wished to have his note taking equipment though it would have inhibited or reduced his senses from experiencing as acutely as they did (1983:286-287). Similarly, a request on the part of his field consultants to leave his notepad behind provided Don Brenneis with a holistic understanding of 'making' *manoramnan* or *tamashabhaw*, an intense and lively social pleasure cocreated through intense talk and singing, and something the apprehension of which could only be deeply limited by intellectualizing the event. This was not just another dimension of fieldwork but a critical chunk of understanding that could not be, initially at least, reduced to words" (Brenneis, personal communication, cf. also Brenneis 1987).[7]

A personal experience at a former fieldwork site may serve as an illustration. In 1981 I carried out my first fieldwork in the Swiss village Urnäsch on an all-male New Years custom or ritual (Bendix 1985). At the time I was still an undergraduate and my focus was on the details of preparation and the ritual disguise and the structure of the performances in front of the houses visited on New Year's Eve by groups of men, on the networks of men collaborating for the event, and on the history of the occasion. I was discovering, without the aid of the as of yet not published *Invention of Tradtion*, a mythologizing of ritual origins that did not match the actual historical record. I heavily shielded myself with fieldwork equipment, in part because my interlocutors were all male, between the ages of 20 and 80, in part because especially the older informants insisted that in addition to recording I also write down their words.

Already in 1981 I encountered somatic components—such as the fever many of the men associated with the days of performance and dutifully noted down that according to some men, this fever took hold of them on Christmas and allowed them to get through the ritual days with a heightened and seemingly boundless energy. However, I was enormously busy getting through my questions, checking the tapes, taking slides and so forth. Projecting to myself and others that what I was doing was indeed work is probably a syndrom other ethnographers have struggled with too.

I returned to Urnäsch for the first time in years on December 31, 2003. I had nothing with me to take notes and no intention to be working while visiting but rather to visit with my major contact from 1981. Being free from duty, so to speak, I experienced a great deal that, at half my current age and somewhat intimidated by my role as ethnographer, I had not been able to feel and perceive. While age and experience certainly have a great deal of influence on ethnographic capacity (and age need not mean improvement!), not being impeded by tape recorder, camera, and a mind constantly wondering what all I should jot down freed up my body and senses in very agreeable ways. Approaching the first group of performing men, the smell of pine and moss exuding from their disguises was acute, mixing with the feel of the falling snow. Their shuffling boots on the snow as they got into position to sing betrayed a physical eagerness and concentration. Approaching another group and putting myself close to the lead figure in the group, I could feel the heat and energy exuding from this body, bouncing and twirling on the snow, as if the thirty plus kilogramms he was wearing in costume, headdress and bells weighed nothing. This 'fever', if you will, multiplied by the six to eight men a group usually consists of, would certainly help to explain how the physical strain of a eighteen to twenty hour day of ritual performance can be managed, hiking through the snow, carrying a lot of costume bulk, singing polyphonic yodels in front of tiny audiences with very high aesthetic expectations. Many of the elements I had earlier taken note of were sensorily evident this time, in audible minutia like the satisfied grunt of a masked performer sipping homebrewed hot wine and immediately being provided with a second glass. The whole day, but especially when I sat near a table of long retired performers in a local restaurant, I picked up sensory cues that I was not able to notice when I was doing the original ethnographic research. These older men spoke little, but peered out the windows to see which group had progressed how far. Inbetween drinking, these retirees would yodel, too, without announcing who would lead and which yodel would be chosen — it was a body that would signal, through a leaning back and seeming broadening of the shoulders, that this man was about to 'take a yodel' as the expression goes locally. The signals of his body communicated with the circle of men around the table, with heads slightly leaned back, eyes but more so bodily attention focused on the person who had made a start and then, once the lead bars were sung and the yodel tune recognized, the others joined in, constructing the expected harmony, eyes mostly half closed, sensing each other with bodies and ears. Though retired as active custom participants, these men performed and their bodies seemed to heat up in the memory of the festive energy experienced in earlier years.

The cues my ears, eyes and skin picked up transported the local meaning of this event in a way that can only enrich the verbal and visual documentation I attempted years earlier. Unencumbered by the tools of ethnography but able to build on much I had learned earlier, the 2003 visit opened a sensory dimension to my understanding of the event that previously I had not known was there and hence not sought to find. Employing one's body and its sensory capacity as a means to augment ethnographic depth is what can be advocated through experiences such as this one. That the knowledge gained through the senses is an addition and not a substitute for other techniques and technologies of fieldwork should, however, be equally evident. Hence speaking of the 'sensual revolution' as some anthropologists specializing in an anthropology of the senses do underestimates the cumulative power of successive layers of different stages of ethnographic insight.[8]

The papers gathered in this issue

The title of the 2004 conference of the *European Association of Social Anthropologists* in Vienna was 'Face to Face: Connecting Distance and Proxemity'. The expression 'face to face' with its visual implications immediately teases an ethnographic curiosity attuned to the breadth of sensory experience. Are not 'distance' and 'proximity' felt and experienced in a sensorially much more complex way? Do face-to-face encounters not rely on sensory information beyond the visual? Indeed, the major categories the congress wanted to address — distance and proximity, identity and alterity in times of rapid movement and transition — are experientially achieved, or at the very least sought, through culturally divergent sensory repertoires. Familiar with aspects of the new and old scholarship on sense perception, Don Brenneis and I decided to propose a workshop for the conference entitled 'ear to ear, nose to nose, skin to skin' which would provide opportunity to present emergent ethnographic work on the role of the senses in cultural practice. Its goal, developed further in the papers reworked and expanded for publication here, was to contribute to the congress's aim of 'recasting the ethnographic presence' and to explore the place of an ethnography of the senses, cast in comparative terms and built on methodological innovation.

As special editors of this issue of *Etnofoor* we thank the journal editors for the opportunity to bring these papers to broader attention in this framework. We thank the workshop participants, not all of whom were able to join this stage of publication, for venturing to present their emergent ideas at the conference; to the contributors we extend further thanks for entertaining our requests for pushing their thinking further.

E-mail: rbendix@gwdg.de

Notes

1 Useful summaries can be found in Howes (2005, 2003:1-58), Earlman (2004) as well as, for that point in time, in Howes' earlier sourcebook (1991). Partial summaries with foci on a narrower spectrum also are contained in Bendix (2000) as well as Bull and Back (2004:1-18).
2 In the last decade, too, though, there has been an increasing interest in what Emily Martin sees as a reductionist explanation of social activities in neural processes of the brain (Martin 2000) — and given the interest in cognitive sciences for the senses, anthropology will do well to offer non-reductionist accounts of sensory workings in cultural practices.
3 One may assume that Febvre's interest arose in an intellectual climate interested in bringing sensory and corporeal practices into view, as for instance Marcel Mauss's essay on body techniques (1935) also stems from that era.
4 Classen whose works on the senses per se (1993) and the senses and cosmology (1998) belong to the core of research often referred to, is co-founder of the Concordia Sensoria Research Group in Canada, a framework within which a great deal of interdisciplinary research on the senses has been initiated.
5 Willerslev's as of yet not published presentation "Anthropology and Ocularcentrism" at the EASA conference 2004 spoke to the kind of debate on different senses' roles in cultural practice.
6 Cf. Cristina Grasseni's workshop on "skilled vision" at the same conference; her as well as Willerslev's challenge to the critics of ocularcentrism will certainly offer opportunities for debates going beyond an anthropology of the senses.
7 The reverse experience must, however, for fairness' sake also be reported. Thus McKim Marriott's account of his first experience of the second part of the Holi festival under the influence of a hashish milkshake is telling in that it left him with largely sensory recollections of the event. Only the following year, in a sober state, did he take notes (1966:203-4).
8 In the case of David Howes' valuable restudy of Malinowski's *Argonauts* (2003:61-123), it is doubtful whether he could have arrived at his sense-based, alternative interpretation of cultural practices such as the *kula* without the preceeding ethnographic insight of Malinowski, Annette Weiner and others who were not or less attuned to a sensual perspective. If anything, this example humbles one to recognize the historical confines as much as the specificity of any individual's ethnography.

References

Ackermann, D.
   1991 A Natural History of the Senses. New York: Barnes and Noble.

Bauman, R.
   1984 [1977] *Verbal Art as Performance.* Prospect Heights, Ill.: Waveland.

Bendix, R.
   1985 *Progress and Nostalgia.* Berkeley: University of California Press.
   2000 The Pleasures of the Ear: Toward an Ethnography of Listening. *Cultural Analysis* 1 (online journal: http://socrates.berkeley.edu/~caforum/volume1/vol1_article3.html.)

Böhme, G.
   2001 *Aisthetik.* München.

Brandes, U. (Ed.)
   1994 *Welt auf tönernen Füssen. Die Töne und das Hören.* Kunst und Ausstellungshalle der Bundesrepublik Deutschland. Schriftenreihe Forum Bd. 2. Göttingen: Steidl.
   1995 *Sehnsucht.* Kunst und Ausstellungshalle der Bundesrepublik Deutschland. Schriftenreihe Forum 4. Göttingen: Steidl.
   1996 *Tasten.* Kunst und Ausstellungshalle der Bundesrepublik Deutschland. Schriftenreihe Forum 7. Göttingen: Steidl
   1998 *Der Sinn der Sinne.* Kunst und Ausstellungshalle der Bundesrepublik Deutschland. Schriftenreihe Forum 8. Göttingen: Steidl. Brandes, U. and C. Neumann (Eds.)
   1995 *Das Riechen. Von Nasen, Düften und Gestank.* Kunst und Ausstellungshalle der Bundesrepublik Deutschland. Schriftenreihe Forum Bd. 5. Göttingen: Steidl.
   1996 *Geschmacksache. Schriftenreihe.* Kunst und Ausstellungshalle der Bundesrepublik Deutschland. Forum Bd. 6. Göttingen: Steidl.

Brenneis, D.
   1987 Performing Passions: Aesthetics and Politics in an Occasionally Egalitarian Community. *American Ethnologist* 14(2):236-250.

Bull, M.
   2000 *Sounding out the City.* Oxford: Berg.

Bull, M. and L. Back (Eds.)
   2004 *The Auditory Culture Reader.* Oxford: Berg.

Classen, C.
   1993 *Worlds of Sense: Exploring the Senses in History and Across Cultures.* Londen: Routledge.
   1998 *The Color of Angels: Cosmology, Gender and the Aesthetic Imagination.* London: Routledge.

Clifford, J.
   1986 Introduction: Partial Truths. In J. Clifford and G. Marcus (Eds.): *Writing Culture. The Poetics and Politics of Ethnography.* Berkeley: University of California Press. Pp. 1-12.

Corbin, A.
   1991 *Wunde Sinne. Über die Begierde, den Schrecken und die Ordnung der Zeit im 19. Jahrhundert.* Stuttgart: Klett-Cotta.
   1995 *Die Sprache der Glocken. Ländliche Gefühlskultur uns symbolische Ordnung im Frankreich des 19. Jahrhunderts.* Frankfurt: S. Fischer Verlag.

Erlmann, V.
   2004 But What of the Ethnographic Ear? Anthropology, Sound, and the Senses. In: V. Earlman, (Ed.), *Hearing Cultures. Essays on Sound, Listening and Modernity.* Oxford: Berg. Pp. 1-20.

Febvre, L.
  1953   *Combats pour l'histoire*. Paris.
Feld, S.
  1982   *Sound and Sentiment: Birds, Weeping, and Poetics and Song in Kaluli Expression*. Philadelphia: University of Pennsylvania Press.
Feld, S. and D. Brenneis
  2005   Doing Anthropology in Sound. *American Ethnologist* 31 (4):461-474.
Grasseni, C.
  2003   *Lo sguardo della mano*. Bergamo: Bergamo University Press. (forthcoming in English, *Skilled Visions*, Oxford: Oxford University Press 2006)
Herzfeld, M.
  2001   *Anthropology: Theoretical Practice in Culture and Society*. Oxford: Blackwell.
Hirschkind, C.
  2001   The Ethics of Listening: Casette-Sermon Audition in Contemporary Cairo. *American Ethnologist* 28(3):623-649.
Howes, D.
  1991   Sensorial Anthropology. In: D. Howes, (Ed.): *The Varieties of Sensory Experience. A Sourcebook in the Anthropology of the Senses*. Toronto: University of Toronto Press. Pp. 167-191.
  2003   *Sensual Relations. Engaging the Senses in Culture and Social Theory*. Ann Arbor: The University of Michigan Press.
  2005   Introduction. In: D. Howes, (Ed.), *Empire of the Senses: The Sensual Culture Reader*. Oxford: Berg. Pp.1-24.
Howes, D. (Ed.)
  1991   *The Varieties of Sensory Experience. A Sourcebook in the Anthropology of the Senses*. Toronto: University of Toronto Press.
  2005   *Empire of the Senses: The Sensual Culture Reader*. Oxford: Berg.
  1984   *Das Schwinden der Sinne*. Frankfurt: Suhrkamp.
  1989   *Der Schein des Schönen*. Göttingen: Steidl.
Koch, H. J.
  2005   *Ganz Ohr: Eine Kulturgeschichte des Radios in Deutschland*. Köln: Böhlau.
Marriott, McK.
  1966   The Feast of Love. In: M. Singer (Ed.), *Krishna: Myths, Rites, and Attitudes*. Honolulu: East-West Center Press. Pp. 200-212.
Martin, E.
  1987   *The Woman in the Body*. Boston: Beacon.
  2000   Mind-body Problems. *American Ethnologist* 27(3):569-590.
Mauss, M.
  1935   Les techniques du corps. *Journal de Psychologie* 32 :271-293.
Naumann-Beyer, W.
  2003   *Anatomie der Sinne im Spiegel von Philosophie, Ästhetik, Literatur*. Wien: Böhlau.
Pratt, M. L.
  1992   *Imperial Eyes: Travel Writing and Transculturation*. London: Routledge. Projektgruppe Zuhören (Ed.)
  2003   *Über das (Zu-)Hören*. Beiträge zur Volkskunde in Niedersachsen 18. Göttingen: Schmerse Verlag.
Rath, R. Cullen
  2003   *How Early America Sounded*. Ithaca: Cornell University Press.

Roseman, M.
   1991 *Healing Sounds from the Malaysian Rainforest*. Berkeley: University of California Press.

Seremetakis, N.C.
   1994 The Memory of the Senses. Historical Perception, Commensal Exchange and Modernity. In: Lucien Taylor (Ed), *Visualizing Theory*. New York: Routledge. Pp. 214-229.

Seremetakis, N. C. (Ed.)
   1994 *The Senses Still: Perception and Memory as Material Culture in Modernity*. Boulder: Westview Press.

Shannon, J. H.
   2004 Knocking some Sense into Anthropology. *American Anthropologist* 106(2):395-396.

Sklar, D.
   1994 Can Bodylore be Brought to Its Senses? *Journal of American Folklore* 107(423):9-22
   2005 The Footfall of Words: A Reverie on Walking with Nuestra Senora de Guadalupe. *Journal of American Folklore* 118(467):9-20.

Slyomovics, S.
   2005 *The Performance of Human Rights in Morocco*. Philadelphia: University of Pennsylvania Press.

Stadelmann, K. and T. Hengartner
   1994 *Ganz Ohr: Telephonische Kommunikation*. Bern: PTT-Museum.

Strang, V.
   2005 Common Senses. Water, Sensory Experience and the Generation of Meaning. *Journal of Material Culture* 10(1):92-120.

Stoller, P.
   1989 *The Taste of Ethnographic Things*. Philadelphia: University of Pennsylvania Press.
   1997 *Sensuous Scholarship*. Philadelphia: University of Pennsylvania Press.

Tedlock, D.
   1983 *The Spoken Word and the Work of Interpretation*. Philadelphia: University of Pennsylvania Press.

Turner, V. W. and E.M. Bruner (Eds.)
   1986 *The Anthropology of Experience*. Urbana: University of Illinois Press.

Urry, J.
   1990 *The Tourist Gaze*. London: Sage.

Wagner, U.
   2000 *Fühlen—Tasten—Begreifen. Berührung als Wahrnehmung und Kommunikation*. Oldenburg: BIS-Verlag.

Wagener, N.
   2003 Von komprimierter Luft zur Erziehung der Sinne. Vom Umgang mit Gehör und Klangwahrnehmung von der Antike bis zur Neuzeit. In: Projekt Zuhören (Ed.), *Über das (Zu-)Hören*. Göttingen: Schmerse. Pp. 15-36.

Willerslev, R.
   2004 Not Animal, Not Not-animal: Hunting, Imitation and Empathetic Knowledge Among the Siberian Yukoghirs. *Journal of the Royal Anthropological Institute* 10(3):629-651.

Zuhören e.V., (Ed.)
   2002 *Ganz Ohr: Interdisziplinäre Aspekte des Zuhörens*. Göttingen: Vandenhoeck and Ruprecht.

Sensing Nature: Encountering the World in Hunting

Garry Marvin, Roehampton University, London

ABSTRACT   In this article I explore issues of the embodiment and being in the world of human hunters in pursuit of animal prey in the context of hunting as sport. The focus is on the immediacy and the experience of hunting rather than an exploration of its social and cultural meaning. This is an attempt to evoke how it is to hunt rather than what it means to hunt. I argue that hunting is a fully embodied, multi-sensory and multi-sensual practice that depends on an immersion into a multi-sensory and multi-sensual world. At the heart of such hunting is a contest between humans and animals based on two sets of senses and senses. My attempt here is explore how the human sensing is experienced and the difficulties of capturing and evoking that experience in an anthropological text.

Ethnographic experience – in the midst of a fox hunt

A cold autumn morning in the countryside of central England. Earthy smells from a freshly ploughed field. A light wind carries other scents and sounds from further away. The rich scent of warm animality rises from perspiring horses at rest. Their riders with flushed faces and their previously immaculate breeches and coats spattered with mud after the last short gallop, converse quietly. A pack of hounds, still gently panting and creating a light fog of breaths swirling among them, is led to the edge of a small wood by the red-coated Huntsman. As the hounds crash through the undergrowth he encourages them in their search for the scent of a fox by calling to them in repeated, slightly pinched, often high-pitched cries or with drawn out wordless sounds. As they move further into the wood he blows on his horn to move them on and to keep them eager. The sound reverberates through the trees. A few birds call in alarm as they flutter noisily out of the wood. One or two hounds whimper and whine excitedly as they begin to find the elusive scent; more of them pick it up as it becomes stronger on a track where a fox passed recently and soon the whimpering, whining and squeaking becomes an excited baying. Echoing the hound chorus with excited calls on his horn the Huntsman gallops in pursuit. Having left the wood the hunted fox has taken a direct line across a grass field and through a narrow opening in a hedge. A little later the hounds, baying in full cry, attempt to scramble through whatever gaps they can find. The ground rumbles with the thundering approach of galloping horses. Their riders push them towards the hedge, some leap safely and gallop on; there are cries of dismay from others whose horses refuse at the last moment or which crash through the hedge, stumble, and unseat them. The hunt is on but moves off into the distance and the stragglers attempt to reconnect with it. Here the countryside is at rest once more and enveloped by the everyday whereas another part is enlivened by the hunt.

Ethnographic interpretation – making sense of foxhunting

For many years a central focus of my research interest has been an ethnographic study of foxhunting in England. As with many anthropological studies of events my concern has been with meaning, with attempting to understand the structures and codes that underpin foxhunting, to tease out its cultural sense. I have continually asked about, discussed and tried to understand, how and why it is constructed and enacted in the way it is. I have also sought to understand the meaning of foxhunting in terms of what meaning it has for the participants – why they do it and what they get out of it. But such an approach and such questions depend, in part, on asking participants to be analytic, interpretive or reflexive before or after the event. All of that is certainly very important but I have become concerned that I am not capturing and understanding, and thus not expressing and representing, a vital element of the event – its immediacy. What is the experience of the event as it is being enacted and how can I gain access to this experience? Certainly it has meaning for the participants while they are participating – it is a meaningful activity – but it is the immediacy itself that is also crucial for understanding the motivations, skills and pleasures of foxhunting and that can only be understood fully in terms of the senses involved and the total bodily engagement with the event and the spaces in which it takes places.

My anthropological aim is to take hunting seriously as a social and cultural activity that involves a complex set of human interactions with the natural world and with the animals that inhabit it. To that end my interest in hunting has broadened beyond foxhunting to encompass a broad range of hunting events and I am seeking to understand what is involved in being in hunting mode in these differently constructed and lived events. At the heart of all hunting of wild animals is a close encounter and engagement with the natural world (however defined) and its animal inhabitants. Hunters must understand and know the world they are entering but, more importantly, they must feel, sense and respond to it. Hunting is a fully embodied, multi-sensory and multi-sensual practice that involves, and depends on, an immersion into a multi-sensory and multi-sensual world. Hunting is more than killing – it concerns a way of being in a particular space and incorporates particular forms of engagements with animals. It involves the hunter contesting his or her abilities with and through animals rather than the enjoyment of their domination. A good deal of the pleasure of hunting is the skill of creating the conditions in which the animal will be encountered whether the hunter is finally able to take a shot or not. Hunters hone their understanding of the senses of animals and then develop their own skills to counter the animal senses. This has a utilitarian or practical aspect in that it enables the hunter to attempt to kill the hunted animal but there is another, more important, dimension to it. It is the immersion into the immediate experience of those senses, the living of those senses and that experience, which seems to give pleasure. In attempting to understand the rich complexity of how it is to hunt, rather than what it means to hunt, I follow important leads set out by Adrian Franklin (2001) writing about hunting and angling in modernity. In particular he suggests that in order to understand the experience of hunting and the experiences of hunters we need to attend to 'their sensual and proximate relation to nature' (2001:57) and to what he calls the 'sensual integration' of hunting, 'the loss of specific sensual control in favour of multi-sensual reaction or intuitive sensing' (2001:69). This article is an initial foray into a territory that needs a much closer and fuller exploration in terms of embodiment – 'an indeterminate methodological field defined by perceptual experience and mode of presence and engagement in the world' (Csordas 1994:12), and here I can only touch on what I think are some of the key issues in understanding the experiential complexities of hunting.

Hunting – engagement and contest

Hunting as a social and cultural practice takes a myriad of shapes and forms and will be experienced differently and have different meanings for different people in different cultures. In this article I will explore a few examples that, while not representative of all forms of hunting, can be used to reveal some of the aspects of its embodiments. It is impossible to offer a full account of the significant differences between specific hunting practices but it is essential to clarify that my concern here will be with hunting as a sporting practice rather than the forms of hunting engaged in by those people who hunt animals with a primary concern for food. Very crudely, a fundamental difference between hunting for food and hunting as sport lies in the nature of the contest between the hunters and the hunted. A person hunting for food must compete with the animals' abilities to escape attention or to flee in order to find and kill them. In this situation the hunter does not seek out that contest for its own sake, this aspect of hunting is simply a necessary, unavoidable and natural element in the relationship between a predator and prey.[1] Here the hunter does all in his or her power to minimize the nature of that contest in order to obtain meat in the most efficient and effective way possible.[2] The sports hunter, however, competes in a very different way. Here the contest itself is central to the event and it is deliberately sought out and elaborated. Rules, regulations and restrictions are imposed and willingly followed to create the challenges that are fundamental for hunting to be a sporting activity. The hunter competes with him/herself in terms of attempting to successfully exercise personal hunting skills, competes with the environment in which hunting takes place and, finally, competes with the animal which is the focus of attention. The primary interest of most sports hunters is not that of obtaining meat, nor even that of killing an animal.[3] Rather it is with an immersion into the very difficulty of bringing about an encounter with the animal, with the experiences generated by the act of hunting and with the pleasure and satisfaction that comes from successfully overcoming these self-imposed restrictions and difficulties. There is certainly the hope and an intention to kill an animal but how that animal is found and how it is killed is far more important than the mere fact that it is killed. In mundane terms, the means is more important than the ends or, put more elegantly by the Spanish philosopher Ortega y Gasset, 'one does not hunt in order to kill but one kills in order to have hunted' (1968:94).[4] The pleasures in hunting are certainly multifaceted but a core pleasure does seem to be that which comes from the exercise of all the skills of hunting up to the moment of killing. Erich Fromm, commenting on the pleasures of the enactment and experience of skills, points out that people who equate the pleasures of hunting with the pleasures of killing, miss something vital:

> The interpretation of the pleasure in hunting as pleasure in killing, rather than in skill, is indicative of the person of our time for whom the only thing that counts is the result of an effort, in this case killing, rather than the process itself (1990:187).

Fundamental to this idea of 'to have hunted' is a way of being or a manner of being in the landscape, of acting and experiencing in the landscape, in order to approach the hunted animal. Here my concern is with the senses that are involved in something that is central to hunting – the contest and the competition between the human and the animal – a contest and a competition between two sets of senses and sensing – the human and the animal. Although this is a contest it is not quite the 'even' or 'matched' contest of most sports because the animal is not cognisant of the nature of the contest even though it might become aware of the presence of the human and attempt to, as it were, out-manoeuvre the hunter. In the sorts of hunting events in which I am interested hunters have to engage with animals that are usually more alert, more attuned to their senses, more responsive to their senses than they are and the hunters must attempt to shape their human senses and behaviour accordingly. This is a contest that centres on two related sets of ideas – those of distance and proximity and those of identity and alterity. The physical distance between the hunter and prey must be reduced to a proximity so that the latter can be killed and identity is significant in terms of the differences between the human and the animal other. Here I will try to tease out some of these elements.

In a recent work (Marvin 2006) I suggest that, although each hunting practice has its own unique social and cultural shape, all forms of hunting can perhaps be divided into one of two general types according to the ways in which those individuals hunting are present in the landscape. I define these as hunting by disturbance and hunting by disguise, with each type involving very different engagements with landscapes and with the hunted animals. The first type is marked by maintaining a clear distinction between the human and the animal in terms of physical, behavioral and emotional distance. Here the presence of humans is clearly signaled and is openly intrusive in the landscape. The creation of noise and movement are essential elements in creating the conditions in which the hunter attempts to engage with the animal. People, often with dogs, might walk through woods noisily, shouting, banging on trees, using whistles, or sweep across open land creating a disturbance and disruption that causes animals to flee so that particular members of the target species can be seen and shot at or in other ways engaged with by the waiting hunters. In contrast, hunting by disguise involves a blurring of the distinction between the human hunter and the animal prey. The hunter attempts to become like an animal and to close the physical, behavioral and emotional distance between them. Here the aim of the hunter is to slip unobtrusively into the hunting landscape and to remain undetected in order to approach and engage with the prey.

Hunting – irruption

I will return to my initial example of the foxhunt as a case of hunting by disturbance because it offers rich material for beginning to think about senses, embodiment and experience in hunting. The actual disturbance created by the riders, horses and hounds is fundamental both to the construction and to the experience of the event. Firstly, those hunting are highly visible in the landscape, they are in a large group, many are mounted on horses and some are wearing bright red jackets that make them stand out even more, and this visibility is one of the ways in which they announce their presence in the countryside. They also announce their presence through sound. Although not a raucous event, foxhunting is not a silent one. Hounds bay, horses whinny, riders chatter, the Huntsman calls to his hounds and blows on his horn, all of them make noise as they move through woodland or across fields. The announcing of presence is extremely important because the fox must be made aware of this invasion into its habitat and encouraged to flee rather than hide. The event is premised on a complex, open, engagement with the hunted fox across the landscape and across time. For hounds to surprise and immediately kill a fox is not foxhunting in its fullest sense for there is no difficulty and therefore no drama, with its corresponding excitement, in such an event.

Foxhunting differs, in significant ways, from other forms of hunting by disturbance because the human participants do not, in any immediate way, hunt foxes. The horse-mounted Huntsman uses a specially trained pack of hounds to do so. It is they who attempt to find the scent of the fox, to follow that scent and then, if they finally catch up with the animal, to kill it. However, this does not make it a natural event centered on a predator/prey relationship. It is a fully cultural event, although intimately and essentially connected with the natural, because it is of human construction. The Huntsman directs the hounds to where he wants them to begin to start searching for a fox and they do this by trying to find the scent of a fox – and this is important; foxhunting does not involve looking for foxes, the primary engagement with them is through scent. The human participants must use animal intermediaries here to compensate for their own inferior sensing abilities. If the hounds are able to pick up the scent of a fox then they will set off excitedly, baying and whimpering, to follow it. In terms of the sensory quality of foxhunting this sound is highly significant. The sounds of hounds baying when following the scent of a fox is referred to as 'speaking' or 'the music of hounds'. Not only do these sounds indicate to the Huntsman and other participants that the hounds have connected with the line of scent, but they are also contribute significantly to the experience of hunting and to the aesthetics of hunting. Those who participate take great pleasure in hearing the ebbs and flows of the soundscape of a pack of hounds in full cry as it moves across the landscape.

If the hounds are able to keep to the scent line of the fleeing fox they will begin to outpace it. Finally they will see it and surge forward to kill it. However, hunts rarely develop in such a linear fashion. Maybe the scent is old and simply disappears – but even if the fox has recently left the area the local weather conditions – rain or a quickly warming sun – may cause the scent to dissipate or evaporate – causing the hounds to come to a halt. The hunted fox might cross surfaces which disguise its scent

– fields with livestock, asphalt roads, stream beds – and result in hounds losing it. A hunted fox might also retreat into a place to which hounds have no access.

A complex array of sensing is involved here – even for the humans. Although only the hounds can scent the fox, the Huntsman must be finely tuned in terms of senses; he must understand or sense what is going on between his hounds, he senses their sensing, and he uses his senses to remain connected with them. Sight is important – he must watch his hounds intently but he must also use other senses. He must listen to them carefully – does the whimper of a particular hound indicate that it really is beginning to find a scent or it is faking it? Is the baying of another really indicating the scent of a fox or is it mere excitement? The Huntsman must also use his voice to encourage the hounds or to bring them back to him – something he also does with his horn. He must both respond to them and ensure that they respond to him. As aficionados of foxhunting express it, he must have 'hound sense'.

At the same time that the Huntsman's senses are directed towards the hounds they are also involved in placing him fully in the event. He must take notice of the wind, rain, mist and sun; register and respond to the changing surfaces of the landscape; and think about the conditions offered by different kinds of vegetation. He must be aware of, and alert to, what other animals in the countryside are doing – does the nervous moving of cattle or sheep indicate that the fox has passed that way? He is also on a horse where he must feel the horse under him and through his entire body; the horse and rider must become as one. In order to stay mounted he must use his body to direct the horse and he must also respond to the movements of the horse. He feels and experiences his movement through the countryside through the movement and bodily experience of being mounted.

There is no space here to go into details about all the activities carried out by individuals associated with foxhunting but a key set of participants are those who are mounted on horses and who follow the moving centre of the hunt (consisting of fox, hounds and huntsman). These participants are viscerally and emotionally connected, in multi-sensual ways, to the event and the landscapes in which in develops. They feel the weather, they watch and listen attentively to the activities of the Huntsman and his hounds (as previously mentioned this 'soundscape' of baying hounds and the Huntsman's voice and horn is a vital element in the creation of excitement), as they respond the pursuit of the fox. The pleasure and excitement for them is not in simply seeing the event but in engaging directly with it. Perhaps the most intense engagement is when they are able to gallop across the countryside jumping hedges, fences, ditches and streams on the way. This is the excitement that most of the mounted participants seek – the complex flow of sensations involved in riding a horse at speed across a challenging stretch of countryside. As Casey has commented in the context of the creation of the placeness of places, this encounter with the countryside is 'an affair of the whole body sensing and moving' (1996:18) through it. The landscape is animated at the moment of hunting and people become animated within it. Landscape here is not something to be looked at but to be moved through and experienced through the body. Again, in Casey's terms, 'its very dynamism is found in its encouragement of motion in its midst, its "e-motive" (and often explicitly emotional) thrust' (1996:23).

Here I have touched on only a few elements of embodiment and experience in the enactment or performance of hunting itself and have left aside aspects such as the close engagement with the placeness of the countryside, the elements that make up the visceral and emotional excitement of hunting and the sensations involved in being part of the hunting and killing of foxes. A fuller account would also need to include all the elements of sight, sound, touch and smell involved in the activities prior to and after hunting. Prior to hunting horses will be groomed, manes and tails plaited, saddlery and tack cleaned, prepared and connected to the horses. Foxhunters will have to attend to their own bodies by dressing themselves in the equestrian clothes required for the event. At the Hunt kennels the hounds must be selected and prepared before they are loaded into a vehicle to take them to where the day's hunting is planned. Horses too must be loaded into vehicles and driven to the meeting point. The commencement of a day's hunting is marked by the Meet at which all the participants come together to spend a short time socializing – greeting one another, talking, eating snacks and drinking glasses of wine, port, or whisky – before the hunting begins.[5] After hunting has finished there is another sensual world to be experienced. Tired horses and hounds must be returned to their stables and kennels where they will be fed, watered, cleaned and bedded down for the night. The human fox hunters will return home, remove their often wet, muddy and certainly sweaty, clothes and attend to cleaning their bodies. Many foxhunters have commented to me on the pleasures that come, at the end of a hunting day, from the sensations of soaking a weary body in a hot bath while drinking a whisky and reflecting on the experiences of the day.

Hunting – immersion

Here I will not be referring to any one specific form of hunting but perhaps we can imagine the case of a person going into the woods to hunt an animal such as a deer or out to the marshes to hunt duck and geese. Forms of hunting that can be classified as hunting by deceit require a movement of a different order towards the animal. Hunting events of this kind are characterized by the human attempting to remain unobtrusive and undetected in the landscape in order to find, follow and approach the hunted animal. This is a close, direct and personal engagement between the human and the animal; it is not, however, an open engagement. Although the hunter does not in any way cease to be human s/he must adopt many of the ways of a wild animal – a process which Ortega y Gasset intriguingly refers to as 'being open to the animal' and 'a vacation from the human condition' (1968:48). Although I do not, in any way, wish to suggest that hunting is in some way an inherent or a natural part of the human condition,[6] many hunters do express the view that the practice and experience of hunting is a movement towards 'nature' and would agree with the suggestion of Erich Fromm that '[i]n the act of hunting, a man (sic) becomes, however briefly, part of nature again' (1990:185). Essential to that process of becoming part of nature is the creation of the hunter as a non-presence to others while at the same time being keenly aware of their own presence. The hunter must sense in order not to be sensed.

I will later discuss how hunters express the nature and the pleasures of this total bodily sensing but here I need to consider how hunters act upon, change and discipline their everyday bodies when in hunting mode. Each hunter is intensely aware of his or her body as an intruding body. The body must be disguised or camouflaged by means of clothes that allow him or her to blend into the environment, to become one with it, to be able to see without being seen. Unlike hunting by disturbance which depends on creating movement, flight, this form of hunting depends on stillness and gradual movement. Here movement has to be disguised; the hunter must learn to walk silently, with stealth, or to sit in wait without moving at all, perhaps in a 'hide'. Adrian Franklin, writing about the skills of angling, captures this perfectly with the simple, but elegant, phrase 'mastering quietness' (2001:67).

Human presence is also carried on the air and lingers on the track that the human intruder has taken. In some forms of hunting the hunter uses a scent that masks his or her own scent and in all forms of hunting the hunter must understand how the air is moving and how to remain down-wind of the quarry. All of this understanding and skill based on sight, hearing and smell is instinctual to the animal, part of its repertoire for survival, and the human must become adept in using and responding to such senses when hunting. The hunter must be fully alert to the animal in order not to alert the animal itself; to attempt to be absent, a non-presence, to the eyes, ears and noses of others in order to defeat the animal. This form of hunting depends essentially on deceit and an out-animaling of the animal. The hunter needs to close the gap as silently and secretly as possible – a characteristic of other predator/prey relationships. The moment of the lethal shot is entirely human – no animal can kill at such a distance – but that moment cannot arrive unless the hunter has been successful in becoming partly animal.

Hunters often speak of having to immerse themselves in, and be fully attuned to, the natural world and to become at one with it. An evocative account of the senses of a hunter and how he places himself in the landscape is given in David Mamet's novel *The Village* (1994). Marty is a deer hunter. As he slowly settles himself into a position in the woods to wait for the deer that he is sure will pass during the day he reflects on what, and how, it is to be in the woods when hunting. To be silent is essential, 'he was silent in the woods, as he always was, and never made an unnecessary sound, or spoke a word at all if he could help it' (1994:194) and he comments that sometimes, when out hunting with an 'an unschooled companion' he would have to raise a finger to his lips if they spoke, to indicate that they should be quiet. Quietness is part of the woods and 'you had to be like it if you wanted to be part of it' (1994:194). Marty's inner commentary lasts from early morning to dusk.

> [H]e'd been out there, his back against the tree, since before dawn, and he was satisfied that he'd moved in nicely, and quiet, the wind in his face, his field of vision good, down the slope, to the bank of the stream, where he commanded a field of view some hundreds of yards to either side, down the stream, and, across the bank, back into the thick woods (1994:195).

He reflects on how he has been sitting, ever more stilled, with even his breathing slowed, 'gradually becoming part of the forest' (1994:196). For hours he sits intensely alert, observing but not reacting to whatever happens around him. He sits until the evening light fades to almost nothing, when the four deer came down the bank. He made out the buck's horns. 'Well, all I have done is wait for you,' he thought, 'but I have waited for you.' As the doe's hooves clattered a stone in the stream he raised his rifle, to see if the scope could catch enough of whatever light there might be, to allow a shot. He saw the buck though his scope, and picked his spot on the buck's shoulder (ibid.).

The narrative of this story ends at the point of sighting. What is not known is whether this fictional hunter actually takes the shot or not. But whether he shoots or not, that part of the encounter between the hunter and the hunted is at an end. The human hunter has been successful in his mode of being, he has hunted successfully, he has achieved the closeness that he desired when he set out in the morning and has had the satisfaction of bodily experiencing hunting.

Concentration, alertness and awareness are fundamental to the hunter's mode of being and in turn generate some of the key experiences, pleasures and satisfactions of hunting. For example a hunter interviewed by Jan Dizard, a sociologist of hunting, commented:

> 'When I am on a walk, my mind wanders and inevitably drifts back to something that's been bugging me or something I ought to have done better. But when I am hunting, I am focused. All I care about is figuring out if that slight noise I just heard is a deer coming into my stand. I am totally absorbed, in a completely different world' (2003:107).

All the hunters I have spoken with mentioned the pleasures of being in a state of heightened awareness of, and intensely attuned and responsive to, the places in which they hunt. This receptivity to the natural world is not a distanced aesthetic response but rather it emerges out of a purposeful engagement with it and a participation in it. Although hunting cannot be understood as mere killing, the intention to kill, the anticipation of killing and actual killing are clearly of immense importance for the experience of each hunter. There is an emotional intensity in hunting that comes from being prepared at any moment to kill an animal and hunters speak about a special engagement with the natural world because theirs is a deadly pursuit. Hunters certainly look for animals and, if they find them, watch them attentively but they are not spectators of nature. Two hunters in a recent anthropological study by Carmen McLeod (2004) of duck hunting in New Zealand convey the sense of intense involvement in the natural that often figures in hunters' accounts of their practices:

> 'People from the city seem to have the idea that nature is something that you go to look at but "don't touch". But a hunter like me wants to get involved with nature – we like to touch and to be part of natural processes – and killing is just one of those processes' (2004:310).

> 'They are involved with more of a ... I can't even put it in words either, you know – they are in their waders, it is cold, it's frosty, they are in situations at times and places where the average person who uses the outdoors doesn't see or doesn't venture. Cold frosty mornings, windy cold horrible weather on a lake in a boat, there's mud, your dog smells ... and there is anoxic mud all over your dog and there is cold water running down your neck and hail

hitting in your face and you are thinking: "gee if we don't get across this lake soon the tide is going to be out and we are going to get stuck in the mud". ... So ...you don't just go and see the Shoveller on Lake Waihola – you shoot one and you touch it and you can see its feathers so you have a much more intimate appreciation, "intimate appreciation" are the words I am looking for ... for the natural world' (2004:311).

The engagement with the dead birds opens the way into a further realm of the sensing body and its experiences in hunting. To balance my account of foxhunting I have here focused only on the act of hunting but, as with foxhunting, there are a range of complex practices both before and after hunting that need to be explored on another occasion in order to complete any analysis.

Prior to hunting the hunter must prepare his or her equipment and hunters report taking pleasure in this physical activity and the sense of anticipation it creates while doing so. For example, if they are used, guns must be cleaned and oiled, decoys prepared and animal callers practiced with. Perhaps special foods and drinks are made to take with them. Certainly most hunters will re-clothe themselves in particular ways for hunting. Many will have to travel to the countryside from their everyday spaces and places of living as they begin the journey out to the animal. If the hunting trip is successful it will result in an animal travelling back to those spaces and places of the hunter.

At the moment of killing, the targeted animal is responded to and engaged with in new ways because it can no longer offer any resistance to the hunter. Often the dead animal is photographed with the hunter; an act of visually recording, marking and celebrating the mastery of the hunter. What was once a free, wild, animal now belongs to the hunter and enters a process of domestication. Usually the animal will be dismantled. It will be skinned or plucked, eviscerated, cleaned and butchered, all activities that involve a complex amalgam of the senses of sight, touch and smell as they encounter flesh, blood and guts. Through such processes the natural animal becomes a cultural product – meat – that will be prepared and consumed in the social and cultural practices of cooking and eating in which smell, taste and texture feature strongly. The animal passes into and makes the human. But not all animals in hunting disappear without a trace. Some will be converted into taxidermised trophies. Here the disembodied animal is reassembled, although in a reduced form, and brought into a semblance of life, even though it is a life that is only skin deep. Like the trophy photograph of the dead animal, this approximation of the living animal is the celebration of the skill of the hunter and both are evocative for the hunter. The animal that was once closely watched and observed is now looked at in another setting and through this visual encounter memories and experiences are evoked. The hunter who was silent in the act of hunting is now able to indulge in the pleasures of speech, as she or he uses the animal to speak to others about how it was to have hunted.

Conclusion – capturing senses?

It is clear that if I want to understand this sort of hunting as a cultural practice in all its complexity I must find a way to pay attention to these multi-sensual ways of experiencing the world. Hunting does not just mean something to hunters, it is something they do. My problem as an anthropologist is with what I can capture at the moment of its occurring and how I can represent it, recreate, or evoke hunting for others who might be interested in understanding it without experiencing it directly. Hunting as it is spoken about before and after the event is perhaps less problematic to record and represent while, of course, being open and sensitive to the issues of writing cultures. Visual anthropology, ethnographic film and ethnographic sound recording offer powerful and evocative domains of representation – but most of us probably work at the reduced level of words to represent the sights, sounds, touch, smell and tastes of what we have experienced of the experience of those with whom we study. A restaurant critic's report of a memorable meal is a necessarily impoverished version of that meal but it can be evocative of that experience. Experience rich anthropology is certainly something to be strived for but its realization seems extremely difficult – how do we capture and evoke scent, taste and touch? In terms of my own research there is still a good deal of experiencing to be done, and understanding to be developed, in order to represent hunting in its full complexity. As an anthropologist I have certainly been closely engaged with foxhunting and foxhunters but I need to expose myself to many other forms of hunting in order to get closer to those practices and experiences. This can be tricky. I have been with Spanish friends on wild boar hunts – I sit silently with them because that is how they are and because that is what they demand of me but I think I am doing something very different from them.

Acknowledgements

I would like to thank Carmen McLeod and Stephanie Schwandner-Sievers who both made immensely useful suggestions. In particular I would like to thank Steven Groarke whose comments about issues, problems and perspectives raised by this 'distasteful' topic have been invaluable.

E-mail: GMarvn@aol.com

Notes

1. This is not to suggest that humans hunting animals is anything other than a human social and cultural event. For an analysis of the differences between animal predation and human hunting see for example Ingold (1986:79).
2. This is an extremely simple rendition of hunting events in which there may well be complex rules about which animals may or may not be hunted and how those huntable animals may be hunted.
3. Here I have not paid attention to the opinions of many sports hunters about only hunting animals that are eatable, the immense importance of consuming the meat of hunted animals and the special significance to them of eating the meat of animals that they have killed personally.
4. Translation from Spanish by the present author.

5 This is a thin description of an immensely important event that marks and celebrates the beginning of a day of foxhunting.
6 For a rebuttal of such arguments see for example Bekoff and Jamieson (1991).

References

Bekoff, M. and D. Jamieson
    1991 Sport Hunting as an Instinct: Another Evolutionary 'Just-So-Story'? *Environmental Ethics* (13):375-378.

Casey, E.S.
    1996 How to Get from Space to Place in a Fairly Short Stretch of Time: Phenomenological Prolegomena. In: S. Feld and K.H. Basso (Eds.), *Senses of Place*. Santa Fe, New Mexico: School of American Research Press. Pp. 13-52.

Csordas, T. J.
    1994 Introduction: The Body as Representation and Being-in-the-World. In: T.J. Csordas (Ed.), *Embodiment and Experience: The Existential Ground of Culture and Self*. Cambridge: Cambridge University Press. Pp. 1-24.

Dizard, J.A.
    2003 *Mortal Stakes: Hunters and Hunting in Contemporary America*. Amherst and Boston: University of Massachusetts Press.

Franklin, A.
    2001 Neo-Darwinian Leisures, the Body and Nature: Hunting and Angling in Modernity. *Body and Society* 7(4):57-76.

Fromm, E.
    1990 *The Anatomy of Human Destructiveness*. Harmondsworth: Penguin Books.

Ingold, T.
    1986 *The Appropriation of Nature: Essays on Human Ecology and Social Relations*. Manchester: Manchester University Press.

Marvin, G.
    2006 Wild Killing: Contesting the Animal in Hunting. In: The Animal Study Group, *Killing Animals*. Champaign and Urbana: University of Illinois Press. In press.

Mamet, D.
    1994 *The Village*. London: Faber and Faber.

McLeod, C.M.
    2004 Pondering Nature: An Ethnography of Duck Hunting in Southern New Zealand. PhD Dissertation. University of Otaga (Dunedin, New Zealand).

Ortega y Gasset, J.
    1968 *La Caza y Los Toros*. Madrid: Revista de Occidente.

Seeing in Motion and the Touching Eye
Walking over Scotland's Mountains

Katrín Lund, Queen's University Belfast

ABSTRACT   In this paper I examine the senses of vision and touch in mountaineering. My aim is to demonstrate how approaches to vision in the Western context have been limited to the observing eye. During fieldwork with mountaineers in Scotland I learnt that how one senses the environment has to be considered in relation to the actual movement of the body and, thus, needs to be examined in relation to how the body measures itself to the ground. The body meets the ground and the touch affects the view because the walker's attention shifts between focusing on the ground and looking into the distance. As a result the gaze into the distance cannot be taken out of the context of how the body treads the ground, which concludes that when approaching vision one needs to examine the eye, that not only sees, but also touches.

Introduction

It was a cold but crispy day in March. We stood at the foot of the mountain looking up, examining the task awaiting us. There was no apparent path to take. From where we stood, the grassy slope seemed vertical. At the end of the slope, I could see a big and rough field of boulders and rocks that would take us up to the ridge. We started walking. The grassy slope offered a soft surface, but its shape proved challenging for my leg muscles. I kept my back straight and kept the next target, the boulder field, in sight. However, the unevenness of the ground sometimes required a thorough examination of how to put one's foot down. I tried to zigzag evenly in order to balance the weight of my body from one side to another. I stopped and looked around. My companion was some way ahead of me. I looked down. I could see that I was already half way up the slope, which encouraged me to keep going. As I got closer to the boulders the ground became harder to get over. Stones were sticking up from the grass and I had to concentrate more thoroughly. But as soon as I reached the boulders, the posture of my body changed, although I still tried to maintain an upright posture. My concentration was on finding balancing foot holes and with the aid of my arms I pulled myself past one boulder after another. I stopped again and looked over and down. The shape of the mountain had changed and now did not allow for views. The ground where we had started was out of sight and the mountain on the other side blocked our views into the distance. It was at this point that I really started to feel at one with the mountains. At the end of the rocks my companion was waiting for me. We had reached the ridge. The most difficult part of the climb was behind us. There was no way back. Tired muscles welcomed the easier gradient over the barren ground. Suddenly we reached the point from where we could see the summit rising in the distance. As we came closer to the summit, the ascent increased again. We had, however, encountered a narrow path that seemed to direct us. The act of balancing my body and all my various muscle tensions was no longer the centre of my attention; the tension between my body and the ground had evened out. My eyes still focused on the ground but with more ease. I did not need to stop to look around anymore. The shape of the grounds allowed me to move with a more flexible posture. I looked down, looked up, looked around, and into the distance. 'You don't have to think when you walk on paths,' my companion called out to me. I agreed, but, like most mountaineers in Scotland know, paths can also be dangerous because they do not always take you where you want to and sometimes they just end. They can also erode the land, especially in places where too many people choose to follow the same paths. The fact is that in mountaineering the mind is constantly engaged; it constantly moves between concentrating on the 'micro environment as well as the larger situation,' as one mountaineer put it. Finally we reached the summit. My body felt lighter, relieved and pleased. The views opened up in all directions. We could see the mountains on the west coast rise in to the distance. With the aid of a map we tried to familiarize ourselves with the views, naming the mountains and recalling and telling each other about our previous experiences of them. We sat down to have a lunch. To the northeast the views on the mountains were blocked by the second mountain we were to climb that day, separated by a steep descent into a glen full of bogs and snowy patches. This would be a hard work but worth it for the sake of the different perspective that the mountain would offer us over to the east. The day had only just started.

This paper is based on fieldwork among mountaineers in Scotland and explores the ways in which views and vistas in the mountains are created alongside the physical activity of walking and climbing. My argument is that in order to understand how the eyes perceive the surroundings it has to be examined in relation to the moving body and how it moves. I claim that incorporated in the movement is a tactile sensation that needs to be considered in order to understand the vistas appreciated by the mountaineer. Hence, along with vision, the sense of touch will be at the forefront of my analysis and I claim that touch, as one of the five senses, has so far been under examined in the ethnographic context. I propose that the sense of touch needs to be approached in relation to *how* the body moves in different contexts. In relation to mountaineering, this kind of approach opens up questions such as: How does the body that touches the ground, as it moves over it, affects the way one perceives the environment? How do the senses of touch and vision interact and emerge through the process of moving? Walking is a bodily movement that not only connects the body to the ground but also includes different postures, speeds and rhythms. These shape the tactile interactions between the moving body and the ground, and play a fundamental part in how the surroundings are sensually experienced.

From 2001 to 2002 I undertook a twelve months long study that focused on hill walking in Scotland.[1] Based in Aberdeen, I followed walkers and mountaineers on their hikes into the mountains, whilst, at the same time, I carried out several interviews. These interviews form the basis of the ethnography in this paper. As a result of my fieldwork, I learned that when mountaineers scaled the hills they express what the eye catches through actual descriptions. They look around and name mountains, glens and lochs like they are in the process of ordering the scenery. Moreover, I also learned that walking in the Scottish mountains is about 'getting to know the country', and this was what most mountaineers agreed on. I, however, want to illustrate that the descriptions only voice *what* is seen; they do not articulate the process through which such descriptions are perceived. It was also frequently pointed out to me that when walking the Scottish hills you learn as much about yourself as you learn about Scotland. This directed me towards thinking about how these two might go together. When one of the mountaineers pointed out to me that getting to know the country and getting to know yourself 'is the same thing', I realized that to assess what the mountaineer sees needs to be examined in relation to the mountaineer's 'reflexive awareness' (Edensor 2001:82) of his or her self. A reflexive awareness, which means, as Edensor (ibid.) has illustrated, that the practice of walking should be examined as an ongoing sensual dialogue between the surroundings and the self. However, as illustrated below, the Scottish Highlands have a history of having been created as a spectacular landscape and therefore the ongoing dialogue is much focused on what the eye catches. Moreover, as the description above reveals, where and how one's eyes move is depending on at what angle, speed and rhythm one moves and how modes of movement change at different inclinations and over the duration of the climb. Furthermore, this ongoing visual dialogue supports Jay's statement that 'the eye is not only, as the familiar clichés would have it, a "window on the world", but also a "mirror of the soul"' (1994:10). In other words, the eye not only observes, it also reflects.

Thus, this essay introduces the reflecting eye, the touching eye. And, by looking at how mountaineers perceive and experience the surroundings on their hikes, my aim is to demonstrate how approaches to vision in the Western context have been limited to the observing eye. In the anthropology of the senses, studies concerning vision (often defined as the 'noblest of the senses') have been addressed to portray the distancing and analytical observer rather than the perceiving person. This has led to the general assumption that the dominant sense in the Western context is vision. Little has been said, however, as to how vision operates in different circumstances. Or, as Ingold has pointed out in his recent review on the anthropology of the senses, 'the reduction *to* vision in the West, has been accompanied by a second reduction, namely the reduction *of* vision' (Ingold 2000:282). In other words, it appears that because vision has been defined as the dominant sense in the Western context, the way we actually perceive through our eyes has been scarcely analyzed. I claim that this reduction both 'to' and 'of' vision is at least partly due to how analyses have been lacking in focus on the moving body. By focusing on movement of mountaineers the aim of this paper is to bring vision into context with the body that is in continuous contact with the ground it touches. Before entering Scotland it will, however, be necessary to examine further how Ingold came to his statement quoted above and how far his critique takes us in order to reconstruct vision as a dynamic and embodied process.

From Ingold's extensive evaluation of the anthropology of the senses, I want to highlight two fundamental points he makes. Firstly, Ingold demonstrates how those who work within the discipline of the anthropology of the senses tend to focus on how the senses were differently ordered or emphasized in various cultures, thereby keeping them as separate entities.

> The common flaw, running through all the work in this field ... lies in its naturalization of the properties of seeing, hearing and other sensory modalities, leading to the mistaken belief that differences between cultures in the ways people perceive the world around them may be attributed to the relative balance, in each, of a certain sense or senses over others (Ingold 2000:281).

Secondly, Ingold highlights that bodily movement has most often been absent in the work of these studies (cf. Sutton 2001). Following Merleau-Ponty's groundbreaking work, Ingold emphasizes the moving and perceiving body, an approach that does not isolate the senses from one another but brings them together 'in the very action of its involvement with the environment' (Ingold 2000:262). It is this involvement that comes prior to any objectification that may take place. Or as Csordas has expressed it:

> Our lives are not always lived in objectified bodies, for our bodies are not originally objects to us. They are instead the ground of perceptual processes that *end* in objectification (Csordas 1994:7).

This is a point of departure for my argument. I agree that in order to discuss sight we need to stay with the involvement of the body. Vision has often been theoretically reduced to its focus, and to the way it objectifies; in other words, to *what one sees* rather than on '*how one sees*'. A focus on what Merleau-Ponty defines as 'a tactile perception of space' (Merleau-Ponty 2002:253), may be useful in this context:

> The very fact that the way is paved to true vision through a phase of transition, and through a sort of touch effected by the eyes, would be incomprehensible unless there were a quasi-spatial tactile field, into which the first visual perceptions may be inserted (ibid.:259).

Thus, it appears that although 'touching is not seeing', as Merleau–Ponty (ibid.:260) claims, one can still touch with one's eyes. And, as I will illustrate further below with examples from mountaineers in Scotland, to understand how this happens the case needs to be made for how the whole body moves, as well as, senses.

I shall start by discussing the concepts of vision and the moving body in a landscape that has historically been constructed as a spectacular one. From there I will highlight the sense of touch by discussing the moving body or the walking body of the mountaineer and how it relates to the environment. This will finally bring me to discuss the touching eye of the mountaineer in a still position at the summit of a mountain. This will bring together my argument about the interrelation between vision, touch and movement in mountaineering.

Seeing in motion

Before considering how the mountaineer looks at the surroundings when in the process of scaling the hills, the Western conceptualization of nature as scenery (Solnit 2000:134; Urry 2000; Macnagthen and Urry 2001; Edensor 2001) needs to be addressed. In the eighteenth century travel writings encouraged tourism, which at that time was in its early stages, and guidebooks told tourists what there was to *see*. The art of how to see was introduced by the clergyman William Gilpin, who in the early eighteenth century established a common use for the word *picturesque* (Solnit 2000:95-96) that emphasized not only forms and compositions in the landscape, but also 'how to frame it in the imagination' (ibid.:96). It was also during this period that the Scottish mountains were created as grounds on which to walk by Victorian gentlemen. Guidebooks for walkers were published which 'charted particular routes, identified specific sites and viewpoints' (Edensor 2001:91) and viewing became an institutionalized aspect of being in nature.

During the mid–nineteenth century the act of scaling the Scottish hills was established as a honourable pastime activity in Scotland. As an activity mainly practiced among circles of gentlemen, the codes of practice of how to traverse the hills did as much to direct the eyes of the mountaineer as his feet. In 1899, in an address to the Aberdeen based mountaineering club, the Cairngorm Club, its president, The Right Hon. James Bryce, informed its members about 'Types of Mountain Scenery' (1900:133). He emphasized three elements that make scenery impressive: height, line, and colour. These are all relative concepts, hierarchically valued and aesthetically institutionalized in western culture. Whilst these instruct the mountaineers about how to see, panoramic illustrations published by the Cairngorm Club journal emphasized what to see or how to combine the heights, the lines and the colours.

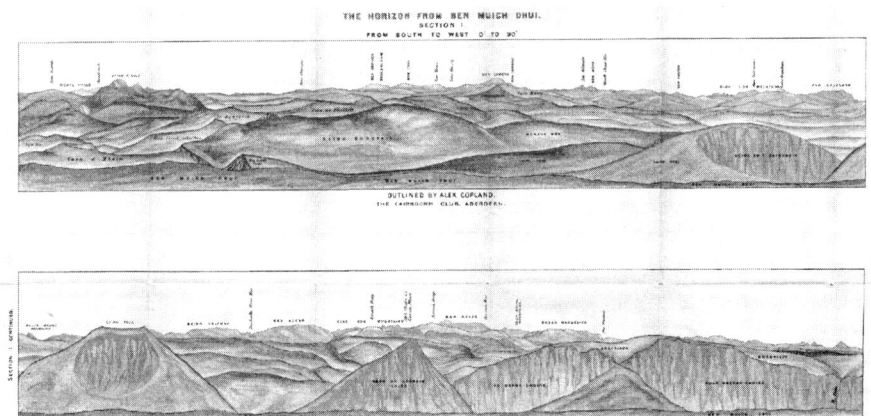

Photo. 1. *The view from Ben Macdui*

These types of illustrations are designed to be experienced as a continuous movement of heights, lines and colours that eventually frame the landscape and make a scenery distant and dramatic. However, the illustration that is constructed by this type of aesthetic framework only appears as it is viewed from a fixed point. The mountaineer is standing at the top of a mountain from which he can view but the means of how he got there or how he may continue his travel is excluded from the scenery and thus the actual bodily movement is excluded. In their accurate measures these types of illustrations may assist mountaineers in learning about the country, but demonstrate more what the mountaineer should see rather than how one learns about the country. As Green (1990:128) has noted, the perceptive relation between nature and those who perceive it can only be 'most effectively measured ... in the *personal experiences* and *identities* of participants'. Therefore, the travel itself and the experience of it need to be further examined in relation to the vistas of the mountaineer. And as I will illustrate below, the travel needs to be analyzed in a much wider context that relates personal experiences in the mountains to the everyday aspects of the life of the mountaineer, or the process through which one learns about oneself.

Furthermore, a landscape scenery made up from lines, heights and colours is a landscape scenery dressed in what Green (1990) has called an 'aesthetic straitjacket'. This is a straitjacket that may, or may not, provide a structure for those who travel through nature with an instructed framework of how to perceive. But, I argue, such a straitjacket provided intellectuals and academics with 'a fixed conception of how we should approach the visual' (Green 1990:33) in the Western context. In agreeing with Green's argument I am not dismissing the aesthetic framework, the picturesque ways of composing the landscape. Rather I am emphasizing what I have argued above that 'pictorial forms of viewing are not always what they seem to be' (ibid.:38) and in order to approach vision, the straitjacket needs to be loosened. As Gilpin himself suggested when he wrote:

> But it is not only the *form*, and the *composition* [emphasis original] of the objects of landscape, which the picturesque eye examines; it connects them with the *atmosphere*, [my emphasis, KL] and seeks for all those various effects, which are produced from that vast, and wonderful storehouse of nature (Gilpin 1808:44).

In mountaineering this *atmosphere* comes about when the mountaineer moves through the landscape, and it is the touch between the body and the ground, on which the mountaineer walks, that affects the whole spectrum of how the surroundings are perceived. It is, however, important to emphasize that there is more to this movement than the physical aspect of it. I am introducing here the movement of the 'lived body' as understood by Merleau–Ponty (2002:272) 'not [only] as objective movement and transference in space, but as a project towards movement or 'potential movement' [which] forms the basis for the unity of the senses'. For further illustration I will bring in a mountaineer's comments.

Billy: I find myself not doing very much spectating when I'm going up hill ... I tend to get my head down and march and it's only when getting towards the top that I start looking around more and stopping to admire the view. And getting on top, if it's not too cold, spending a while on top and it's great just to sit and look around once you have finished the up hill slog – to sit around and ... and look at the view.
Katrín: Is that what you do on the summit?
Billy: Depends on the walk I'm on. If it's a big long ridge walk then there might not be a lot of time to be sitting around ... if it's a small hill I'm quite happy to sit at the top ... and do so until it gets cold

Katrín: And when you are admiring the view what are you admiring?
Billy: I'm looking at the distant peaks, I'm looking at the terrain below, the different colours, a lot of different colouring in the Scottish landscape, the sky, the way I've come or the way I'm going to go … sometimes *I'm just sitting*.

Although Billy may be 'just sitting' as he describes it, I want to argue that this 'just sitting' does not indicate a lack of movement. Rather, the 'sitting' is a part of the process of walking towards an object or a goal that includes the changing rhythms and postures of the body. He describes how he marches along the route and when the gradient hill slows down the speed of his body he starts looking around and admiring the views. There appears to be a process of interaction going on between the body and the landscape through which the moving body responds to the different shapes and forms of the landscape as it measures itself in relation to the ground. This process is indicated through the different speeds and postures of the body. The procedure continues as he sits down and admires the surroundings, the picturesque, in a still position like the mountaineer that is supposed to connect and order the landscape according to the instructions in the image above. He does, however, also look at where he came from and where he is going and, thus the momentarily pause is in itself full of movement. Ingold makes a distinction between the act of walking and sitting and argues that these call for a different use of the senses. His claim is that 'sedentary perception of the world' is 'mediated by the allegedly superior senses of vision and hearing and unimpeded by any haptic of kinaesthetic sensation through the feet' (Ingold 2004:323). I shall not dispute the fact that the sensational engagement may alter as the bodily postures change, but instead I am making the point that the sitting position does not push the sensory experience towards face level only because the physical movement stops temporarily. The 'lived body' continues to move in the sitting position rather than exclude haptic forms of sensation.

The sedentary position does, however, also indicate a sense of stillness because of how the rhythm of the walk is brought to a different phase. But as Serematakis emphasizes, stillness does not indicate a lack of movement but rather a change of directions or a movement of 'sensory self-reflexivity' (1996:7), which indicates

> …a different movement within time that captures everyday temporal experience from another oblique angle as if the sensory array is shifted from one point of consciousness to another, from one side of the body to another, which gives rise to a new or alternative perceptual landscape. It is a moment of poetry. It can be a moment of vision (Serematakis 1996:14).

Billy does not describe how he sees but rather what he sees – a messy mixture of different aspects that appear in the landscape: terrain, mountains, colours and sky. Billy does not describe a landscape in which colours, lines and heights may or may not be connected to form an authorized picturesque but, more importantly, he describes how these elements are brought together by the atmosphere. It can be a moment of poetry and vision, or may I suggest, a moment of a poetic vision. Furthermore, Billy's route, which appears as a part of his scenery, emphasizes the importance of the actual movement of walking and the haptic form of sensation as the feet touch the ground. But at the same time as the route is a part of his picturesque, so is the picturesque a part of his route. This is what alters the framework, and as Serematakis claims, 'gives rise to new or alternative landscape'. This is a framework in which the mountaineer and the landscape he views cannot be separated from each other because as Husserl stated: 'We [would] get into the difficulty of [having] *two* realities facing one another, whereas only *one* is and can be there' (Husserl, in Van den Berg 1952:161). To further explore the new or alternative landscape that may emerge for the mountaineer I will now discuss the physical movement of walking and examine further how this landscape is influenced by the touch of the feet on the ground.

Touching the ground and changing perspectives

> Where does it start? Muscle tense. One leg a pillar, holding the body upright between the earth and sky. The other a pendulum, swinging from behind. Heel touches down. The whole weight of the body rolls forward onto the ball of the foot. The big toe pushes off, and the delicately balanced weight of the body shifts again. The legs reverse position. It starts with a step and then another step and then another that add up like taps on a drum to a rhythm, the rhythm of walking (Solnit 2000:3).

It is with this technical but rather sensitive description that Solnit starts describing the astonishing sequence of the bodily techniques that bring our everyday lives into different directions. It sets the rhythm. The activity, although mostly dismissed by social and cultural anthropologists, has been regarded as the one, which created *homo sapiens*, the only animal to move around in an upright position. There is, however, as Mauss pointed out, 'no such thing as a natural way of walking' (Mauss, in Ingold 2004:335). His observation was that walking, like other bodily techniques, was culturally specific as a result of training and being 'functional to a specific aim' (Edensor 2001:96). This indicates that walking is never an aimless task although sometimes in its most mundane forms it may appear as such.

The aim of walking in the British countryside was established in the eighteenth century alongside the gaze into the picturesque. Before that time, walking had been associated with danger that prevented people from going out, where the 'roads were atrocious and plagued by highwaymen and their pedestrian equivalents, footpads' (Solnit 2000:83). Walking had, however, been recommended for health reasons since the sixteenth century but these were walks that were exercised along the stretching corridors of the residence palaces and mansions and later moved into the surrounding gardens (cf. Solnit 2000). When the garden gate opened up, an untouched nature appeared and became accessible. 'Where the eye went the walker would soon follow' (ibid.:88) and the romantic notion of nature was 'forged through the contrast with nineteenth century industrial cities and their sense-scapes' (Macgnathen and Urry 2001:5). Walking was still carried out for health reasons but now out in the open air where scenery was uninhibited. Solnit writes:

...the eighteenth century created a taste for nature without which William and Dorothy Wordsworth would not have chosen to walk long distances in midwinter and to detour from their already arduous course to admire waterfalls. This is not to say that no one felt a tender passion or admired a body of water before these successive revolutions; it is instead to say that a cultural framework arose that would inculcate such tendencies in the wider public, given them certain conventional avenues of expression, attribute to them certain redemptive values, and alter the surrounding world to enhance those tendencies (Solnit 2000:85).

Thus, the taste for nature in Britain was created in the south of the Scottish borders and the Scottish Mountains were created by 'men from the south' (Murray 1987:207). The Scottish context of creation did, however, add an air of scientific motive to these romantic and aesthetic values. This was an explorative motive established by military map makers and ordnance surveyors who designed the groundwork by measuring and mapping the Scottish wilderness, followed by scientists, zoologists and geologists, and scholarly inclined gentlemen explorers. Scaling the Scottish hills soon became a honourable pastime activity. The first mountaineer in Scotland, according to W. H. Murray, was Sheriff Alexander Nicolson, who was born in the Isle of Skye in the year of 1827 but moved to Edinburgh as a student. 'His writings in *The Scotsman* and *Good Words* (a widely read magazine) made it plain that he climbed without scientific motive purely for enjoyment, and from deep, aesthetic appreciation of the mountain scene' (Murray1987:207). Consequently, as the inhospitable surroundings of Scotland's Mountains were transformed into more tangible landscape the aesthetic aspect became the one that was expressed. The motive of exploration has however always been, and still is, closely linked with the aesthetic notion. This is reflected in the mountaineers saying that not only is scaling the Scottish hills about learning about the country but also about learning about oneself. The element of exploration is not only inherent in the tradition that created the mountains as grounds on which to walk, but is also maintained by the unruly shapes and rugged grounds that the mountainous surroundings offer for walking. I thus want to claim that, although the Scottish mountains were originally created as walking grounds by 'men from the south', walking in the Scottish mountains has a different traditional and cultural shape to it than rambling across the rolling hills of the English countryside which Edensor (2001) and Urry (2000) write about. Mountains demand a different kind of bodily interaction with the landscape, which alongside with the motive of exploration, calls for different types of self-awareness and reflection.

Edensor (2001) and Adams (2001) also both stress the notion of the body that moves in the countryside freed from the strains of the city; the body that escapes the fast changing, over-socialized and overwhelming present to 'restore' and 're-establish' connection to the past and create continuity. There is no doubt that hill walkers in Scotland do restore connections to the past through their practices but the question I shall raise is: whose past are they restoring and how they do it? How is the sense of continuity established? 'In the continuum of landscape, mountains are discontinuity – culminating high points, natural barriers, unearthly earth' (Solnit 2000:134). Therefore, the act of mountaineering requires most often highly specific bodily skills and codes of practice (see Lorimer and Lund 2003), accompanied by the drive to explore and master the experience of continuity by getting to a top of a hill.

Catriona: ...sometimes I will go to the hills and walk simply because I need to sort something out and that seems to be the dominant thing. Sometimes it will take about an hour or so to sort things out and I am just a part of whatever is going along and I can just put that behind me. Particularly on a clear day on the top and you can just see forever in all directions. I sometimes feel like dancing.

Catriona's experience reflects what, according to Edensor (2001:86) has been called the 'walking cure' through which walkers 'alienated by modern urban living' (ibid.:87) walk their 'way into physical and mental condition' (ibid.). It does however appear that Catriona does not make the same distinction between the urban and the rural, between the past and the present, as Edensor wants to have it. She brings what she needs to sort out with her into the mountains and when she is at the top and encounters the all surrounding views she wants to dance. It is also curious that, differently from Billy, she does not say what she may be looking at in terms of features in the landscape but rather she says that she 'can see forever in all directions'. She does not explain what this 'forever' includes. Nonetheless, it appears that her perspective has changed but she does not tell how. Gabriella describes a similar process but emphasizes more the bodily aspect and says:

Gabriella: ...somehow climbing is a way of improving yourself, you know it is definitely a raise but you are only rising against yourself. It is something that is quite enjoyable to test – you are trying to improve yourself. And if you manage it you are quite pleased with yourself – do you understand what I mean?
Katrín: So this goes together, the mental side of you and the physical?
Gabriella: Yes, but sometimes as well, depending on how you feel, rather than just testing yourself you just want to enjoy it. You don't want to put yourself up against a challenge. You just want to do it in ... [she hesitates] ... Yeah, it depends on other aspects of your life – so if you are quite stressed by your work the hills can be a way of either testing you but it can also be releasing – or the other way around if you just want to have an easy, relaxing day, without having another thing to stress yourself up about you are better of with doing something comfortable.
Katrín: So do you think that walking is about getting to know yourself?
Gabriella: Mmm, yes that is what it is about, that is true, it is about getting to know how you feel, trying to see if you are happy with what you are doing, ... when you are on the hill, it clears your mind and so you can see things better. It gives you better perspective on things in life ... it almost ... all the problems that you have in everyday life become a lot smaller ...

In this quote, Gabriella hints at how the process of learning about oneself may be experienced. She does that through thoroughly describing how walking in the mountains is about the process of measuring the body to the ground, not in terms of examining the terrain and the features in the landscape as external objects but the other way around, in terms of exploring herself. The terrain and the features she needs to overcome are not just objects in the way of the body but are embodied as she moves over the ground and every step ahead can be a matter of thorough decision. She tries to *see* what she is happy with doing. In order to traverse the ground she needs to examine her ability, skills and feelings towards the conditions the mountains offer. Van der Berg describes this relation between the body of the mountaineer and the landscape from the physical relations that emerge and writes:

> The body [...] is realized as *landscape*: the length of the body is demonstrated by the insurmountable steep bits necessitating a roundabout way, the measure of his stride by the nature of the gradient which it is just possible or not just possible for him to climb, the size of his foot is proved by the measurements of the projecting points which serve as footholds (Van der Berg 1952:170).

Thus, traversing the ground on feet, or walking, materializes itself as a metaphor that mediates 'changes in people's bodies and experience, as well as alter their relationships with [...] the world' (Jackson1983:134). It therefore appears that the mountaineer is not simply escaping the strains of the everyday, as Edensor and Adams put it above, but he or she is rather measuring the body to a type of surroundings where a special kind of bodily awareness is required through which the body changes its shape. As Gabriella phrased it for me on a later occasion: 'you ...feel that you melt in with the landscape'. And, when the summit is reached a new perspective has emerged and an altered 'perception indicates a [change in] *direction*' (Merleau-Ponty 2002:13); continuity comes into sight. Walking thus mediates relations of continuity between the walker and the landscape. It is not that the body is compared with the landscape but it is *realized* as landscape 'continuous with the animate and articulate world of Mind' (Jackson 1983:131).

There is, however, the fact that for this process to take place the mountaineer must be able to visualize the landscape that surrounds him or her. The eye must meet the object so that it can be mastered through the bodily movement. To be able to realize the body as a landscape the mountaineer must see, as well as hear and smell and, most importantly, touch. It also appears that through the process, in which the mountaineer and the surroundings emerge, a degree of distance is needed for measuring. This brings me to my final discussion or that of the touching eye that sets out to gaze over the surroundings.

The touching eye

We are back at the beginning where the body of the mountaineer seeks a momentary rest at the summit where the rhythm of the walk and the position of the body change. The body slows down and usually moves into sedentary position but the body is still moving although with a sense of stillness attached, such as in the case of Billy who was 'just sitting'. This is the point where the mountaineer takes a position and looks at the surroundings and it may appear that the sensory experience becomes focused on the eyes, at face level, as Ingold (2004) suggests. If, on the other hand, the walking process is considered to be an ongoing process, in which the body continues to move, - although with the air of stillness attached, then it appears that the spatio/temporal movement of the sensing body continues. The stillness, however, means that the body is differently aware which, in Serematakis words (1996), creates an 'alternative perceptual landscape' perceived through the touching eye. Susan Stewart writes

> Of all the senses, touch is most linked to emotion and feeling. To be 'touched' or 'moved' by […] things implies the process of identification and separation by which we apprehend the world aesthetically (Stewart 1999:31).

When we encountered Billy in a sedentary position he described how he saw distant peaks, colours and terrain, and combined the panorama with the route he had ascended and would be descending. At the same time that he is a part of the surroundings there is also a separation being made through how he gazes over and into the distance. He sees different colours, terrain and sky and yet, at the same time, he is moved by these features as he touches them with his eyes.

So far, my focus has been on how 'activating the body will alleviate the tendency towards immobilization and depression in the mind' (Jackson 1983:138) and how walking may materialize as a metaphor of movement into the future. There is, however, as Jackson (ibid.) points out a geographical aspect to walking or as de Certeau expresses it: '[t]he long poem of walking manipulates spatial organizations, no matter how panoptic they may be' (De Certeau 1984:101). This is so because it is the person that walks who manipulates the space and at the same time organizes the view. This is where the processes of learning about the country and learning about oneself emerge because as Husserl stated: there is only one reality. It is here where the tactile sensation is integrated in the view. Jim, a young mountaineer tells me:

Jim: It's strange, but you can never fully 'know' a hill until you've climbed it. For example, you can stand on your first Glencoe summit and look around you at perhaps 40 or 50 peaks, all fairly anonymous. Once you've climbed them, and you revisit that first hill, you stand at the top and you name them all. You often remember the walk up those hills by some of the most trivial things – sometimes it will be from the view, other times it will be '… the walk where I forgot the gloves' or '… where I watched the ptarmigan' or '…when you stayed over at my house and we left early'. It's odd, but we all remember the walks in different ways.

And later he says:

Jim: When you climb a hill it imprints something on your mind and that will never be erased.

Differently from Billy, Jim is connecting actual features in the landscape. He is in Glencoe and he has got to 'know' the hills. He is in the process of getting to know the country. What appears, however, is that the ways in which Jim and Billy gaze over have much similarities. Connecting geography is about a momentary separation through which a mountaineer may look at heights and distances, but at the same time encounters and locates past experiences that appear in the landscape. Thus, at the same time that there is a process of separation going on, the mountaineer is still emerged into the surroundings when recalling previous moments of being in the hills. When looking into the distance the mountaineer experiences 'a moment […] of intimacy' (Urry 2000:81) with the surrounding hills. These hills possibly store only fragments of the mountaineer's life in their grounds, but these fragments call forth experiences that can be shared with the hills. These external views connect the spatial grounds of the mountaineer and provide a new kind of internal perspective. At the same time that the mountaineer may be moving into the future one is also looking into the past. What becomes evident is that the space experienced is not 'ordered and systematic, but of [embodied] memory, provocative and strange' (Kwint 1999:7); the external view is as much about seeing it as touching it with the eyes and with the body. It is a touch that in the words of Susan Stewart crosses 'the threshold between what is unconscious and what is conscious, what is passive and what is active, what is dead and what is living' (Stewart 1999:36).

There is, however, more to this view than what the mountaineers sees at a distance because the process of measuring oneself to the grounds continues in this context of separation; learning about the country is about learning about oneself. Hector, an older mountaineer with long experience of climbing states:

Hector: That first time you look down on the world at a distance has an effect on a lot of people that is permanent …stepping back and seeing things from a distance is being able to step back and seeing your own life from a distance.

According to Hector the process of internal and external examination continues at the top of the hill. In this process, entities are not separated but remain integrated because, as indicated by Merleau-Ponty 'inner perception is impossible without outer perception' (2002:xvii). The 'quality, light, colour, and depth', which the mountaineer looks at in the distance 'are there only because they awaken an echo in our body and because the body welcomes them' (Merleau-Ponty, in Stoller 1989:37). The landscape offers a multiplicity of vistas: external and internal, which are in constant dialogue and, as a result, the views constantly change. Such views cannot be taken out of context of the walk itself. Like Gabriella stated, 'you have to see what you are happy with doing', in other words, measure the body to the grounds. Thus, the views are also depending what the mountaineer wants to see, as another mountaineer, John, explained to me when I asked him about how hill walking is about learning about oneself: 'Ahhh, that depends doesn't it? It depends on how much you want to learn about yourself …'. And he points out that the process may often be a harsh lesson because as with 'any reflective experience we [may] see things that we don't like about ourselves'.

The process of involvement with the surroundings is in part dependant on how the mountaineer chooses to touch and be touched by the environment. Thus, the chosen route needs to match the body of the mountaineer and during the course of walking this measurement continues. The bodily involvement continues as the mountaineer's eye gaze over the surrounding landscapes. This is echoed in John's answer when I asked him why he had chosen to use pastels to make drawings in and of the mountains:

John: ...I started using pastels, I supposed I liked pastels because I could kind of get involved with them, they were fairly messy things, you got them on your fingers and kind of really get involved with them in a very physical kind of a way. I like that, I suppose that is what I like to do with my mountains as well, I like to get involved in a physical kind of way.

Photo. 2. *South from Arkle*

In Merleau-Ponty's words: 'It is by lending his body to the world that the artist changes the world into paintings' (in Stoller 1989:38). It is in a similar manner that the mountaineer organises the spatial framework of the mountains through the reflexive act of walking that requires the touching body, touching feet and the touching eye. Moreover, if the interaction between the body and the grounds does produce a successful result, it produces a situation where the internal and the external gaze are brought into a perspective that creates continuity.

Conclusions

The aim of this article has been to provide further direction into studies towards sensory experiences with a special emphasis on the senses of vision and touch. Building my approach on Ingold's (2000) recent critique of the anthropology of senses, my aim has also been to underline the importance of ethnographic work in the context of sensory experience. By using examples from the Scottish Mountains I have illustrated how the sense of vision and the mountaineer's gaze cannot be separated from examining the body that moves and touches the ground. In this context I have emphasised how bodily movement needs to be examined in a spatio/temporal context and not merely as technique carried out by the objectified, physical body. Such a way of looking at movement provides us with a sensual body, the moving body that does not separate the senses but unites them through the act of being part of the surroundings.

My focus has been on the sense of vision and touch in this instance and, thus, I may be accused of still keeping the senses apart. It is, however, important to emphasise that the activity of walking in the Scottish hills has both historically and culturally been associated with the notion of spectacle and it can also be argued that the tradition has shaped mountains as features that provide focal points both away from them and towards them. In this particular Western context it can be argued that the sense of vision has been established as the dominant way of perceiving. However, as I have illustrated in this paper, when brought into context with the moving body, perspectives constantly shift to and from the body in relation to how the body moves over and measures the grounds it touches. How these shifting perspectives fluctuate needs to be examined in relation to the speed, the rhythm, the postures and the pauses of the mountaineer, as all these aspects are a part of the dynamic that bring together the body and the landscape. As the changing rhythms and postures alternate the ways in which the body touches the surroundings also provide different vistas, both temporal and spatial. Thus, although, the senses of sight and touch have been at the forefront of my analysis, due to the historical and cultural processes that have shaped the ethnographic context of hill walking in Scotland, I argue that the approach does not need to ignore different types of sensing. I suggest that by moving the sensual experience more towards the moving body, may provide us with a scope for looking at the body that senses – sees, touches, smells, hears and tastes – and how all these senses are integrated by the way in which the living body moves.

E-mail: k.lund@qub.ac.uk

Notes

This paper has benefited from discussions with several people: Lisette Josephides, Tim Ingold, Michael Jackson, Jo Lee, Fiona Magowan. I want to thank my postgraduate students Sean Foley and Naomi Mozard for their positive comments and Jonathan McIntosh for both his comments and corrections. I am especially indebted to encouraging and constructive comments from the editors, especially Don Brenneis.
1   The fieldwork was funded by the Economic and Social Research Council in Britain (ESRC), ref: R000223603. It was based on participant observation with mountaineers on their hikes in the Scottish Highlands. These were followed up with formal and informal interviewing as well as several focus group discussions.

References

Adams, P.
   2001 Peripatetic Imagery and Peripatetic Sense of Place. In: P. Adams et al. (eds.), *Textures of Place: Exploring Humanist Geographies*. Minneapolis: University of Minneapolis Press.
Bryce, J.
   1900 Three Types of Mountain Scenery. *The Cairngorm Club Journal* III(15).
Certeau, M. de
   1984 *The Practice of Everyday Life*. Berkeley: University of California Press
Csordas, T. J.
   1994 Introduction: The Body as Representation and Being-in-the-World. In: T. J. Csordas (ed.), *Embodiment and Experience*. Cambridge: Cambridge University Press.
Edensor, T.
   2001 Walking in the British Countryside: Reflexivity, Embodied Practices and Ways to Escape. In: P. Macnagthen and J. Urry (eds.), *Bodies of Nature*. London: Sage.
Feld, S.
   1991 Sound as a Symbolic System: The Kaluli Drum. In: D. Howes (ed.), *The Varieties of Sensory Experience: A Sourcebook in the Anthropology of the Senses*. Toronto: University of Toronto Press.
Gilpin, W. A. M.
   1808 *Three Essays: on Picturesque Beauty; on Picturesque Travel; and on Sketching Landscape: with a poem, on Landscape Painting*. London: Strahan and Prefton.

Green, N.
    1990   *The Spectacle of Nature: Landscape and Bourgeois Culture in Nineteenth–Century France*. Manchester: Manchester University Press.

Ingold, T.
    2000   *The Perception of the Environment: Essays on Livelihood, Dwelling and Skill*. London: Routledge.
    2004   Culture on the Ground: The World Perceived through the Feet. *Journal of Material Culture* 9(3):315-340.

Jackson, M.
    1983   Thinking Through the Body: An Essay on Understanding Metaphor. *Social Analysis* 14:127-48.

Jay, M.
    1994   *Downcast Eyes: The Denigration of Vision in Twentieth–Century French Thought*. Berkeley: University of California Press.

Kwint, M.
    1999   Introduction: The Physical Past. In: M. Kwint et. al (eds.), *Material memories: Design and Evocation*. Oxford: Berg.

Lorimer, H and Lund, K.
    2003   Performing Facts; Finding a Way over Scotland's Mountains. In: B. Szerszynski et. al. (eds.), *Nature Performed: Environment, Culture and Performance*. Oxford: Blackwell Publishing.

Macnaghten, P and Urry, J.
    2001   *Bodies of Nature*. London: Sage.

Merleau-Ponty, M.
    2002   *Phenomenology of Perception*. London: Routledge. [1962]

Murray, W. H.
    1987   *Scotland's Mountains*. Scottish Mountaineering Club Guide.

Serematakis, N. C. (ed.)
    1996   *The Senses Still: Perception and Memory as Material Culture in Modernity*. Chicago: University of Chicago Press.

Solnit, R.
    2000   *Wanderlust: A History of Walking*. New York: Penguin.

Stewart, S.
    1999   Prologue: From the Museum of Touch. In: M. Kwint et. al. (eds.), *Material Memories: Design and Evocation*. Oxford: Berg.

Sutton, D. E.
    2001   Introduction: A Proustian Anthropology. In: D. E. Sutton (ed.), *Remembrance of Repasts: An Anthropology of Food and Memory*. Oxford: Berg.

Stoller, P.
    1989   *The Taste of Ethnographic Things: The Senses in Anthropology* Philadelphia: University of Philadelphia Press.

Urry, J.
    2000   *Sociology Beyond Societies: Mobilities for the Twenty-First Century*. London: Routledge.

Van Den Berg, J. H.
    1952   The Human Body and the Significance of Human Movement (A Phenomenological Study). *Philosophy and Phenomenological Research* XIII:159-183.

and spatial. Thus, although, the senses of sight and touch have been at the forefront of my analysis, due to the historical and cultural processes that have shaped the ethnographic context of hill walking in Scotland, I argue that the approach does not need to ignore different types of sensing. I suggest that by moving the sensual experience more towards the moving body, may provide us with a scope for looking at the body that senses – sees, touches, smells, hears and tastes – and how all these senses are integrated by the way in which the living body moves.

E-mail: k.lund@qub.ac.uk

Notes

This paper has benefited from discussions with several people: Lisette Josephides, Tim Ingold, Michael Jackson, Jo Lee, Fiona Magowan. I want to thank my postgraduate students Sean Foley and Naomi Mozard for their positive comments and Jonathan McIntosh for both his comments and corrections. I am especially indebted to encouraging and constructive comments from the editors, especially Don Brenneis.

1   The fieldwork was funded by the Economic and Social Research Council in Britain (ESRC), ref: R000223603. It was based on participant observation with mountaineers on their hikes in the Scottish Highlands. These were followed up with formal and informal interviewing as well as several focus group discussions.

References

Adams, P.
    2001 Peripatetic Imagery and Peripatetic Sense of Place. In: P. Adams et al. (eds.), *Textures of Place: Exploring Humanist Geographies*. Minneapolis: University of Minneapolis Press.

Bryce, J.
    1900 Three Types of Mountain Scenery. *The Cairngorm Club Journal* III(15).

Certeau, M. de
    1984 *The Practice of Everyday Life*. Berkeley: University of California Press

Csordas, T. J.
    1994 Introduction: The Body as Representation and Being-in-the-World. In: T. J. Csordas (ed.), *Embodiment and Experience*. Cambridge: Cambridge University Press.

Edensor, T.
    2001 Walking in the British Countryside: Reflexivity, Embodied Practices and Ways to Escape. In: P. Macnagthen and J. Urry (eds.), *Bodies of Nature*. London: Sage.

Feld, S.
    1991 Sound as a Symbolic System: The Kaluli Drum. In: D. Howes (ed.), *The Varieties of Sensory Experience: A Sourcebook in the Anthropology of the Senses*. Toronto: University of Toronto Press.

Gilpin, W. A. M.
    1808 *Three Essays: on Picturesque Beauty; on Picturesque Travel; and on Sketching Landscape: with a poem, on Landscape Painting*. London: Strahan and Prefton.

Green, N.
- 1990 *The Spectacle of Nature: Landscape and Bourgeois Culture in Nineteenth–Century France*. Manchester: Manchester University Press.

Ingold, T.
- 2000 *The Perception of the Environment: Essays on Livelihood, Dwelling and Skill*. London: Routledge.
- 2004 Culture on the Ground: The World Perceived through the Feet. *Journal of Material Culture* 9(3):315-340.

Jackson, M.
- 1983 Thinking Through the Body: An Essay on Understanding Metaphor. *Social Analysis* 14:127-48.

Jay, M.
- 1994 *Downcast Eyes: The Denigration of Vision in Twentieth–Century French Thought*. Berkeley: University of California Press.

Kwint, M.
- 1999 Introduction: The Physical Past. In: M. Kwint et. al (eds.), *Material memories: Design and Evocation*. Oxford: Berg.

Lorimer, H and Lund, K.
- 2003 Performing Facts; Finding a Way over Scotland's Mountains. In: B. Szerszynski et. al. (eds.), *Nature Performed: Environment, Culture and Performance*. Oxford: Blackwell Publishing.

Macnaghten, P and Urry, J.
- 2001 *Bodies of Nature*. London: Sage.

Merleau-Ponty, M.
- 2002 *Phenomenology of Perception*. London: Routledge. [1962]

Murray, W. H.
- 1987 *Scotland's Mountains*. Scottish Mountaineering Club Guide.

Serematakis, N. C. (ed.)
- 1996 *The Senses Still: Perception and Memory as Material Culture in Modernity*. Chicago: University of Chicago Press.

Solnit, R.
- 2000 *Wanderlust: A History of Walking*. New York: Penguin.

Stewart, S.
- 1999 Prologue: From the Museum of Touch. In: M. Kwint et. al. (eds.), *Material Memories: Design and Evocation*. Oxford: Berg.

Sutton, D. E.
- 2001 Introduction: A Proustian Anthropology. In: D. E. Sutton (ed.), *Remembrance of Repasts: An Anthropology of Food and Memory*. Oxford: Berg.

Stoller, P.
- 1989 *The Taste of Ethnographic Things: The Senses in Anthropology* Philadelphia: University of Philadelphia Press.

Urry, J.
- 2000 *Sociology Beyond Societies: Mobilities for the Twenty-First Century*. London: Routledge.

Van Den Berg, J. H.
- 1952 The Human Body and the Significance of Human Movement (A Phenomenological Study). *Philosophy and Phenomenological Research* XIII:159-183.

Race, Place and Taste
Making Identities Through Sensory Experience in Ecuador

Emily Walmsley, University of Manchester

ABSTRACT Sensory experience is cultural, social and material and it therefore acts as a powerful means of binding people together, or of highlighting their differences. Taste, in particular, is an emotionally charged marker of either familiarity and belonging, or strangeness and alienation. This article uses taste and its interrelated senses as a focus for exploring the construction of subjectivities in a context where racial differences are reproduced through everyday cultural practices such as cooking and eating. In Ecuador, where this ethnography is located, race is understood in terms of place and thus regional cuisines and their associated tastes and smells often become representative of a localised black, indigenous or mestizo culture. Drawing on Howes' (2005) idea of 'emplacement,' this study uses sensory experience to highlight the way in which identities are both discursively and materially constructed, and become embodied without becoming fixed.

Introduction

Sensory experience mediates social relations in immediate and unspoken ways. It indicates sameness and belonging when an experience is familiar and meaningful to all; it marks otherness and difference when it is new to some, and has diverse associations for others. As a culturally embedded, socially shared and physically embodied phenomenon, sensory experience provides a visceral dimension to identity that impinges directly on our daily lives without necessarily entering into dialogue. It challenges Cartesian dualisms between body and mind, and nature and culture, and it integrates the material world of things with the discursive world of words, signs, symbols and meanings.

The senses are not a significant subject of study in and of themselves but rather, as David Howes notes, they are an effective media for experiencing and making sense of other fields of social life (2005:4). In this paper, I will show that by paying close attention to taste (and its interrelated senses) we can gain significant insights into the production of cultural identities – particularly those that are made through the intersecting social constructions of race and place. The ethnographic analysis developed here refers to Esmeraldas, a small city in northwest Ecuador, which has a predominantly black population. The historical associations between cuisine and the local black community provide rich material for exploring the sensory role of taste (and food more widely) in creating difference and belonging.

Taste, along with smell,[1] has become gradually recognised as a worthwhile focus of ethnographic study over the past fifteen years. Beginning with Paul Stoller's (1989) notorious case of 'bad sauce' in Niger, some anthropologists have begun to appreciate that taste and smell warrant attention because they are culturally experienced and therefore socially meaningful features of everyday life (for example, Borthwick 2000; Howes 1991 and 2005; Seremetakis 1994; Stoller 1997; Sutton 2001). This new focus has comprised a direct challenge to the western, modernist view of the senses that prioritises vision and sound – supposedly more objective, rational and therefore important ways of knowing – over taste and smell – deemed too subjective and emotive for social analysis. In overcoming this bias, ethnographers have considered not only whether alternative sensory hierarchies may operate in other societies, but also whether the subjective, emotive impact of smells and tastes might not in fact say something about social relations more generally. Thus, Stoller, for example, interpreted the intensely bitter, inedible 'bad sauce' that he was served in the Songhay compound as a powerful expression of anger and frustration by the person who prepared it – a young, female incomer, subject to racialised and gendered abuse within the compound. In no position to put these feelings into words, she ensured that they would not be ignored by anyone who ate her sauce (Stoller 1989:15-22).

As with all the senses, taste and smell must be understood as culturally defined experiences that are physical, embodied processes. A particular taste or smell may invoke revulsion in one person but bring enormous pleasure to another. While this reflects, at one level, their individual preferences, at another, it indicates their divergent social backgrounds. Sensory knowledge is ingrained in people through their socialisation in particular cultural settings. This early embedding of sensory associations leads to visceral responses to tastes and smells throughout a person's life, which identifies him or her with the cultural environment in which he or she was raised. However, while these associations and embodied responses tend to be enduring, they do not preclude the acquisition of new 'tastes' or the supplanting of old ones. Different environments and relationships engender new sensory knowledge and in so doing invest previously unfamiliar tastes and smells with social and emotional meaning. Sensory experience therefore draws attention to the processual nature of cultural identities: tastes and smells can be powerful markers of difference or of belonging, but they are not fixed as one or the other. Their meanings are shifting, contingent, multiple and diverse.

Taste and smell are crucial to the construction of identities because food – the stuff of all sensory experience – is so central to our daily lives. And food, in turn, is laden with cultural significance because it is the object of constant transformation by social and natural processes. Arjun Appadurai writes that, 'The daily pressure to cook food (combined with the never-ending pressure to produce or acquire it) makes it well suited to bear the load of everyday social discourse' (1981:494). But not only is it continually being acquired and prepared: food is also continually being consumed, or if it is not consumed, it will inevitably decay. Thus Lévi-Strauss's 'culinary triangle' incorporated not only the raw and the cooked, but also the rotting ([1978] 1990). It is the on-going transformation of food through these different molecular states that gives it such a powerful and immediate sensory presence in everyday life. Deborah Lupton captures the significance of this process vividly:

> Food intrudes into the 'clean' purity of rational thought because of its organic nature. Food is unclean, a highly unstable substance; it is messy and dirty in its preparation, its disposal and its by-products; it inevitably decays, it has odour. Delicious food is only hours or days away from rotting matter, or excreta. As a result, disgust is never far from the pleasures of food and eating. (1996:3)

This sensory urgency of food, its concurrent potential for deliciousness and revulsion, was very present in both public and private spaces of Esmeraldas. My field notes refer recurrently to the strong smells that emanated everywhere from consumed or discarded foodstuffs. 'Esmeraldas is all stench and fragrance,' I wrote in one entry:

> People and houses and air. Hands carry the sweet lingering smell of mango, lime, coriander, or the pungent odour of '*mariscada*' (fishy) skin that's been preparing seafood. In the street, delicious smells of *chuzos*, *empanadas* and *corviche* compete with the stench of rubbish cast into cracks and ditches, onto pavements and roadsides.

As an ethnographer the sensory experience of food invaded my everyday life even when I was not cooking or eating. But while I brought my own understandings to these smells – and likewise tastes – and prioritised them in my perception of the city, it was very notable that Esmeraldans themselves also lavish attention on their food and its sensory qualities. They are always quick to proclaim its '*sabrosura*' (deliciousness) and to relish the odours that drift from kitchens and street stalls, tempting them with a foretaste of dishes to come. It is this centrality of cooking and eating in their daily lives, and the conscious pleasure they derive from it, that has made the local cuisine a potent symbol of Esmeraldan, and thereby black, identity.

Before explaining further this relationship between race and place, however, it is worth considering why food and sensory experience offers particularly rich, if unusual, material for understanding the construction of racial identities – in Esmeraldas and potentially throughout the region. Race is an ambiguous issue in most of Latin America: it rarely figures in official discourses of the nation but, as many scholars have now recognised, it is clearly a salient reality of everyday life.[2] Centuries of *mestizaje* (cultural and biological mixture) since colonial times between indigenous, African and European peoples has been followed, in the Republican period of nation-state building, by the spread of dominant ideologies tying modernity and progress to the need to 'whiten' national populations (cf Appelbaum et al. 2003). In Ecuador, as elsewhere, this has produced an image of the ideal Ecuadorian citizen as urban, *mestizo* and hispanicised: that is, as a supposedly productive member of the modern, developing nation. Black and indigenous peoples lie outside this discourse, standing for the backward, uncivilised Other against which the ideal citizen is defined (Cervone and Rivera 1999; Rahier 1998; Stutzman 1981).

There exists, therefore, an on-going tension in Ecuadorian society between the official ideology of 'racial democracy' and the everyday reality of an embedded racial hierarchy. The rhetoric of racial democracy asserts that all Ecuadorians are, or will become, mestizo, thereby obviating the need for a language of racial differences (and discrimination). Implicit in this discourse, however, has been the view that race mixture will improve the nation because it will 'whiten' the darker sectors of the population: in other words, it will overcome the black and indigenous presence rather than incorporating it as such. This tension between the official rhetoric and the everyday reality of racial attitudes, along with the prevalence of *mestizaje*, has created enormous ambiguity in the ascribing and assuming of racial differences, as multiple degrees of mixture produce highly subjective, contingent and shifting identities. Nevertheless, race remains a defining, if often unspoken, feature of social relations. Those who self-identify as indigenous and black mostly recognise the discrimination they face in daily life and, increasingly, express pride in their cultural difference.[3] As this discrimination and these differences are mostly disguised by national discourses, a more productive area in which to explore the salience of race is in the language and embodied practices of daily life. For this reason Mary Weismantel, writing about the Andean region of Ecuador, recognises that the everyday materiality of race is as significant as any politicised discourse. It is in the interactions, she writes,

> between bodies and the substances they ingest, the possessions they accumulate, and the tools they use to act upon the world… we can really see race being made, and making the society around it. This kind of race is neither genetic nor symbolic, but organic: a constant, physical process of interaction between living things. Little surprise, then, that it has a distinct smell. (2001:266)

This paper draws on this idea of organic race by focusing on the sensory experiences of food in Esmeraldas as one factor in the construction and reproduction of local black identities.[4] It will look at how these experiences are talked about and how they are felt: that is, how Esmeraldans interact with these substances that they ingest. This draws attention to the embodied aspect of racial identity formation and, in so doing, attempts to overcome the conceptual divisions between discourse and practice, mind and body, nature and culture – divisions that limit a fuller understanding of the intersubjective, lived experience of belonging. First, however, it is necessary to contextualise the analysis by outlining in more depth the relationship between race, place and cuisine in Ecuador.

Race, place and cuisine: mapping sensory and racial geographies

Ecuador is a country of extraordinary ecological and social diversity and as a result, its landscape can be imagined in many different ways. In order to understand how racial identities in Esmeraldas are reproduced through local food practices it is useful to foreground two particular geographies of the nation: the sensory and the racialised. These become mapped onto each other to produce embodied racial identities that are spatially located and materially experienced through diverse culinary processes.

Altitudes range from sea level to 6,300 meters in Ecuador, and its land area (straddling the Equator) covers the Pacific coastal plain, Andean mountains and Amazon basin. There is therefore considerable diversity of climate, ecosystems and, consequently, food products grown and reared within the country. Different ingredients are associated with particular regions: potatoes and cereals belong to the high Andean mountainsides, for example, and sugar cane to the lower Andean valleys; tropical fruits to the Costa (Pacific coastal plains) and hard fruits to the Sierra (highlands); seafood to the coast, and guinea pig to the mountains. These foodstuffs do not, of course, remain only within their places of origin but are constantly transported for sale in trucks and vans all over the country. Local markets thus in many ways replicate the sensory geography of the nation. Within a single town square products from different corners of the Costa, Sierra and Amazonia are brought together on stalls, mats, tricycles or in baskets. Walking down the makeshift aisles, customers are assailed with myriad smells – some potent, some merging, some familiar, some strange, but all paralleling the blaze of different colours and textures that characterise every market. These smells and sights not only lure or repel, however; they also remind customers of other places, times and people. In a highland stall, the pungent, too-sweet odour of an overripe mango bespeaks a season on the coast when mangoes are so plentiful the locals eat them all day long. In a coastal stall, the smell of fresh, dark earth clinging to a new delivery of potatoes is the smell of the Sierra, of high-altitude mountain slopes where the wind blows cold and the sun beats down hard on the bare land. Coming across this smell in the intense heat of an Esmeraldan market always induced waves of nostalgia in me. However fleetingly, it would make me long for those higher, cooler climes.

Food markets in Ecuador, as in many parts of the world, are memorable and complex sensory experiences. They are crowded with diverse colours, shapes, textures, smells and above all, noise. In Ecuador it is the noise in markets, separated out into the sounds of different voices, that completes the sensory geography of the nation. Accents vary significantly from one province to the next, and even within provinces, and thus the regional origin of wares can be marked not only by their smell and image but also by the voice of their vendor. The smell of rich fresh earth on potatoes is often accompanied by the soft, clipped tones of highland farmers who have driven their crop down from the mountains overnight. And conversely, tropical fruits, with their glowing colours and cloying fragrances, are often sold with the louder, faster, slurred words of a distinctively coastal voice.

An Ecuadorian market thus draws attention to the role of intersensoriality in the production of meaning through everyday lived experiences. Smells, sights, tastes, textures and sounds signify each other according to the particular context and the particular sensory knowledge of the individual experiencing them. This points to a central theme in the study of culture and the senses, which is that of 'emplacement.' Howes defines this as the 'sensuous interrelationship of body-mind-environment' and suggests that by bringing the paradigm to the fore we are able to 'reposition ourselves in relationship to the sensuous materiality of the world' (2005:7). As the geography of the markets suggests, the idea of emplacement is particularly relevant to analysing the associations between place, identity and sensory experience in Ecuador. To appreciate this 'sensuous interrelationship' further, however, we must follow not only the movement of foodstuffs around the country, but also the movement of people as they travel from one sensory environment to another.

Inter provincial bus journeys provide a good illustration of this experience. Each time a bus picks up or drops off passengers their progress is marked by food vendors selling local snacks along the way. As a bus draws up near their roadside stoves and stalls, the vendors rush to proffer their wares through the windows or to clamber aboard, pushing their way down crowded aisles holding baskets and trays aloft that fill the bus with new sweet and savoury smells. In each valley of the highlands, at each stage of descent into the coastal plains, and in each province of the Costa, different snacks and foods are offered by women, men and children who trade their wares with accents that identify them quickly with that place. Not only the accents, smells and tastes change with the journey but also the air, the climate, the music on the radio, and the distance of the views. Among ethnographers of Ecuador, Weismantel (2001) stands out for her evocative descriptions of these sensory shifts, and their significance for making sense of each place. There is a well-known junction in the highlands where the Pan-American Highway meets the road coming up from the coast. The slowed busses are a captured market for the vendors, especially, it seems, those of particular local pastry:

> In the high voices of highland women, they cry out that they have *allullas* for sale, letting their voices linger on the sounds: "Ah – zhhhhuuuu – zhhhhaaaas!" The very word *allullas* signifies the region doubly, for its two *ll*'s highlight the characteristic highland "zh"... To the groggy passengers, those soft, buzzing *zh*'s signal their arrival in the Sierra just as much as the cold gusts of air blowing into the bus.' (Weismantel 2001:99)

At an equivalent crossroads in the lowlands, where the road from the Sierra ends its steep descent, 'the hot, sticky riders buy mangoes and sugar cane, and colas sold from ice buckets that sweat in the heat. The rapid, indistinct Spanish of the coastal vendors, who "swallow their words", is as rich and soft as the flavour of the mangoes' (ibid:99-100). Likewise, travelling to Esmeraldas from Quito (the capital in the highlands) is a dramatic six hour journey from one cultural, geographical, climate zone to another. Whenever I took this bus trip, the Esmeraldans on board grew clearly more animated as we left the mountain slopes behind and edged towards their home territory. On entering Esmeraldas, they would slide their windows open to call out to acquaintances in the street and to let back in the greetings yelled out in return, mixed up with the sounds, smells and hot air of their vibrant, chaotic, seaside city. For Esmeraldans, this sense of 'emplacement' marks their homecoming. For others, it signals difference, strangeness and unfamiliarity – the increasing distance and 'displacement' from their own home. The sensory experience of Esmeraldas has other connotations, then, for them.

These connotations may sometimes have their roots in the national discourses that align certain regions and spaces in Ecuador with different radicalised groups. As in many other Latin American countries, race is often imagined here in terms of place.[5] The dominant discourses that present the mestizo individual as the ideal modern citizen also locate this individual in the country's large urban centres (for example, Quito and Cuenca in the Sierra, and Guayaquil in the southern Costa). The nation's economic and political power is concentrated in these cities, leaving the more remote rural areas, small towns and outlying provinces – such as Esmeraldas – as relatively peripheral to processes of national development. Most of the black and indigenous populations have historically been located in these areas and today, despite much migration, the two groups are still thought of as belonging to such spaces by most other Ecuadorians.

This enduring association between race, region and power has been referred to as the 'racial/spatial order' in Ecuador (Rahier 1998), echoing Michael Taussig's (1987) use of the term 'moral topography' to frame a similar regionalised racial discourse in Colombia. In constructing racial Otherness through discourses of spatial distancing, areas that are deemed black or indigenous have been represented as backward, stagnant and uncivilised (Stutzman 1981). Thus, geographically, culturally, economically and politically they are considered remote from the hispanicised, modernising, and white mestizo centre of the nation. This distancing and Othering of non-white, non-mestizo Ecuadorians has helped to reproduce negative racial stereotypes in national discourses. Dominant representations imputed to black people, for example, include laziness, licentiousness, innate violence and hyper-sexuality. As Jean Rahier has noted, for white and mestizo Ecuadorians, blacks have been commonly represented as all 'that which one does not want to be' (1999:104).

Esmeraldas lies within one of the two regions designated as 'black' in this racial/spatial order.[6] The city is the capital of Ecuador's most northwestern province – also called Esmeraldas –, which borders Colombia in the rich ecological zone of the Chocó. From the sixteenth to the nineteenth centuries the impenetrable forests of this region provided a safe haven for communities of runaway slaves from the highlands and from mines further north on the Colombian Pacific coast. After abolition in Colombia in 1852 large numbers of freed slaves moved south to join communities that had been established along the network of rivers in Esmeraldas (West 1957). By the early twentieth century the majority of Esmeraldans were of African descent and lived alongside a declining indigenous population and a small white and mestizo elite (Jurado Noboa 1995; Rueda Novoa 2001). In recent decades, however, a short-lived but dramatic banana boom, the construction of a road connecting Esmeraldas to the interior, and the building of an oil refinery and port next door to the city has brought about a large influx of non-black immigrants from other parts of Ecuador. In the past fifty years the city itself has grown seven fold, while a quarter of the Esmeraldan population today has been born outside the province (Preciado Estacio 2000:42). This demographic change has led to significantly increased *mestizaje* within the city and, concurrently, a heightened sense of racial difference between black Esmeraldans and others.

One important area in which this difference is felt and expressed is in the local cuisine, and it is here that the sensory geography of Ecuador becomes mapped most clearly onto its racial topography. The distinctive aspects of Esmeraldan cuisine – such as its extensive use of coconut milk, plantain and seafood, and the distinctiveness of its locally-grown herbs – have become symbolic markers of the local black culture that are experienced sensuously through the everyday practices of cooking and eating. The key ingredients are sourced locally, often from non-commercial farms or from the wild, thereby maintaining a connection between the urban black population and their historical roots in the rural communities. However, as the markets indicate, many other food products from all over Ecuador and beyond are now available to Esmeraldans, and so their cuisine is not only distinguished by its local ingredients but also by how these are brought together and prepared with others. Thus, tomatoes, potatoes, carrots, flat-leaf coriander and Maggi stock cubes may not derive from Esmeraldas – or even from the Costa in general – but today they are incorporated into coconut-, plantain- or seafood-based dishes that are represented as typical of the black Esmeraldan culinary culture. This localised use of non-local ingredients reminds us that food is indeed 'well suited to bear the load of everyday social discourse' (Appadurai 1981), but that it is able to do so because it is such a malleable bearer. A single food item can signify many things in different contexts and thus, as Alison James emphasises, '[it] provides a flexible symbolic vehicle for self-identity' (1996:80). The same can be said not only for foodstuffs but also for the sensory experiences that derive them.[7]

Emplacement therefore remains a key paradigm for understanding what the tastes and smells of certain foods mean to particular people in a designated cultural and geographical setting. The interrelationship between mind, body and environment specified by Howes harnesses the malleability of food and its sensuous qualities to make them meaningful in one way to one group of people, and in another way to others. Coconut, seafood and certain herbs, for example, are not exclusive to Esmeraldas but their use in cooking, the flavour they produce and the texture of their materiality has become closely associated with blackness in the modern, increasingly mixed-race context of this particular city. The flavour of their cuisine is especially emphasised by Esmeraldans as it is seen to indicate both the culinary skill of black women and the enormous sensory pleasure derived from eating this food. Local popular discourses hereby imply that there is a kind of sensual superiority about black Esmeraldan culture that places it above other regions and racialised groups in Ecuador. In so doing, it goes some way to reworking and contesting national discourses that marginalise blackness, stereotyping it as inferior to the dominant mestizo culture.

Entrando en la sazón: tasting, smelling, feeling the flavour

Much of the language used by Esmeraldans to talk about their cuisine centres on the word '*sazón*', meaning flavour or seasoning. Whether a dish's *sazón* is good or not is seen to directly reflect the culinary skill and sensibilities of the person (usually a woman) who cooked it. The word is therefore often used in the possessive sense, as in '*su sazón*' (*her* flavour-ing) or '*tiene buena sazón*' (she *has* good flavour-ing). It is more common to hear that a woman '*tiene buena sazón*' than that she '*sabe cocinar bien*' (knows how to cook well). To have good *sazón* requires skill and knowledge at every stage of preparing a dish, but it also refers particularly to the way in which distinct ingredients are combined. The *refrito*, for example, which is at the base of every cooked meal, requires dicing and grinding together garlic, cumin, bell peppers and fresh herbs – either coriander, or one of the local herbs such as *chiyangua*, *chirarán* or *oreganón* – and simmering them for the right amount of time in oil and *achiote* colouring. Not all these herbs, however, go into the *refrito* of every dish, and in cases where they are added later separately, it is important either to tear or cut them up into the right size, or to add them whole.

The other key ingredient for many Esmeraldan dishes is coconut milk, and the form and method by which this is extracted and then added to the food is critical for ensuring the right *sazón*. The coconut is halved and its flesh grated (using either an empty clam shell, or a metal spoon, or a serrated blade fixed onto a strip of wood that attaches to the seat). The gratings are then squeezed by hand, producing a creamy, condensed liquid called the *'esencia'* (essence). This is put aside while the gratings are mixed with warm water, liquidised and then squeezed again – by hand or through a sieve – to produce a more diluted liquid known as the *'agua'* (water). For an *encocao* (a very liquid coconut-milk stew) pieces of seafood, chicken or meat are cooked in the *agua*, which is poured into the *refrito* early on in the preparation: the *esencia* is added at the last minute to give the stew a creamy texture and stronger coconut taste. For other coconut-milk dishes, such as the *ensumacao*, only the *esencia* is used, giving the food a more intense flavour.

These are the basic methods for cooking a dish that is easily identifiable as Esmeraldan. A very important feature of these methods is that they always entail the use of fresh ingredients. The real quality of a dish's *sazón*, however, depends ultimately on the subtle skills of each cook – skills that are seen to represent her both as an individual and as a black Esmeraldan woman. Some of the clearest examples of this arise during the *Feria de Comida Típica* (Traditional Food Fair) that is held for a week each year as part of the city's August festivals. Sixty or seventy makeshift food stalls are set up in a central square, each one selling dishes that are deemed local, typical and authentic – such as the *encocao*. In 2002, I spent much of the Feria at the stall of Celia Zamora, a teacher in her late forties who is an excellent cook and often uses the occasion to supplement her meagre salary. One afternoon, when the fair was filling up with customers, I asked a group of men why they had chosen to eat at Celia's stall instead of any of the numerous others selling exactly the same dishes. One of them, a black man called Felipe, who was tucking in an *encocao de guaña* (a local river fish) with relish, replied:

> 'Well, you see, you try to work out exactly who's doing the cooking. Celia's a friend of mine, and being the black woman she is she'll have tasty food (*como negra que es, tiene buena sazón*).'
>
> 'Why tastier because she's black?' I asked.
>
> 'It's traditional (*Es lo típico*)', he said. 'It's the people who are really from here who know how to prepare these dishes well, using the fresh herbs in the right way and all that. It's something intrinsic to this place (*Son cosas intrínsecas de aquí*). It comes from the ancestors.'

In this brief dialogue, Felipe reiterated the commonplace association of race and region and linked it directly to culinary skill and the taste of Esmeraldan food. It is the people like Celia 'who are really from here,' he said, by way of re-emphasising their blackness, who know how to use the fresh herbs correctly and create the right kind of flavour. Race, place and taste signify each other in both directions, then: the woman's blackness marks her as having good *sazón*, while her good *sazón* – knowing 'how to prepare these dishes well' – identifies her as Esmeraldan and, as a person who is 'really from here,' as black.

Another example in a contrasting context produces a very similar account. Nayades Tenorio, also a teacher, refuses to have a stall at the Feria (which she claims is a rip-off for tourists) but sells food on a daily basis on a street corner in the city centre. From Nayades' stall – called *Comedor Don Tuly*, after her husband – hot, fresh plates of *comida de casa* (home food) are sold for about one US dollar a go. It is one of the most renowned and frequented street stalls in the city and Esmeraldans will travel across town to eat there. When I asked Nayades why it was so successful she quickly replied that it was the freshness of the food and her consistently good *sazón* that kept the customers coming back for more. Immediately, however, she went on to say that, while individual women can be known for the tastiness of their food, black *esmeraldeñas* in general are renowned for having *buena sazón*: 'We have a special touch (*un toquecito*)', she said, 'which comes from always using fresh, local herbs, even when we're cooking for business – like at my stall, we never use chemical flavourings, ever.' But knowing how to cook well, she added, is also '*algo nato en el negro*' (something innate in the black person).

It was for this same reason that my friend Elsa, another black woman born and raised in the city, advised me that when I ate out in the street I should always choose the stall of '*una negra*' over that of '*una blanca*' (a white woman) because the flavour and quality of the former's food is likely to be much the better. And, in the case of a local dish such as an *encocao*, by no means should I ever consider eating from the stove of a non-black woman. Here she also echoed Nayades (and many other Esmeraldans) when she told me that anyone can cook an *encocao* if they try, but it will not turn out quite the same: as black people, she said, 'we have *un toque magistral* (a masterly touch)' for flavouring such dishes. After all, these dishes 'are customs that are entwined with the black Esmeraldan race' (*van como entrelazados con la raza negra esmeraldeña*).

For Nayades, the touch that enables a black woman to cook so well was 'innate' (*algo nato*). For Felipe, in Celia's stall, the black *esmeraldeña*'s tasty food was 'intrinsic'. According to Elsa, the special touch and flavour were things that came out 'from deep inside you' (*dentro de uno*): like her dancing style, the *esmeraldeña*'s *buena sazón* was something that she simply 'felt' (*se la siente*). Similarly, when my neighbour Goyi tried to teach me to make a *tapao* (also very distinctive, exclusively Esmeraldan fare), she insisted that to get the seasoning just right I had to be able to 'feel the flavour'. It was not a question of exact amounts of salt, pepper, herbs or spices that could be replicated each time, but rather, '*Tienes que <u>sentirlo</u>*' (you just have to <u>feel</u> it). Goyi's words provide a clear message that these dishes cannot be learned in a cookery book, for there is no fixed recipe for a *buena sazón*. I heard such comments expressed in similar ways on many occasions in the city and they suggested that not only is the tasting and smelling of Esmeraldan cuisine an embodied, sensuous experience, but that the knowledge and skill that produces it is also conceived as such. The cognitive and the bodily dimensions of cooking with *buena sazón* are not clearly separated in this discourse. *Esmeraldeñas* are seen as 'knowing' how to prepare dishes well but they do not, apparently, call upon this knowledge consciously when they cook because it comes out 'from deep inside'.

This kind of discourse could, in one sense, be seen as naturalising the cooking skills of black Esmeraldans as a racial characteristic. However, bound up with the language of 'innateness' and 'intrinsic-ness' there is a recurring emphasis on the passing of this culinary knowledge down through generations of black Esmeraldans. The cuisine is seen as a tradition that ties this community to this place – as Felipe said, only 'those who are really from here' are those who know how to cook local food properly. The stress in this discourse is therefore as much on the importance of teaching children how to prepare the food as it is on the supposed natural ability of *esmeraldeñas* to do so in adulthood. Much of an Esmeraldan child's socialisation takes place within the kitchen and so he or she learns about local flavours, smells and cooking methods from a very early age. This knowledge becomes ingrained in these children and eventually taken for granted by them. It comes to serve as embodied cultural capital that informs their sensory experiences later in life and their ability to prepare local dishes with just the right flavour. It was maybe this process of ingraining that Nayades was referring to when she told me proudly that her teenage daughter was finally '*entrando en la sazón*' (literally, entering into the *sazón*).

The ethnographic glimpses given here illustrate how blackness, in certain contexts, is constructed through the sensory experience of food. It is important to note, however, that in doing so they are also showing how constructions of race are intimately bound up with constructions of gender and sexuality. It has been widely recognised that race can only be fully understood in terms of other subject positions, and the present discussion of cuisine and *buena sazón* in Esmeraldas provides a very clear example of how race and gender, as well as race and region, become constituted in and through each other. The emphasis on sensuousness that emerges in local discourses of Esmeraldan blackness is paralleled by the importance given to *gozando* (relishing) the flavour and texture of each dish. To *gozar* properly often requires eating with ones hands, crunching chicken bones to extract the marrow, sucking juices out of clam and crab shells, turning fish bones over in the mouth to savour every morsel of flesh. Great value is thus given both to producing and to appreciating the taste of Esmeraldan food. But it is almost always women who are said to 'have *buena sazón*' and it is usually women's food that is said to be so '*sabrosa*' (tasty, delicious).

In gendering this racialised attribute the stress on sensuousness slips readily into a stress on sensuality, which feeds easily into wider, national discourses that hypersexualise black women (cf. Rahier 2003). In the common phrase that an *esmeraldeña* has good *sazón*, is 'her' *sazón* referring always to her food, – sometimes to herself? The word *sabrosa* is used to describe many aspects of Esmeraldan life and so, when it is readily used to refer to an *esmeraldeña*'s cooking, is it obliquely saying something about her too? Such questions arise in the context of a city where a drink such as Cott Cola (a national version of Coca Cola) is advertised on a wall downtown with the words, '*La Negra Que Provoca*' (the tempting or provocative black drink/woman); and a Colombian brand of dark beer is sold under the slogan, '*La Negra Rica*' (the delicious black drink/woman). This merging of themes of consumption, sensory pleasure, blackness and female sexuality is not only reproduced through dominant national stereotypes. It also recurs in Esmeraldan discourses, as illustrated in these lines by an eminent local, male poet:

Alta fruta madura	Ripened fruit up high
sobre tu rama.	on your branch.
¿Cómo alcanzarte, negra	How can I reach you, black woman
del alma?	Of my soul?

> *Carne más miel te pusieron,* Honey-like flesh they gave you,
> *caramba!, caramba!*
> *¡Ay cómo morderte entera,* Oh, to consume you in just one bite,
> *mulata!* mulata![8]

The fruit is ripe, the flesh honey-like: texture and flavour figure strongly in this and many other ascriptions of black, female Esmeraldan identity. Sensory experience is not only a means through which Esmeraldans construct their own racial identities, therefore, but also a means through which these identities are objectified – here in sexualised terms – by others. Meanwhile, the value given to a woman having *buena sazón*, and the fact that she is expected to achieve this by always cooking with fresh ingredients, also reaffirms her gendered familial role – one that places her firmly beside the stove.

Sociality, food and the senses: making *esmeraldanidad*

The previous section shows how blackness is strongly associated with, and constructed through, the sensory qualities of Esmeraldan cuisine. This is expressed explicitly in a city in which, over the past five decades, the local population has evolved from one of predominantly black descent to one that incorporates many non-blacks and an increasing number of mixed-race families. This demographic shift has resulted in certain local practices such as food acquiring more symbolic importance in the face of the contrasting cultural practices of incomers. It would limit the analysis, however, to suppose that such local practices remain exclusively 'black,' and that immigrants and their descendants do not learn to participate in them, while also bringing their own influences to them. This returns us again to the plasticity of both food and sensory experience as vehicles for social meaning and identities: in one context, the taste and knowledge of Esmeraldan cuisine is highly symbolic of blackness; in another it serves to incorporate incomers and their descendants into the increasingly mixed-race local identity of *esmeraldanidad* (Esmeraldan-ness). The sensory geography of Ecuador remains a powerful discursive tool, but, like its racial topography, it is constantly changing on the ground.

In order to understand more clearly the diverse meanings of food and its sensory qualities in the Esmeraldan context it is useful to recognise that 'no one sensory model can tell the whole story' but that, rather, multiple sensory orders always coexist (Howes 2005:11-13). This has occasionally been considered in terms of the effects of 'culture contact' in colonial and postcolonial situations where indigenous sensory values have continued to circulate alongside and interact with new, foreign, or 'modern' ones (for example, Roseman 2005; Law 2005). In Esmeraldas, the sensory models that have coexisted over the past fifty years may not be so dramatically divergent, but they are nevertheless significant to particular sectors of the population. A large proportion of recent immigrants, for example, come from the Sierra (highlands) where the contrasting climate and cuisine create a very different sensory relationship between the body and its environment. Talking to a number of first generation Serrano immigrants it was clear that many of them maintained a palpable sense of 'displacement' in Esmeraldas, where the heat, the smells, the noises and the taste of local ingredients constantly reminded them of their different cultural and geographical origins.

By contrast, their children, as second-generation immigrants, invariably felt more at home – *enseñado* – in the city, and while they recognised their roots in the food prepared by their parents, the taste of coconut and local herbs also gave them a sense of 'emplacement' in Esmeraldas. This kind of parallel culinary familiarity – produced through kin relations on the one hand and the social experience of place on the other – was also often invoked by second generation Manabas, whose parents had come from the neighbouring coastal province of Manabí and comprised another significant proportion of immigrants. Despite the proximity of Manabí to Esmeraldas, the province's cuisine is quite distinct and Manabas are as proud of it as Esmeraldans are of theirs. This difference figures prominently in everyday life in the city, where the markets and corner shops supply Manaba ingredients (in particular, toasted, ground peanuts and certain vegetables and herbs) and the cooking smells emanating from Manaba households at midday often contrast with those of other homes in the neighbourhoods. And yet the children of Manabas born and bred in the city are as familiar with an *encocao* – cooked by the relatives of their friends, neighbours, schoolmates – as they are with the soups, stews and sweets prepared by their own mothers and grandmothers. It was often their familiarity and enjoyment of both cuisines that members of this generation referred to in explaining to me that they felt they belonged to both places. Take René, for example, a young taxi driver who was born in Esmeraldas to Manaba parents. His mother registered his birth in Manabí (to ensure that he would be *manabita*) and brought him up on *sabroso* Manaba dishes, but when asked, he tells people that he is Esmeraldan: and his favourite food, he admitted, was an *encocao*. And then there was Luís, a second generation Manaba who runs a vegetable stall in the market who told me that he combines '*las dos cosas*' (the two things) – Manabí and Esmeraldas – inside him. His mother's Manaba cooking is delicious but he does not miss it: 'Esmeraldan food,' he said, 'especially the *encocaos*, is just as good, isn't it?'

Esmeraldans of Manaba and Serrano origin clearly come to identify strongly with a cuisine that, in certain contexts, is also emblematic of black culture. At the same time, Esmeraldans of local black descent now incorporate some Manaba and Serrano ingredients and dishes into their own daily diets. The *corviche*, for example, a deep-fried snack made of ground plantain and peanut with a well-spiced fish filling, is often seen as quintessentially Manaba but it can be found for sale on numerous street corners throughout Esmeraldas. Likewise *encebollado* – a Manaba fish and onion soup – and *tostado con achochos* – toasted maize mixed with scraps of tomato and a round, white bean that is very specific to the Sierra. The list is long but the significance of it is that tastes – in terms of both sensory experience and culinary preferences – in the city today are diverse, even as some foods remain highly symbolic of racial and regional differences. Not only does this illustrate that multiple sensory models co-exist in the city, but it also highlights that an individual's sensory knowledge is never fixed or limited but always capable of adapting and expanding.

Sensory knowledge is developed through the sociality of food practices, which are produced through the sharing of tastes, smells and embodied culinary techniques.

Again, this is well illustrated in the case of Esmeraldas where diverse culinary traditions are brought together regularly both within homes – where local and immigrant families have intermarried – and between them, when plates of food are sent to other households as a gift or when a group of neighbours cook and eat a meal together in the street. These last two practices are very common in the city and they are an important means through which individuals are introduced to different ways of preparing food and to its sensory qualities.[9] The shared experience of tasting and smelling a dish are highly significant in binding them together physically and emotionally. As Fiona Borthwick (2000) explains, the separation between self and other is not clear cut in the moment of smelling and tasting, for the same particles are entering different bodies. Smells, especially, she stresses, cannot be divided off and experienced individually because they overcome such divisions by their very nature: 'boundaries are meaningless to a free floating airborne chemical' (2000:131).

Given that smells and tastes are necessarily shared, they come to have powerful associative links with those other people with whom they have been experienced. For this reason, Nadia Seremetakis, who so subtly analyses the role of food's materiality in processes of socialisation and remembering, notes that commensality should be defined not simply as the social organisation of food and drink consumption, but also as *'the exchange of sensory memories and emotions, and of substances and objects incarnating remembrance and feeling'* (emphasis in original, 1994:37). To relate this back to the Esmeraldan context, we can see how the practice of shared cooking and eating, which creates common sensory ground, can incorporate individuals of diverse origins into a collective Esmeraldan identity: one that is not exclusively aligned with blackness. Becoming familiar with local tastes and smells, and associating them with people from that place, can gradually produce a sense of emplacement and belonging in Manaba and Serrano immigrants. At the same time, the sensory qualities of foods from their places of origin will serve as a reminder of their one-time displacement. For Esmeraldans of local descent, these other tastes and smells continue to act as a marker of the racial and cultural diversity of their city today.

Concluding comments

The links made between sensory experience, sociality and identity in this paper no doubt resonate with similar cases all over the world, and in so doing they may draw attention to the usefulness of this focus for understanding social relations and cultural practices more widely. Esmeraldas, however, clearly provides a very rich case study for exploring the relationship between, in particular, the materiality of food (as found in its sensory qualities) and the social construction of belonging and otherness. The ethnography presented here highlights that these constructions are embodied as much as they are discursive, and that the material and symbolic aspects of identities constantly shape each other as they are reproduced. This can be seen in the role of tastes and smells – simultaneously physically and culturally defined experiences – in binding individuals to other people and to places.

The associations between the senses, sociality and subjectivity – neatly framed in Howes' idea of 'emplacement' – are also significant in tracing the shifts and ambiguities in identities. One way to get a hold on these is to recognise that, in any one context, there are multiple sensory models coexisting, conflicting, overlapping and merging. In Esmeraldas, this helps to make sense of the recurring slippage between representations of blackness and representations of *esmeraldanidad*, where, for example, the taste of a seafood *encocao* may be emblematic of black Esmeraldan culture in one discourse, and symbolic of incorporating non-black immigrants into a collective Esmeraldan identity in another. In the same way, distinctive and merging sensory models reflect, on the one hand, the coexistence of a heightened sense of racial difference in the city as a result of recent immigration, and, on the other, the growing cultural hybridity that has come with increased *mestizaje*. Thus, the significance of a black woman's *buena sazón* may indicate the opposition constructed between those 'who are really from here' (to quote Felipe again) and those who are not. But at the same time, the close identification of second generation Manabas and Serranos with the flavours of Esmeraldan cuisine indicates that a more mixed, inclusive idea of *esmeraldanidad* also operates widely in the city.

Notes

1 Taste and smell are closely interrelated senses that cannot be considered in isolation of each other. For a further, useful discussion of synaesthesia see David Sutton (2001:86-102).
2 Some anthropological studies that have confronted and analysed this reality in depth include Wade (1993) on Colombia; Whitten ([1974] 1994), Rahier (1998) and Weismantel (2001) on Ecuador; de la Cadena (2000) on Peru; Sharman (2001) on Costa Rica; and Twine (1998), among many others, on Brazil.
3 The indigenous movement in Ecuador, under the umbrella organisation CONAIE (la Confederación de Naciones Indígenas del Ecuador), not only expresses pride in their non-mestizo culture but also seeks to acquire greater political representation. Since the early 1990s the movement has strengthened dramatically and is now a significant player in national politics. Black organisations have not developed to the same extent, thus indicating significant differences in the way in which racial otherness is experienced by black and indigenous populations.
4 Other anthropologists who have noted the significance of the material form that race relations take in Latin America are Colloredo-Mansfeld (1999) and Orlove (1998).
5 For example, for Colombia see Taussig (1987) and Wade (1993); for Costa Rica, Sharman (2001); and for Peru, de la Cadena (2000).
6 The other region is the Chota-Mira valley in the northern Sierra, where many slaves were held during the colonial period and where they remained as independent farmers after abolition. However, despite the strong association of blackness with these rural areas, it is clear from historical records that there have also been small black populations in major cities, such as Quito, Guayaquil and Loja, since the colonial period (Savoia 1992).
7 A good example of this from my fieldwork was coffee. I was not able to buy fresh coffee in the city: Esmeraldans tend to drink the instant version, despite the fact that coffee is grown in the surrounding countryside. So I brought a coffee maker out from England and my mother sent me regular instalments of freshly ground beans (European supermarket brands blending beans from all over the world). Making this coffee each morning was my one sensory link with home – a comforting one that provided me with an emotional as much as a

dietary boost for the day. But for the woman who lived three floors above me, and who smelt these freshly percolated fumes as they filtered unhindered up the stairwell, it was a strong and nostalgic link with her past there in Esmeraldas. 'Oh, that smell, Emily,' she declared on several occasions. 'It takes me right back to my childhood. We used to buy sacks of coffee beans down by the docks and grind them here at home, then make the most wonderful *cafecitos* (little cups of coffee).'

8   These are the opening lines of the poem '*Frutal*' by Antonio Preciado (1998:178).
9   For a further discussion of these practices and their role in both creating a sense of belonging among Esmeraldans and marking their diverse cultural origins, see Walmsley (2005).

References

Appadurai, A.
   1981   Gastro-Politics in Hindu South Asia. *American Ethnologist* 8(3): 494-511.
Appelbaum, N.P., A..S. Macpherson and K.A. Rosemblatt. (Eds).
   2003   *Race and Nation in Modern Latin America*. Chapel Hill/London: The University of North Carolina Press.
Borthwick, F.
   2000   Olfaction and Taste: Invasive Odours and Disappearing Objects. *The Australian Journal of Anthropology* 11:127-140.
Cadena, M. De la
   2000   *Indigenous Mestizos: The Politics of Race and Culture in Cuzco, Peru, 1919-1991*. Durham/London: Duke University Press.
Colloredo-Mansfeld, R.
   1999   *The Native Leisure Class: Consumption and Cultural Creativity in the Andes*. Chicago/London: The University of Chicago Press.
Howes, D. (Ed.)
   1991   *The Varieties of Sensory Experience: A Sourcebook in the Anthropology of the Senses*. Toronto/Buffalo/London: University of Toronto Press.
   2005   Introduction. In: D. Howes (Ed.), *Empire of the Senses: The Sensual Culture Reader*. Oxford/New York: Berg, Pp. 1-17.
James, A.
   1996   Cooking the Books: Global or Local Identities in Contemporary British Food Cultures. In: D. Howes (Ed.), *Cross Cultural Consumption: Global Markets, Local Realities*. London/New York, Routledge, Pp. 77-92.
Jurado Noboa, F.
   1995   *Historia Social de Esmeraldas: Indios, Negros, Mulatos, Españoles y Zambos del Siglo XVI al XX, Vol. 1*. Quito: FEDIAM.
Law, L.
   2005   Home Cooking: Filipino Women and Geographies of the Senses in Hong Kong. In: D. Howes (Ed.), *Empire of the Senses: The Sensual Culture Reader*. Oxford/New York: Berg, Pp. 224-241.
Lévi-Strauss, C.
   1990   A Short Treatise on Culinary Anthropology [1978]. In *The Origin of Table Manners: Mythologiques. Vol 3*. Chicago: University of Chicago Press.

Lupton, D.
   1996 *Food, the Body and the Self.* London/Thousand Oaks/New Delhi: SAGE Publications.

Orlove, B.S.
   1998 Down to Earth: Race and Substance in the Andes. *Bulletin of Latin American Research* 17(2): 207-222.

Preciado, Antonio.
   1998 *De Sol a Sol.* Quito: Libresa.

Preciado Estacio, A.
   2000 *Esmeraldas: Marco Referencial para su Estudio, y Caracterización Socioeconómica.* MA thesis, Universidad de Chile (Santiago).

Rahier, J.M.
   1998 Blackness, the Racial/Spatial Order, Migrations, and Miss Ecuador
   1995-96 *American Anthropologist* 100:421-430.
   1999 Representaciones de Gente Negra en la Revista 'Vistazo', 1957-1991.
Iconos 7, Pp. 96-105.
   2003 Racial Stereotypes and the Embodiment of Blackness: Some Narratives of Female Sexuality in Quito. In N.E. Whitten (Ed.), *Millennial Ecuador: Critical Essays on Cultural Transformations and Social Dynamics.* Iowa City: University of Iowa Press, Pp. 296-324.

Roseman, M.
   2005 Engaging the Spirits of Modernity: Temiar Songs of a Changing World. In D. Howes (Ed.), *Empire of the Senses: The Sensual Culture Reader.* Oxford/New York: Berg.

Rueda Novoa, R.
   2001 *Zambaje y Autonomía: Historia de la Gente Negra de la Provincia de Esmeraldas. Siglos XVI-XVIII.* Esmeraldas: Municipalidad de Esmeraldas/TEHIS, Pp. 212-223.

Savoia, P.R. (Ed.)
   1992 *El Negro en la Historia: Raíces Africanas en la Nacionalidad Ecuatoriana.* Quito: Centro Cultural Afroecuatoriano.

Seremetakis, C.N.
   1994 *The Senses Still: Perception and Memory as Material Culture in Modernity.* Boulder/San Francisco/Oxford: Westview Press.

Sharman, R.L.
   2001 The Caribbean *Carretera*: Race, Space and Social Liminality in Costa Rica. *Bulletin of Latin American Research* 20:46-62.

Stoller, P.
   1989 *The Taste of Ethnographic Things: The Senses in Anthropology.* Philadelphia: University of Pennsylvania Press.
   1997 *Sensuous Scholarship.* Philadelphia: University of Pennsylvania Press.

Stutzman, R.
   1981 *El Mestizaje*: An All-Inclusive Ideology of Exclusion. In N.E. Whitten (Ed.), *Cultural Transformations and Ethnicity in Modern Ecuador.* Chicago: University of Illinois Press, Pp. 45-94.

Sutton, D.E.
   2001 *Remembrance of Repasts: An Anthropology of Food and Memory.* Oxford/New York: Berg.

Taussig, M.
   1987 *Shamanism, Colonialism and the Wild Man: A Study in Terror and Healing.* Chicago/London: The University of Chicago Press.

Twine, F.W.
   1998   *Racism in a Racial Democracy: The Maintenance of White Supremacy in Brazil.* New Brunswick/London: Rutgers University Press.

Wade, P.
   1993   *Blackness and Race Mixture: The Dynamics of Racial Identity in Colombia.* Baltimore/London: The Johns Hopkins University Press.

Walmsley, E.
   2005   '"Feeling the Flavour": Food, embodiment and belonging in an Ecuadorian coastal city', Paper presented at the Departmental Seminar, School of Anthropological Studies, The Queen's University Belfast.

Weismantel, M.J.
   2001   *Cholas and Pishtacos: Stories of Race and Sex in the Andes.* Chicago: The University of Chicago Press.

West, R.
   1957   *The Pacific Lowlands of Colombia: A Negroid Area of the American Tropics.* Baton Rouge: Louisiana State University Press.

Whitten, N.E.
   1994   *Black Frontiersmen: Afro-Hispanic Culture of Ecuador and Colombia.* [1974] Prospect Heights, Illinois: Wavela.

The Smell of Greenness
Cultural Synaesthesia in the Western Desert*

Diana Young, Australian National University

ABSTRACT This paper explores the correspondence between colour and odour made by Pitjantjatjara people in the Western Desert of Australia. Although anthropologists have construed sound as the most important sense in structuring social events in Indigenous Australia, Aboriginal people also consider odour to be crucial. When the first rain drops hit the ground after a long dry spell, the smell of land is a smell of the new green growth to come. This odour is manufactured using odiferous plants and animal fats and applied to resurface human bodies, providing a conduit of communication with the Ancestral realm. Through this case study the paper will also address the differences between 'cultural' and 'clinical' synaesthesia'.

Introduction

Arriving in the Ernabella area during early March after a summer of heavy rains, I rapidly learnt two things from my Pitjantjatjara hosts about the land and their relationship to it. We drove miles to collect branches from an odiferous plant, a lone and what seemed to me, rather scrubby shrub of irmangka-irmangka, which is a member of the fuchsia family. Like the whole land, Anangu said, this bush was becoming alive again, about to acquire a nascent greenness – *ukiri*. As we drove along my new acquaintances taught me phrases about the country and all these seemed to concern its greening up.

This paper concerns the connection that Anangu, Pitjantjatjara and Yankunytjatjara Aboriginal people living in the Western Desert of Australia, make between greenness and a particular odour. These are inextricably bound together in people's expectations about the vivacity of the surface of the land or 'country' and the sequence of changes that unfold across its surfaces. Olfaction is here evoking transition in space and in ritual but it is also linked with another sensory dimension, the visual (cf. Gell 1987; Howes 1991). The connectivity, or as I will show, more strictly, a correspondence between two or more senses usually considered as separate is described in western aesthetic and scientific terms as synaesthesia. As I will show, in the Western Desert the correspondence of greenness and odour is a socially created and transmitted synaesthesia that Anangu consider effects a transformation in the whole body. This is rather different from the conventional synaesthesia of western psychology that is fundamentally concerned with imagery in the brain. Before discussing the ethnographic details I will therefore first explore further the various theoretical approaches to this connectivity between the senses in psychology. In this article about the senses I want to contrast the ethnographic details with conventional western notions about synaesthesia to create a dialogue between the two.

Synaesthesia

In western psychology synaesthesic perceptions are construed as those that present a correspondence between senses that are conventionally considered as separate; sound triggering visual imagery for example. The search for universal correspondences between the senses, and especially between sound and colour, has occupied Newton, Goethe, and the Symbolists, including Kandinsky and Baudelaire. Before the recent efflorescence of laboratory based research, much writing concerning synaesthesia argued for it as metaphorical – sweet sounds, loud colours, fragrant melodies and so on (for example Marks 1978; Classen 1993). Synaesthesic metaphor is used extensively in Japanese haiku poetry (Odin 1982) and work by the European Symbolists, in the poetry of Rimbaud for example. This poetic entanglement of sensory realms forms the basis of symbolism for commentators such as Marks and Hallpike (Marks 1990; Hallpike 1979). For these authors the brightness of music or the sweetness of laughter are universal correspondences, not simply culturally learnt connections. Hallpike particularly stresses synaesthesia as concrete physical experience forming the basis of symbolism.

There are also individuals who are apparently innately synaesthesic.[1] Such people experience a perception in one sense, music for example, in two sensory modes; in this case as sound accompanied by coloured imagery of some kind. Furthermore a synaesthete has an irrepressible and consistent life long experience of such specific correspondences across the senses; for that person the letter 'a' has always been yellow or the number seven has, for as long as they can remember, been violet (Harrison 2001:35). For cognitive scientists such persons are not only offer a possible 'proof' that metaphorical synaesthesia has some neurological basis, but are also fascinating. Crudely, this is because perception is construed usually as based on external stimulation of the brain. In synaesthesia one 'input' triggers two 'outputs' making it particularly enticing as a subject for neurologists.[2] A leading neurologist recently suggested that similar processes to synaesthesia might be critical for creativity, enabling the capacity to form analogical connections, and underlie the capacity for metaphor (Ramachandra 2004).

A test devised to find 'true' synaesthete is in effect a memory test, although the genuine synaesthete, because of the spontaneity of their synaesthetic sensations, does not have to remember as such. Tested with a range of colour – word associations synaesthetes produced a far higher degree of accuracy in matching these over time than non-synaesthetes (Baron-Cohen et al. 1993). The role that their synaesthesia plays in remembering has been emphasized in some studies. A synaesthete may fail to remember a name, but know that the name associated with the person is greenish. 'S', the extreme synaesthete of Luria's famous case study, was so bombarded with his own synaesthesic mental imagery that he often confused memory with the present (Luria 1968).

Much of this more recent psychological research into synaesthesia has been designed to ascertain if the experience of synaesthetes is learnt, culturally inherited metaphor or 'genuine', which is innate, synaesthesia. Psychologists consider the latter as a neurological foible and unconnected to any social or embodied context (Baron-Cohen and Harrison 1997). Evidence to support this is obtained by examining the processes in the brain that produce synaesthesia, something that has been enabled by new brain imaging techniques such as Positron Emission Tomography (PET) and functional magnetic resonance imaging (FMRI). Despite this empiricism there are only tentative theories as to how synaesthesia is actually produced.

Colour – word synaesthesia has become the typical 'standard' type as it seems to be the most common. An overview of recent neurological accounts of such synaesthesia includes environmental shaping and genetic disposition (Baron-Cohen and Harrison 1997). In environmental theories childhood play with coloured alphabets is said to account for later synaesthesia associations between words, letters and colours. Such theories are convincingly dismissed by among other things, the variation even within families of synaesthetes of the colours of letters (Baron-Cohen and Harrison 1997:115). Research with neonates suggests that all babies are synaesthesic but that most loose the ability as they mature, whereas synaesthetic individuals retain neurological connections between some of the senses (Maurer 1997). Baron-Cohen has theorized synaesthesia as occurring when some process of neurological break down occurs during the perception of discrete senses (Baron-Cohen et al. 1993).

A further interesting complication that lends weight to the theory that everyone has vestigial synaesthesia is that synaesthesia can be induced by narcotics. Examples from South American cultures are those most widely documented. For instance the Desana create tunes carrying an erotic message on a flute that are said to be male in odour, red in colour and hot in temperature (Classen 1990).

The commonest sort of synaesthesia then, at least in the parameters of most psychological research, is a correspondence between sound and colour (Baron-Cohen et al. 1993). I am not aware of any research among predominantly pre-literate societies such as those of the Western Desert. In the western studies, more rarely are odour or taste the trigger, or the response (Cytowic 1989). Odours also produce shapes for some synaesthetes (Harrison 2001:170). However there are some psychological studies that show that the colour of comestibles influences their smell. One study 'exposing subjects to the scent of cassia or vanillin facilitates the perception of the colour green while at the same time inhibiting the perception of red or violet' (Allan 1971, quoted in Howes and Classen 1991:279). This has a synaesthesic resonance. Another study shows that colour influences the perceived intensity of odour if they it is the 'right' colour; orange coloured drinks smell more of oranges than clear drinks for example (Zellner and Kautz 1990).

The theory that cross-sensory 'mapping' occurs in synaesthesia, as apparently evinced in the colour – taste experiment of Kautz and Zellner cited above, has not been situated in a social context. However suggestions that this mapping shows vestigial synaesthesia in the non-synaesthesic population might concur with the ethnography presented below (Harrison 2001:220). Psychological researchers such as Harrison and Baron-Cohen consistently make a distinction between inherited metaphor as culturally learnt and synaesthesia proper which is somehow neurological/genetic. This tension between the individual's cognitive experience and that of the social group is one that has hindered anthropological accounts of synaesthesia and of colour.

There are claims then, derived from psychological studies, that constraints exist as to the pairing and direction of synaesthesic imagery. There may be a cultural factor in the rarity of odour or taste as a trigger since almost all psychological or neurological studies of synaesthesia have involved westernized literate subjects. Furthermore, as the anthropologists of the senses have shown, the classical Aristotelian hierarchy of the senses in which sight, hearing and smell are superior to touch and taste has prejudiced fieldwork (Howes 1988; Synott 1991). It may be that odour and colour for example are closely linked in Austronesian contexts. Experimental Psychology operates within a Cartesian concept of personhood that is not shared by small-scale societies such as that of Australian central desert people (Howes 1988, 1991; Wilkins and Evans 1998). As other commentators have discussed, here the social self and the social body are not so bounded and the manifestation of synaesthesia should surely accordingly differ.[3]

Harrison notes the recent insistence of a Russian researcher that synaesthesia is not a 'biological function' at all but a social and cultural phenomenon (2001:243). In short, this researcher argues that synaesthesia is just 'a different way of thinking' (Harrison 2001:243). He also points out that the psychological and social or cultural functions concerning synaesthesia are not mutually exclusive. The emphasis on the individual in such research does not answer how a socially agreed synaesthesia such as the Andean example above, induced by narcotics, works. Through the ethnography that follows I want to argue that synaesthesia must be socially based or at least socially influenced and may indeed be a different way of thinking.

Greenness and odour among Anangu in the Western Desert of Australia

The earth in the Western Desert is red but after heavy or prolonged rain, and the immediate germination of opportunistic seeds, the ground begins to turn a brilliant green. As the first raindrops hit the ground a strong smell is released. The more forceful the smell the longer the time that has passed since previous rain. Like all odour it is difficult to describe; eucalyptus with a top note of dust and shit – perhaps dog, camel or human. This is my description; Anangu merely describe it as a good smell – *panti wiru*, and one that makes it easier to breath. The smell of eucalyptus is an iconic odour for Anangu. The fragrance emitted by blood wood and red river gum trees intensifies during rain as the volatile oils from their leaves are washed from the ground. Anangu link the particular smell of the eucalypt oil washed from the earth as rain falls, and odours they regard as similar, with the transformation of country to green.

Thus for Anangu bright greens are synonymous with water and times of plenty, as well as with the anticipation of the land filling with potential as it fills with water, commencing a cycle of burgeoning growth after rains. The newly greened earth attracts grazing kangaroo, emu and other desirable game. Green growth – *ukiri* and meat – *kuka* are both '*wanka*' translated as alive or raw, until they are dry – *pilti* or cooked – *pauntja*, a crucial connection of greenness and life. Greenness is indicative of the well being of land and all creatures who live on it including humans. Intensely bright green plants especially are expected to possess a strong smell while the odour itself is expected to promote greenness. Greenness is also ingested. A person can herself become green by consuming very green plants with a strong smell and by rubbing the odour of greenness on her skin. Plants said to be 'really green' are associated with the smell and results of rain, that is the greenness and blossom of new growth and by extension with renewal, with young things, young persons and with fecundity.[4]

The bright green of new plant growth occurs only where there is moisture. '*Ukiri wiru*' or in English 'really green' is a phrase people often use about country, or plants. There are places that are always green and these are often sacred ones. Bright green is thus not only symbolic of wetness and growth but is indexical of both of these. A rain dreaming site pointed out to me in passing at Pipalytjara near the border with Western Australia, was bright green and has also been the site of, or very near to, a mine for crysophrase, a green stone sometimes used by men attached to their spear throwers instead of white quartzite.[5]

The region of the Western Desert right in the centre of the Australian continent is a harsh one. The area between the Peterman and Mann Ranges is described as suffering badly in drought years (cf. Duguid 1972, quoted in Layton 1989), while the Musgrave Ranges where my fieldwork was carried out further south and east, provides a better watered environment than the country to the west (cf. Tindale 1972, Hamilton 1980).[6] Before settlement, the hunter-gatherer's knowledge of water, especially of dependable water holes, was paramount for survival. Access to a reliable potable water supply is the single most important criteria enabling permanent settlements to exist now in the Western Desert and the provision of water is sometimes given precedent by Anangu, over the preservation of sacred sites.[7] Creek beds remain dry for most of the year although digging down into their beds at known spots yields water. Even water holes thought of as permanent may dry up.[8] A water source is often indicated by the localized greenness in otherwise dry red country.

The landscape features were created by Ancestors during a period known in Pitjantjatjara as *tjukur(pa)* and glossed in English as the Dreamtime or Dreaming. The actions of the Ancestral Dreamings as they moved across the land were transformed into such features and the Ancestors themselves, at last went into the ground or up into the sky. Through the songs, dances, stories and material culture of living human beings bequeathed from the Ancestors and passed on through every generation, the actions of particular Ancestors and the Ancestors themselves are brought back into the present during ceremonies – *inma*. For Anangu, people are closely bound to the land through the sites of their conception and birth, through their parents' and grandparents' sites. An individual may accumulate more rights through marriage and through residence and possess many totemic connections (Young 2001b).

Each individual is thus linked not only to an extensive network of kin but to a site or sites in the landscape, and thence to the Ancestor or Ancestors associated with that site and her travels to and from that place. Such relationships between people and sites are highly complex and form the basis of much political and social activity (e.g. Dussart 2000). That one's own country is green or idealized nostalgically in the mind's eye as such is mentioned incidentally by Myers. Myers writes of a Pintupi friend who was feeling 'homesickness' for country; 'I close my eyes and I can see that place. It's very green. There's a rock hole and a hill where I used to play. My brother pushed me down…. It makes me homesick' (1991:120, my emphasis). Despite the fluctuations in the appearance of a place its imagined state is green.

Bodies and the senses: odour and transition

For Anangu the land itself is thought of as an animated body, and one that is cognizant of the actions of those who inhabit it. Indeed human bodies, animals and plants and the earth are all considered as potentially permeable to one another (McDonald 2001). Surface changes in the appearance of the land are indexical of the enormous power that the ancestors exert from beneath and through the ground (Young 2001b). This vitality is paralleled in the animals and plants that live in country and in human bodies that, like other animals, absorb the qualities of what they consume or what permeates through their skins. In times of drought when the land dries up it has a similar, sometimes catastrophic effect on animals and on humans. People and animals also take on the qualities of the country they move through affecting that country in turn (Young 2001a).

Bodies, just like country must have freely flowing substances to be healthy. Blockages may occur and much traditional medicine seeks to alleviate such blockages as I will discuss below. The emphasis among the women with whom I worked seemed to be on blockages of blood and the free flow of saliva, sweat and breath.[9] Such concepts about the social-ness of a body, defined primarily in relation to others are very different from the implicit individualism in the psychological experiments on synaesthetes cited above. In these the assumption is of the synaesthetic subject as a bounded, discrete entity with her or his synaesthesia as an a-social mind/brain based experience. In the Western Desert synaesthesia, as I am calling it, affects the whole body, which is to a large extent mutually constituted with the land and with other people, and can be permeable to both.

For Anangu, the relationship of one's body to the land is an intimate one. People lie or sit directly on the earth when relaxing or working and continue to sleep on it too. The marks that feet make in the earth and the deliberate pattern making of dances are meaningful contact with the porous earth. Human bodies are the locus of ritual action and here too tactility is important, rubbing fat and tracing designs on skin and into the earth, following the lines of paintings and photographs not just with ones eyes but with ones fingers also (Young 2001b).

Until the recent writing on such tactility, linguistic and musicological studies have emphasized the auditory as the most important mode of sensory cognition in Western Desert societies (cf. Wilkins and Evans 1998). Since much of what is taught to others in societies such as that of the Pitjantjatjara and Yankunytjatjara is by watching and copying, this presents an incomplete analysis. Odour has received little attention from anthropologists in Aboriginal Australia although a song is said to have a flavour – *mayu* (Ellis et al. 1978). Warner does record of the Murgin of Arnhem Land that the bones of the dead were dried in the sun to lose their odour. When brought back to camp for their final rites they were then resurfaced with red ochre, acquiring its smell as well as it redness (Warner 1937:438). The highly emotive, evocative nature of odour makes it a vehicle for recollection and grieving so that while the odour of the corpse was in the past smeared on the mourners (Howes 1991:132, Berndt and Johnston 1942). It is now the odour of the mourner themselves that plays this part among Anangu.

A person's odour is indexical of their emotional state particularly at times of emotional stress or 'emotional transition' such as at funerals and during Dreaming ceremonies – *inma*. On such occasions, women pull up their clothing over their noses to smell themselves. One must not wash one's body or hair during the days of participation in Dreaming *inma*, only at the finish of it, whereas going to church *inma* necessitates showering and washing one's hair and perhaps using shop bought scents. For church there is clearly some intended rupture with previous events, making oneself a blank slate in the way rain cleans tracks from the ground. In Dreaming *inma* the body is accumulating power from the land evoked through the media of song and dance and via body odour combined with the smell of the 'bush buta' – *irmangka-irmangka*. Pitjantjatjara people's concept of the human body is very different from that assumed by psychology. In Western Desert cultures there is no mind–body split. Furthermore even personal mental imagery – an individuals sleeping dreams – maybe socially directed and become objectified as new ceremonies (Dussart 2000) or new dreaming sites (Young 2001b). An individual's odour thus has a social dimension where smelling the same as others has agency in that it effects how the ceremony as a whole – whether funeral, Christian *inma* or other *inma*, may evolve.

The nullification of a person's social smell occurs in petrol sniffing. Petrol sniffing is a continuing problem in many settlements including Ernabella. Sniffers place a can at the neck of their clothing. The gesture is so similar to that of someone inhaling their own body odour that it must be a deliberate replacement of body odour as social connectivity, with petrol. The odour unites sniffers as a group in themselves. Anangu speak of a person who sniffs as 'a sniffer' in a way that they never do of any other 'occupation'. People are defined usually by their relatedness to others but sniffing apparently lessens a person's social value, since they are unable to extend due care to others, and is mentioned along with their familial position. For example, a friend told me of her dead child, '[my] son number two was a good boy, but he was a sniffer'. Sniffing reduces inhibitions and induces complex waking mental imagery in users that is possibly synaesthesic.[10] The importance of using a careful shined recycled can, stripped of all its labels, to hold the fuel perhaps also indicates a linkage between vision and odour.

Next I will discuss substances that are valued for two or more sensory attributes. I begin with a plant that possesses a strong odour and is also, Anangu consider, very green and beneficial; wild tobacco. I will then discuss 'bush medicine number one'. In these plants and their subsequent processing, Anangu have created a correspondence between odour and greenness by fusing together the odour of rain and the following transformation of the country to greenness into one contemporaneous sensory 'event' that I will argue is synaesthesic. The potency of greenness corresponding to the odour of rain is associated with the Ancestral potency latent in the land.

Wild tobacco

Although the majority of food stuffs are purchased from settlement stores, hunting and gathering from the land remains an ideal for Anangu, both as a reconnection with the vitality of the land but also for what it may serendipitously yield. For women being out in the bush away from the considerable social pressures of settlement life is a welcome opportunity for many diversions. Such trips always occur in cars (Young 2001a).

Along with kangaroo meat, wild tobacco – *mingkulpa* is the most important and desired of bush produce.[11] *Mingkulpa* is an addictive chewing tobacco. The plants grow at the base of rocky outcrops often under the shade of fig trees at the mouth of caves or at the edges of creek beds. The seed germinates in cooler weather and also after fire (Latz 1982, Goddard 1985:96). After winter rains existing plants become green again with great rapidity. Anangu refer to an area where *mingkulpa* grows in profusion as a 'garden' in English and although these areas are not cultivated, people repeatedly returned to them.[12] The tobacco plant, harvested when it is very green, it is often simply referred to as '*ukiri*' – green. Plants that have become brown, that is dry – *pilti* in the ground as happens when rain has not fallen for some months, are of no use. Raw wild tobacco – *minkulpa wanka* has such a strong smell that women say it is dangerous for children to inhale in a confined space such as a car. The first time one tries *mingkulpa* it makes you feel sleepy and, women say, 'act drunk'. Chewing *mingkulpa* keeps ones mouth moist, staves off pangs of hunger and thirst. You must chew it, swallow and spit. Women hawk copiously and frequently. This is especially important when singing during ritual to ensure the throat is kept moist and open. Both the need and desire for *mingkulpa* when travelling about is illustrated in this passage:

> "Oh yes! I'm chewing tobacco at last! I've been without it for ages!"… And he'd sleep with it, holding it in his mouth. He doesn't sleep without it … When day breaks, they would get up and tuck it behind the ear and carry it round with them. And would travel around contented, with it held in the mouth. They'd feel satisfied. They put some in the mouth, and travel around looking out for game" (Sam Pumani recalling pre-contact times in, Goddard 1985:98).'

Mingkulpa contains nicotine and is combined with ash, which promotes its rapid absorption into the bloodstream through the thin skin of the lips and mouth and behind the ear, where quids are stored (Latz 1982:234). The ingestion and the absorption through one's skin of wild tobacco turns you 'green' and moist and new, in direct analogy with the rain greening up the country – body. Chewed *mingkulpa* is also said to smell like rain and is used in rain making along with pearl shells attached to a length of string with which to 'pull in' the rain clouds (Ackerman 1994).

The bark – *likara* of the red river gum tree which grows along the banks or in the beds of creeks is the ideal material for making ash – *tjunpa* for *mingkulpa*.

> 'Field notes, June 1997
> Stand of minkulpa near the trees. The girls uproot whole plants, very green hairless leaves. When Dora, driving along the creek bed, spots another plant in the distance, '*ukiri ukiri* – really green' and sends Maria for it who tips it up, Dora clucks about the wasted seeds
> The bark we gather from under low fallen gum branches of the huge red river gum trees. It is eight millimetre or so thick, yellowish, pinkish, brownish, 'really white' says Dora of it.

She makes a fire and chars some bark pieces and as they cool the edges change from black to white. This ash she uses to mix a fresh quid of tobacco.'

The bark of another eucalypt, blood wood, is also used to obtain ash but mostly when the tree is a sacred one, which is when the tree is an ancestral body. The ash must be 'really white', if grey (not an English colour term that is frequently used) it is cast aside and called 'rubbish – *raputji*'. This whiteness is spoken of as though it were already present, immanent, in the raw bark but just how white it will be, only becomes apparent as the blackened bark cools. Ash made from a type of mulga leaf, an acacia tree found commonly in the bush here, can also be used with *mingkulpa*.

In the past men and women used *mingkulpa* but now it is mostly women and old men who chew it whilst other men and some young women smoke store bought cigarettes. The two substances may, though, be combined. Piturpa, a smaller species of tobacco plant, grows on rocks and Anangu call it 'another mingkulpa – *mingkulpa kutjupa*', but is, I was told 'not strong – *pulka wiya*', and seldom seems to occur in the quantities that *mingkulpa* does in the Musgrave Ranges.[13]

Women say that they can gather food 'anywhere' round Ernabella. In contemporary life, it is residence in the local settlement that gives one the right to do this. The rules though are not rigid and habitual use of an area qualifies one to take its produce. A woman became very annoyed when, on telling her visiting daughter, her sister's child, about a stand of tobacco, the daughter and her party stripped the whole lot from the ground, even uprooting the plants rather than breaking them off. They had, she said, taken advantage of her generosity. They were greedy. On another occasion, when great quantities of *mingkulpa* were presented at the end of a large ceremonial gathering of women near Fregon, the Ernabella women became angry. Although they did not live there, they made other claims to that country through their grandparents and therefore to the *mingkulpa*, which they said, those who had no right to do so, were giving.[14] Raw *mingkulpa* was in this case a problematic mediator of social relations. Generally women are not profligate with their own supplies of dried processed tobacco that is keenly prized. Although ash is more freely given, women hide their own *mingkulpa* store, but the quid carried between lips and teeth is visible. Women ask one another, as relatives, holding out an open palm, for a piece of the *kaputu*, the quid or ball of chewed *mingkulpa*, and the quid or part of it passes from mouth to mouth in a mutuality of greenness – taste – odour. This interplay between sharing and re-establishing closeness through all the various stages of gathering, processing and consuming *mingkulpa* materializes the tension between individual autonomy and the need to constantly establish relatedness to others that Myers has written of among the neighbouring Pintupi and which applies equally to Anangu (Myers 1991).

Wild tobacco then is a way of absorbing the smell of rain and keeping one's body substances moist and free flowing. It provides an embodied connection to country, a means of becoming green, hydrated and fertile like green land. The white ash is cooling (Hamilton 1980) and white is also symbolic of running water and rain.[15] The tobacco with its astonishingly green and heavily odiferous leaf, like the odiferous herbs discussed below, seem to embody the epitome of vitality in the land as when people say the plants are '*wanka*' with its multiple meanings of green, healthy and raw and not '*pilti*' – dried out and dead (Goddard 1996). By the time the *mingkulpa* has been processed – dried out and crumbled up – it is no longer spectacularly green but its greenness is immanent. The mimesis of the green smell of the land occurs also in the application of 'bush medicine', fragrant fat, rubbed into skin, ingested as tea or ground into a poultice.

Bush medicines

There are a number of odiferous plants that are used as skin rubs, when combined with fat, or boiled in water, as tea. Knowledge of these and their processing is the province of women. These plants Anangu also describe as 'really green' or '*wanka* – alive'. The most important and ubiquitous is the native fuchsia, occurring as small shrubby trees, which are said to green up after rain and are known as *irmangka-irmangka*, to the Pitjantjatjara.[16] These shrubs grow only in this region of central Australia and even here are only locally common (Latz 1982:171), their presence often betrayed by the sets of tyre tracks leading toward them from the road.

Irmangka-irmangka is 'bush medicine number one'. When I asked women if I might learn more about other bush medicines I was told this again and again. It is used to cure muscle ache, especially that induced by a woman's dance executed by bracing the knees. It is a decongestant said to smell like eucalyptus and like Vicks chest rub. While white (cool) ash and the green tobacco are mixed together for internal consumption to produce the flow of saliva and the taste of greenness, white store bought fat 'buta' or any fat that comes to hand, and the fuchsia leaves and stalks are cooked to make fragrant skin grease.

> 'Field notes, August 1997 in camp out bush
> No fat – so N. used Flora margarine, one and a half tubs of it in her frying pan over the fire, and some pieces of herb – really luminous parrot green – before all subsided into the hot fat. N. remarks on this as a 'lovely green' and a 'lovely smell' and strained the lot, with my slotted spoon, into an empty milk powder container.'

The resulting fragrant fat is used as a cosmetic on a daily basis particularly when a woman returns to her country after spending time in the city and has run out of supplies. Then it is rubbed into the traveller's arms and legs and she becomes like the land again, reconnected with her own place – *ngura*. This aromatic fat is used also for more serious health problems where the patient is sung over by other women. A special rolling or slapping motion called *kuluntananyi* removes blockages in the flow of blood around the body. The smell of 'bush buta' – *irmangka-irmangka* is the smell of life, the smell of the healthy land – body and facilitates easy breathing when rubbed into the neck, chest also the crown of the head both to cure sore throats and headaches. The decongesting aspect also relates to ideas about 'breath', the wind being conceived as the breath of the country.

Women stressed over and over again the good smell – *panti wiru* of the 'bush buta'. Making a gesture with their hands in front of their bodies, moving down nose, throat, chest, and lungs, women indicate the clearance of congestion. 'Bush buta' is also used during women's ceremony – *inma* to coat the exposed skin of all present. This is only done for *inma pulka*, that is, important Dreaming ceremonies, not for love magic or *watiku mukaringkulpai* (wanting or loving a man). In the context of ceremony the application of the scented fat seems to be both protection and some kind of spiritual conduit, where everyone present smells the same, can breathe easily and is recognized by the Ancestors. This additional olfactory dimension may also promote insightful emotive understanding of the ritual (cf. Andermann 1991:207). The fat also has some protective dimension perhaps against the ambiguous ancestral power evoked through the ritual. In a similar protective role to the skin it is reputed to stop mosquitoes biting.

As well as offering protection to skin, *irmangka-irmangka* can be ingested. *Irmangka-irmangka* tea made by boiling the herb in water, Anangu also call 'really green' and is similarly, but in my experience less popularly, used as a decongestant. In a parallel with wild tobacco mixed with the shop bought variety, *irmangka-irmangka* tea has a few shop-bought tea leaves added to it and cures a sore throat.

There are several other plants which women say are 'like irmangka-irmangka'. That is, they are said to have similar odours and are used for similar purposes. Aratja, another fuschia species, can also be used as an inhalant and as a tea but is far less common in the Musgrave Ranges than *irmangka-irmangka* (Cleland and Johnston 1937:212).[17] In other Western Desert societies this fuchsia performs the same role that *irmangka-irmangka* does for Anangu (Latz 1982: 173). Another green fragrant plant with healing properties that smells like the land when it rains is kalpari.[18][19] This herb seemed to have a very brief growing season and is not common in the area. The plant favours disturbed ground after fire and sets seed a month or so after rains (Latz 1982:164). Its scent is said to be like eucalypts as well as like *irmangka-irmangka*. The stiff green spikes are probably also casually connected to love magic. Kalpari can also be used to make a medicinal wash for skin rashes (Goddard 1985:140). Red river gum leaves themselves, can be pounded and cooked with fat to make 'bush buta' I was told. These huge trees are often the only visible trace of a creek from a distance lining its banks as well as sometimes growing in the creek bed itself. Their roots grow deep into the bed of the creek and are full of water even in the dry season, yielding clear potable water. The anthropologist Charles Mountford, arriving in the newly set up Mission also a sheep station at Ernabella in the Musgraves in 1940 noted the following in his fieldnotes:

'Men and women arrive complaining of kata pika [literally: 'head sick']. A cure-all lotion used around the station is a mixture of olive oil and eucalyptus. This was poured on the hands of the sufferers and in most gave instant relief. Evident (sic) that this used as body/ head rub oil and a quick way of obtaining grease. (Mountford 1940:228).

This substance, dispensed in 1940 by the Mission superintendent, was, probably unknown to him, efficacious on two counts. One was certainly its greasing factor, but the other was surely its scent.

A further insight into the equivalence of green aroma with idealized bodies is revealed in the recollections of a former Mission staff member. Gum leaves are used to represent people in young girls' tales both in a game called *milpatjunanyi*, played with a bent stick or wire that is used to beat time into the ground while narrating:

> 'They would use the rib side of the gum leaf up to designate men, and they'd use the smooth side to designate... women. They did have half castes, they had a sort of pinkish leaf that was fading... When it was losing its colour and that would be half caste. It wouldn't be a bright one, and then they had the young leaves, the little ones for children.' (Ernabella staff member Mary Bennett interviewed in 1995 Ara Iritija Archival project, record 1507).

In another example of green things being attributed a captivating odour I was told of budgerigars who arrive in numbers after rain. 'That little green bird' whose greenness is glimpsed in flashes as it flies is a sudden outstanding green like that of bush tobacco among other duller greens and has, it is said, a lovely smell when cooked, 'like chicken'.

Conclusion

My argument here has been that greenness and a particular odour are culturally constructed as inseparable materialized in wild tobacco and *irmangka-irmangka*. This is not a mere perceptual linkage but a correspondence and is complicated by its embodied nature. That is, greenness is held to correspond with a particular smell and this smell corresponds with greenness and each of these enhances the other. Using these green – odiferous substance brings about changes in the body and its receptivity to the land. I am arguing that this is as much 'synaesthesia' as the clinical cases of individuals with coloured imagery triggered by words on a page or by sounds that I delineated at the opening of this paper in that a particular smell and green-ness are considered to correspond and enhance one another. I am not however suggesting that Anangu are 'innately' synaesthesic. Rather the productive potential of connecting odour and greenness are a strategy for people to mimic the idealized states of the land when it is at its most powerful and fertile.

The Pitjantjatjara ethnography demonstrates the gap between anthropology and cognitive studies. The ethnography shows a culturally productive synaesthesia mediated by particular substances, unlike the stress on the individual in western psychological literature. Here there is a desire to find synchrony among synaesthetes – in the colours of vowels for example – but only at a neurological level to try to prove some universal correspondences across the senses. The Pitjantjatjara case shows synaesthesia as a basis for shared mimesis rooted in the bodily experience of being in the land. It may be that wild tobacco or *irmangka-irmangka* do promote visual imagery and this might be questions for future research. Undoubtedly Anangu conceive of greenness as enhanced by the right companion smell and visa versa that confirms the Zellner and Kautz experiment and a theory of synaesthesia as sensory 'mapping'. The smell of greenness can bring about an exchange of energies, the 'flow of life' is effected (McDonald 2001:21). The qualities of the consumed or absorbed are duly acquired through the mutual dependency and permeability of all forms of life.

Howes has written of olfaction as effecting not only a transition in space, as one crosses a threshold for example, but a transition from one state of being to another (1991:131). The smell of greenness is the fugitive odour released by the start of rains, the beginning of a new cycle and all it promises. Anangu use these aromatic green plants, themselves reanimated by the rain, to mediate between humans, ancestors and the landscape. The odiferous greenness is another conduit to ancestral power, and perhaps also a protection. This odour is the odour of life, cooling and clearing, enabling one to breathe more easily. The cooled white ash mimics the cooling effect on the land and the rain that will make water flow just as combining the green pungent tobacco with ash as a quid makes the saliva flow in the body.

I have attempted to show how the substances that combine odour and greenness are evoking a particularly important transitive state, collapsing into one sensory event the release of the smell of rain and the greening up of country. It is this fulcrum with its potentiality that is contained in green odiferous substances. Possibly the repetitious use of such substances that mimic this transitive moment ensures that the moment of potentiality will reappear in the land to which people are symbiotically connected. People themselves are ideally like the land when it is in this state and connected to the Ancestral power that makes the rains. The fragrant green moment is the one from which all subsequent transformations of the land's surface unfold. The particular combination of odour and greenness therefore contains a dynamism and movement that is part of Anangu concepts about the vivification of country and bodies and the flow of substances in and between both. The greenness – odour synaesthetic correspondence underpins fundamental concepts about the creation of time and the nature of personhood.

Returning to psychology, current theories of synaesthesia are not mutually exclusive (Harrison and Baron-Cohen 1997). If we take the widest theoretical definitions of synaesthesia in psychology, this ethnography shows perhaps mapping or vestigial synaesthesia or synaesthesia induced by consuming various substances. But whereas synaesthesic experiences in the psychological studies are a-social and spontaneous – 'unlearnt' – and related only to individual disembodied brains, in the Western Desert the experience is very much embodied and socially transmitted. Furthermore, the pairing of odour and vision is unusual in the cognitive samples. We are left then with more questions than answers. Even 'innate' synaesthesia must surely be socially influenced and the question of the role of substances that apparently induce synaesthesic imagery remains unexplored in the cognitive literature as a social and cultural phenomenon. Synaesthesia may indeed be just a different way of thinking.

Notes

* The Economic and Social Research Council (ESRC) supported the doctoral research from which this paper is drawn and a postdoctoral research fellowship from 2002-2003 award number T026271266. I would also like to acknowledge Regina Bendix and Don Brenneis for their helpful comments on an earlier version of this essay.

1. A series of studies by Baron-Cohen and associates produced a prevalence of one in 2000 people with innate synaesthesia and this figure is now widely quoted. This result was based on a study of synaesthetes who responded to an advertisement placed in a local newspaper in Cambridge by the researchers. They also found a ratio of six to one female to male synaesthetes (Baron-Cohen et al. 1993, 1996). In the Unites States Cytowic has suggested that one in 25,000 are synaesthesia with a ratio of two and a half to one female to male (Cytowic 1997:33).
2. See a recent example in Gray 2004.
3. For example Myers 1991 and 1988.
4. Cf. Conklin 1955 on the Hanoonoo and Baines 1985 on the Ancient Egyptians.
5. Billy Wara was making spear throwers like this to sell in 1997. I am unclear as to whether spear throwers like these were used in the past or whether this was a creative expression of the desirability of green-ness.
6. The doctoral research from which this paper is taken took place in the Anilalya Homelands near Ernabella, South Australia on the Anangu Pitjantjatjara Lands, from March 1997 to September 1998. Since I am female and In Western Desert societies the separation of the genders remains a feature of everyday and ritual life, I worked mostly with women and children.
7. Gertrude Stotz, personal communication 1998.
8. See for example Layton 1989 and Young 2001b for a discussion of water sources in the region.
9. Compare for example McDonald 2001.
10. See Maggie Brady 1992:86-89.
11. *Nicotiana excelsior.*
12. Gardens are much admired although infrequently kept alive for more than a few months by Anangu partly because people move about so much and irrigation is therefore haphazard. The garden that we had outside the hut where we lived on a homeland was frequently commented upon by visitors and admired from cars on the road nearby, for its greenness. This garden, like others made by Anangu and by white people, is still remembered and pointed out although it is, now some years later, abandoned.
13. *Nicotiana Gossei*. Marijuana, which is now widely available on the Anangu Pitjanjatjara Lands, is also known as another mingkulpa/ '*mingkulpa kutjupa*'. This 'other *mingkulpa*' though is said to make Anangu sad and introspective, by implication careless of others, and is blamed often for the apathy and suicide of young people. There have been increasing numbers of such deaths in recent years.
14. Tindale relates a similar incident in 1957 on the western border of South Australia between *Pitjantjatjara* men and neighbouring 'Nakako tribe' who took the former's *mingkulpa* (1974:97).
15. Another relevant example of this is the guano of a tiny bird, the zebra finch – *nyii nyii*, whose presence indicates a near by water source, was used in the past as a cure for head aches because its white droppings contained a cooling effect (Goddard 1996).
16. *Eremophila alternifolia.*
17. *Eromopholia freelingii.*
18. *Dysphania kalpari.*

References

Ackerman, K. with J. Stanton
    1994 *Riji and Jakoli: Kimberley Pearl Shell in Aboriginal Australia.* Northern Territory Museum of Arts and Sciences Monograph series 4. Darwin: Northern Territory.

Andermann, L.
    1991 Sense among the Ndembu. In: D. Howes (Ed.), *The Varieties of Sensory Experience. A Source Book in the Anthropology of the* Senses. Toronto: University of Toronto Press. Pp. 203-209.

Baron-Cohen, S., M. Wyke and C. Binnie
    1987 Hearing Words and Seeing Colours: An Experimental Investigation of Syaesthesia. *Perception* 16:761-767.

Baron-Cohen, S., J. Harrison, L. Goldstein and M. Wyke
    1993 Colored Speech Perception: Is Synaesthesia What Happens When Modularity Breaks Down? *Perception* 22:419-426.

Baron-Cohen, S., et al.
    1996 Synaesthesia: Prevalence and Familiality. *Perception* 25:1073-9.

Baron-Cohen, S. and J. Harrison
    1997 *Synaesthesia: Classic and Contemporary Readings.* Oxford: Blackwells.

Baines, J.R.
    1985 Color Terminology and Color Classification: Ancient Egyptian Color Terminology and Polychromy. *American Anthropology* 87(2):282-97.

Berndt, R. M. and T. Harvey-Johnston
    1942 Death, Burial, and Associated Ritual at Ooldea, South Australia. *Oceania* XII(3):190-213.

Brady, M.
    1992 *Heavy Metal. The Social Meaning of Petrol Sniffing in Australia.* Canberra: Aboriginal Studies Press.

Classen, C.
    1990 Sweet Colors, Fragrant Songs; Sensory Models of the Andes and the Amazon. *American Ethnologist* 17(4):722-35.
    1993 *Worlds of Sense. Exploring the Senses in History and Across Cultures.* London and New York: Routledge.

Cleland, J.B. and T. Harvey-Johnston
    1937 Notes on Native Names and Uses of Plants in the Musgrave Ranges Region. *Oceania* 8(2):208-342.

Conklin, H.C.
    1955 Hanunoo Color Categories. *South Western Journal of Anthropology* 11:339-344.

Cytowic. R
    1989 *Synaesthesia; A Union of the Senses.* New York: Springer Verlag.

Duguid, C.
    1972 *The Doctor and the Aborigines.* Adelaide: Rigby.

Dussart, F.
    2000 *The Politics of Ritual in an Aboriginal Settlement: Kinship, Gender and the Currency of Knowledge.* Washington and London: Smithsonian Press.

Ellis, C. J., A. M. Ellis; M. Tur and A. McCardell
    1978 Classification of Sounds in Pitjantjatjara Speaking Areas. In: L. Hiatt (Ed.) *Australian Aboriginal Concepts.* Canberra: Australian Institute of Aboriginal studies.

Gell, A.
   1977   Magic, Perfume Dream. In: I.M. Lewis (Ed.), *Symbols and Sentiment: Cross Cultural Studies in Symbolism*. London: Academic.

Goddard, C.
   1985   *Punu: Yankunytjatjara Plant Use*. Alice Springs: IAD Press.
   1996   *Pitjantjatjara/Yankunyjatjara to English Dictionary*. Revised second edition. Alice Springs: IAD Press.

Gray, J.A.
   2004   *Consciousness: Creeping up on the Hard Problem*. Oxford and New York: Oxford University Press.

Hallpike, C.R.
   1979   *The Foundations of Primitive Thought*. Oxford: Oxford University Press.

Hamilton, A.
   1980   Timeless Transformations; Women, Men and History in the Australian Western Desert. Unpublished Ph.D. Dissertation, University of Sydney.

Harrison, J.
   2001   *Synaesthesia: The strangest Thing*. Oxford: Oxford University Press.

Harrison, J. and S. Baron-Cohen
   1997   *A Review of Psychological Theories in Synaesthesia: Classic and Contemporary Readings*. Oxford: Blackwells.

Howes, D.
   1988   On The Odor of the Soul; Spatial Representation and Olfactory Classification in Eastern Indonesia and Western Melanesia. *Bijdragen Tot de Taal, Land- en Volkenkunde* 144:84-133.
   1991   Olfaction and Transition. In: D. Howes (Ed.), *The Varieties of Sensory Experience; A Source Book in the Anthropology of the Senses*. Toronto: University of Toronto Press. Pp. 128-147.

Latz, P.
   1982   *Bush Fires and Bush Tucker. Aboriginal Plant Use in Central Australia*. Alice Springs: IAD Press.

Layton, R.
   1989   *Uluru. An Aboriginal History of Ayers Rock*. Canberra: Aboriginal Studies Press.

Luria, A.
   1968   *The Mind of a Mnemonist*. New York: Basic Books.

Marks, L.E.
   1978   *The Unity of the Senses. Interrelations among the Modalities*, London: Academic Press.
   1990   *Synaesthesia: Perception and Metaphor. Aesthetic Illusion*. Berlin: Gruyter.

Maurer, D.
   1997   Neonatal Syaesthesia: Implications for the Processing of Speech and Faces. In: S. Baron-Cohen and J. Harrison (Eds.), *Synaesthesia: Classic and Contemporary Readings*. Oxford: Blackwells.

McDonald, H.
   2001   *Blood Bones and Spirit. Aboriginal Christianity in an East Kimberley Town*. Victoria: Melbourne University Press.

Mountford, C.P.
   1940   Unpublished Journal of an Expedition to the North West of South Australia, Vol I and II. State Library of South Australia.

Myers, F.
   1988   The Logic and Meaning of Aanger among Pintupi Aborigines. *Man* 23:589-610.
   1991   *Pintupi Country Pintupi Self. Sentiment place and politics among Western Desert Aborigines.* Berkely: University of California Press.

Odin, S.
   1982   Blossom Scents Take up the Ringing. Synaesthesia in Japanese and Western Aesthetics. *Soundings* 69:256-81.

Ramachandran, V.
   2004   The Emerging Mind. *BBC Reith Lectures.* London: Profile Books.

Synott, A.
   1991   Puzzling over the Senses: From Plato to Marx. In: D. Howes (Ed.), *The Varieties of Senosry Experience. A Spurce book in the Anthropology of the Senses.* London/Buffalo/Toronto: University of Toronto. Pp. 71-76. Tindale, N.
   1972   The 'Pitjandjara'. In: M.G Bicchieri (Ed.), *Hunters and Gatherers Today.* New York: Holt, Reinhart and Winston. Pp. 217-68.

Warner, W.L.
   1937   *A Black Civilisation.* New York: Harper and Row.
   2003   *Piercing the Ground.* Freemantle: W.A. Freemantle Arts Centre Press.

Wilkins, D. and D. Evans
   1998   The Knowing Ear: An Australian Test of Claims about the Semantic Structure of Sensory Verbs and Their Extension into the Domain of Cognition. *Arbeitspapier* 32. Institute of Linguistics, University of Köln.

Young, D.
   2001a   The Life and Death of Cars: Private Vehicles on the Pitjantjatjara Lands, South Australia. In: D. Miller (Ed.), *Car Cultures.* Oxford and New York: Berg. Pp. 36-57.
   2001b   The Colors of Things. Memory Materiality and an Anthropology of the Senses in the North West of South Australia. Unpublished Ph.D. Dissertation, University College London.
   2004   Water as Country in the Western Desert, unpublished paper, ASA Durham.
   2005   The Colors of Things. In: P. Spyer et al. (Eds.), *A Guide to Material Culture.* Oxford: Sage.

Zellner, D. and M.A. Kautz
   1990   Color affects perceived odor intensity. *Journal of Experimental Psychology: Human Perception and Performance* 16(2):391-397.

Acute Pain Infliction as Therapy*

Elisabeth Hsu, University of Oxford

ABSTRACT This essay begins with the observation that acute pain infliction is central to the therapeutic process in Chinese acupuncture. The common biomedical explanation for this is 'counter-irritation', yet this essay suggests that an acute pain event can cause a bodily felt, immediate social connectedness between patient and healer, which might be therapeutic. Since acute pain can effectively be communicated to others by non-verbal means, it has the capacity to break down habitual boundaries between persons, decentre both the person in pain and those in his or her close vicinity and enable instantaneous trans-individual communication. The collective presence of communally felt pain makes possible an embodied experience of sociality. Based on an anthropological definition of acute versus chronic pain, the essay suggests that life cycle events typically structure intrinsically (or potentially) painful situations into acute pain events. Concluding, this essay suggests that in medicalised societies the decline of acute pain events in life cycle rituals has led to the silent rise of chronic pain syndromes.

An ethnographic account of *de qi* in acupuncture treatment

Pain infliction is central to the therapeutic process in acupuncture. Such treatment usually involves needling between four and ten acupuncture points (or loci) that are located at clearly defined positions on the body surface. In medical practice, the acupuncturist who has memorized their positions finds their precise location by tapping in their vicinity on to the patient's skin; points are often in grooves or by the side of a protuberant bone structure. Then, after having determined the precise place, he or she presses on to the skin with one hand, and with a skilful movement, which should avoid causing pain, inserts the needle with the other. Nowadays, needles are usually made of steel; although they are fine, they are not easily bent. Once inserted, they should not be left sticking in the skin, but doctors should work on them, particularly if a condition is treated that involves supplementing (*bu*) or discharging (*xie*) *qi*.[1] The acupuncturist may push or pull the needles at different velocities (*xuji buxiefa*), shift and wave them (*yiyao buxiefa*), or twirl and rotate them (*nianzhuan buxiefa*), apart from engaging in a wide range of other techniques (Lu et al. 1987).

When the doctor inserts the needle and works on it, there is a moment of slight tension, stillness, and concentration between doctor and patient, which finally is dissolved by the patient exclaiming: 'Dele, dele – I got it [the *qi*]'. This is the moment of acute pain infliction: often synchronically the patient shivers slightly or catches a breath of air and the doctor sighs with relief or sometimes grunts with satisfaction (Hsu 1993/94). For the needling to be effective, I was told, the patient has to feel pain. The pain is of a particular kind, it should not hurt in the sense of *tong* (to hurt). Rather, the pain experiences that needling is supposed to evoke are *suan*, which means 'sour' or 'sore', or *ma*, which refers to a prickly and tingling feeling, or *zhang*, which means 'to swell' and 'to expand', and may refer to a feeling of warmth and heat expanding from the needled point. This is taken as a sign that 'one has got *qi*' (*de qi*). Doctors are also meant to feel in their finger tips whether or not one gets *qi*, and some explained, in accordance with accounts from the medical archive (cited in for example Qiu and Zhang 1985:156), that it felt like a fish that snaps the hook of an angler.

I carried out ethnographic fieldwork in Kunming, the capital of Yunnan province, in the People's Republic of China, in 1988-89, as a student of acupuncture at the Yunnan Traditional Chinese Medicine College, where I learnt Chinese medicine in Chinese with Chinese classmates. The first six months I spent in the class room learning the basics of Chinese medical theory (Hsu 1999: chapter 6), but from the second semester onwards, I spent three mornings a week on the acupuncture ward. I engaged in what I later called 'participant experience' and set out to gain competence in the esoteric knowledge and practice I planned to write about as an anthropologist. I believed that by acquiring the embodied skill myself I would gain a fuller understanding of it (Hsu forthcoming).

The method of 'participant experience' lent itself well to the study of touch that evokes pain, for not only was I learning the refined methods of inflicting pain on others with fine needles, I also experienced this sort of pain infliction on myself. Acupuncture represents a highly sophisticated technique, which works our largest sensory organ, the skin, for healing purposes by, as argued in this essay, generating an enhanced feeling of sociality. It is always difficult to communicate one's sensory experiences (as will be discussed below), and the fieldwork method of 'participant experience', which involved touching and being touched, made possible an ethnography that may escape the participant observer. Since acupuncture attends to the sensory vastness of the skin, an ethnographer's insights are in the course of learning this technique much enhanced by him- or herself engaging in the processes of needling and being needled.

When I was needled the first time (during an undergraduate fieldwork period in Chengdu in March 1986), I realised that the needle did not only inflict a locally sensed pain but also affected my breathing. I had attended the acupuncture clinic despite a cold and a blocked nose, and was constantly sniffing. My teacher, slightly irritated by this, suggested treating me with acupuncture. I had no idea that acupuncture was effective for treating colds, but why not give it a try? He sat me on a stool, had me lower my head, pushed my hair from my nape, and skilfully inserted two needles into the two loci called *fengchi*. This instantly took my breath and I gasped for air. The pain was excruciating, and I asked my teacher to take out the needles. He explained that treatment consisted of bearing them for twenty minutes, and assured me the pain would eventually diminish. By then I had noticed that I had started to breathe deeply. At first, I thought this was a body reflex to reduce the pain. However, after some minutes, which seemed to me an eternity, it was impossible to tolerate the pain any further and I insisted on having the needles removed. My nose was indeed cleared, albeit only for a short while, an hour or so.

Despite this rather dramatic experience, I sometimes took acupuncture treatment in later years. It was never as drastic as the first time. When needled, it felt more like a tingling or prickling, which could be quite pleasant, and, sometimes, particularly in Europe, I barely could feel the needles. Nevertheless, I variously observed myself changing rhythm and depth of breathing. Incidentally, Chinese acupuncturists say that *de qi* affects *qi* (which has connotations of 'breath'), and its movements.

The concept *de qi* (to get *qi*) explains differences in therapeutic effectiveness after delivery of the same treatment. When two doctors needle exactly the same acupuncture loci but one is effective, and the other not, the technique of latter's hand (*shoufa*) is to blame. A good *shoufa* brings about the arrival of *qi*. In contemporary acupuncture, *qi* is thought to flow in channels (*jingluo*) and one works on the needle to effect an arrival of *qi*. Once this is achieved, one can regulate the flow of *qi*.

While the acupuncturist makes 'getting *qi*' responsible for efficacious treatment, the anthropologist puzzles over the social significance of this form of acute pain infliction during the therapeutic process. Incidentally, the same idiom, *de qi*, or rather, a closely related expression, *qi zhi* (*qi* has arrived) is found in self-cultivation and medical manuscript texts that are two thousand years old. Vivienne Lo renders a passage in a text on the sexual arts called 'Uniting of Yin and Yang' (*He yin yang*) as follows:

> Stab upwards but do not penetrate in order to stimulate *qi*, when the *qi* arrives (*qi zhi*), penetrate deeply and thrust upward in order to distribute the heat. Now once again withdraw so as not to cause its *qi* to dissipate and for her to become exhausted (2001:43).

Evidently, *qi zhi* refers in this text to the climax of sexual union, but the same expression was used in the context of acupuncture treatment already in antiquity (Ren 1986:256). Accordingly, *qi zhi* and *de qi* must refer to the climax of needling in acupuncture treatment. This climax, one would assume, is in one context marked by extreme pleasure (although the above text on the sexual arts does not explicitly state this), while the words *suan*, *ma*, *zhang* are generally used to express slightly painful experiences. One may wonder why the same idiom *qi zhi / de qi* denotes in one context extreme pleasure and in the other acute pain, and is reminded of how sadomasochists collapse the distinction between the two:

> In my experience, practitioners consistently report that S/M is not about pain, but pleasure. The appeal, they say, is that it collapses the distinction between the two: both in the end are 'sensation' and there is no such thing as good or bad sensation (Rosenblatt 1997:312).

It seems to me that the idiom *qi zhi* or *de qi* refers to what S/M practitioners call a 'sensation', which implies neither pain nor pleasure. The idiom seems to designate a moment of climaxing not only in sexual union but also in the therapeutic moment of synchronous action. In both cases, two persons are involved and after climaxing in pleasure or pain, there follows relaxation, or a catching of breath.

Another colleague, Gry Sagli, who works on Chinese medicine and its reception in Norway, quite independently of other researchers' interest in *qi zhi* and *de qi*, was also intrigued by the concept and extensively discussed it in her PhD thesis (Sagli 2003:215-218). She studied the reception of Chinese medical concepts among Norwegian practitioners, and their patients, and how in the course of cultural transmission these concepts and corresponding practices are transformed. She pointed out a wide spectrum of different ways of relating to Chinese medical concepts, which ranged from the one extreme of denying them any reality to the other of their unquestioned acceptance. The channels (*jingluo*), for instance, are entities of Chinese medical theory for which no bio-physiological explanation has been found. *Qi* and *xue* (blood) are supposed to flow through these channels, and most acupuncture loci are found along them. While doing fieldwork in China, I immersed myself so much into my studies that I sometimes felt much the same as my colleagues, who were completely convinced of their reality. It was only a matter of time, we agreed, before biomedical research would prove their existence. Needless to say, once I returned to Britain, my belief in the reality of these channels quickly dissipated. It is therefore not surprising that many Norwegians have the same critical attitude to the channels as I experienced for myself among the people in Britain. In a European setting, what needs to be explained is why people start believing in the reality of the channels.

Sagli made the interesting observation that some of the people she worked with would sense a pulling along the channels, once they were needled, and that those who had this 'sensation' were more inclined to believe in the reality of these channels. This is plausible. Yet Sagli also found that patients who experienced *de qi* readily accepted the reality of the channels. This surprised her. After all, *de qi* was not felt along a channel but only in a particular point. How is it possible that acute pain infliction can affect one's perception and cognition? Why should such acute pain experience facilitate acceptance of new concepts? Is it that pain is 'real', and the reality of pain is transposed onto the concepts that predicted the experience of this reality? Or, is it that this sort of pain infliction opens up the person to all kinds of new ideas?

A note of caution is necessary in this context: acupuncture treatment (*zhenjiu*) that involves *de qi* is not to be confused with acupuncture analgesia (*zhenjiu mazui*), which is a modern invention that became known and was instantly widely implemented during the Great Leap Forward in the late 1950s (Zhang 1989). The modern invention of acupuncture analgesia was used for pain suppression during minor surgical interventions, as for instance thyroidectomy. Acupuncture analgesia surgery was performed in operation theatres that an audience of often foreign visitors observed, from a bird-eye's view, standing in a gallery behind glass. This audience of foreigners was meant to be persuaded that not merely acupuncture analgesia, but any Chinese medical treatment was effective.

The confusion between the two rationales of therapy was perhaps intentional: it is an irony of history that a 'modern' invention, acupuncture analgesia, was used for proving the usefulness of an ancient medical practice, 'traditional' Chinese medicine and 'traditional' acupuncture (Hsu 1995, 1996). Acupuncture analgesia, although barely practised in China anymore (fieldwork 1988-89), is nowadays respected by Western biomedical professionals as being effective in about thirty per cent of pain management cases. Certain endorphins are released by needle insertion and this relieves pain and/or entirely suppresses it (for example Pomeranz 1996).

The pain researchers Ronald Melzack and Patrick Wall (1996:236-40), who also discuss 'traditional' medical techniques such as cupping, cauterisation and acupuncture, suggest that these techniques treat pain by means of pain infliction, so-called 'counter-irritation'. The concept 'counter-irritation' may partly explain therapeutic success, but it cannot possibly explain it entirely. Acupuncture, for instance, is not only used for managing pain but also for treating such disparate disorders as common colds, fevers, coughs, digestive problems, irregular menses, oedema and other swellings, and many more. In those cases, one cannot take recourse to the idea of 'counter-irritation'. Rather, as argued below, acute pain inflictions may be effective in that they generate physical, emotional and cognitive dispositions in the patient which have the potential to enhance, or even effect, healing.

Acute pain infliction as therapy

The question that arises here is: how can acute pain infliction be therapeutic? Above, the concept of *de qi* and the therapeutic centrality of acute pain infliction for Chinese acupuncture treatment was discussed. In what follows, two further ethnographic examples are given that mention pain infliction during therapy; one is from New Guinea, the other from Namibia. A third observation from Nepal suggests that acute pain infliction causes so-called 'presence' which is thought to be therapeutic.

In his most recent book *A Failure of Treatment*, Gilbert Lewis (1999) describes how among the Gnau of New Guinea a capable and well-respected man, Dauwaras, suddenly lost control over his knees and fell. After he rose, he fell again and injured himself. What appeared to be a seemingly harmless stumbling was in fact a terminal disease. Among the Gnau, a man who considers himself seriously ill will retreat into the darkness of his hut, cover himself with dirt and impose a long list of food taboos on to himself for avoiding the attention of the spirits he thinks could harm him. This is what Dauwaras eventually did. His kin and neighbours suspected he had been hit by the spirit Malyi, and consequently performed the great ritual of Malyi in many rites, which were held at intervals throughout weeks if not months. Yet the ritual could not restore Dauwaras' health, and in the end he died.

It is impossible to communicate Lewis' moving account of Dauwaras' illness here, and I will draw attention only to a minor detail which concerns the initial treatment of Dauwaras' knee. This is to rub nettles on to the knee. Dauwaras' knee is repeatedly treated with nettle massage. Why nettle massage? From a biomedical viewpoint one could say that this massage enlivens blood circulation or one could speak of a case of pain management through 'counter-irritation', but what about the social aspects of this practice? Noteworthy in this context is the cross-cultural similarity between the stinging of the nettles in the Gnau context and the tingling of the needles in the Chinese one, processes that both are considered to instigate recovery and can be regarded as some form of acute pain infliction.

Among the !Kung in the Kalahari desert of Namibia it is not primarily the sick person but the person who acts as healer who experiences acute pain during a healing session, and the sessions climax in a moment where pain is inflicted on everyone present. These healing sessions are generally held at night. The sick person lies beside the fire around which the community gathers. People sing and sing, rhythmically swinging and clapping their hands, while one, two, several among them are overcome by *num*, which as Richard Katz (1982:94) explains, is the primary force of their universe.

Those overcome by *num* are in a state of *kia*. One could speak of 'trance', although Katz prefers not to use the term because he considers it too vague; it refers to very different 'states of altered consciousness', such as spirit possession, hypnosis, meditative states, and many more. Rather than using terms like 'trance', or even worse, implicitly normative notions like 'altered states of consciousness', he advocates detailed description of how these states are experienced. This is how a !Kung healer describes *kia*: 'When I pick up *num*, it explodes and throws me up in the air, I enter heaven and then fall down. I open up; I burst open, like a ripe pod' (Katz 1982:44).

In this process of opening up, which notably invokes a botanical metaphor, fear and acute pain can sometimes arise. A healer comments on his first experience of *num*: 'I was very surprised when *num* came to me. It made me cry out in pain' (ibid.:97). The pain is caused by invisible arrows, which are felt in the *gebesi*, the centre of the stomach: 'In *kia*, around your neck and around your belly you feel tiny needles and thorns which prick you. Then your front spine and your back spine are pricked with these thorns. Your *gebesi* tightens into a balled fist. Your breathing stops (ibid.:46).'

In this state of *kia* it is important to pull – to pull and pull – the illness out of the sick person, and to negotiate with the spirits by shouting loudly into the air. It is interesting to note that pain affects one's perceptual and cognitive faculties and alters them; or, as some put it, even enhances them. One becomes capable of 'seeing': 'As a healer in *kia*, you see everybody. You see that the insides of well people are fine. You see the insides of the one the spirits are trying to kill, and you go there. Then you see the spirits and drive them away' (ibid.:106). One notices again that pain affects the cognitive faculties. It is a pain that healers experience in a state of exaltation. However, in the moment when the illness is pulled out of the sick person's body, acute pain is inflicted on him or her and everyone else through ear-piercing cries and shrieks:

> The pain involved in the boiling of the healers' *num*, in the putting of the *num* in the one being healed, in the drawing of the other's sickness into their own body, and in the violent shaking of that sickness out from their body is acknowledged by the healers by crying, wailing, moaning, and shrieking. They punctuate and accent their healing with these sometimes ear-shattering sounds. As the breath comes with more difficulty, until they are rasping and gasping, the healers howl the characteristic *kowhedili* shriek, which sounds something like 'Xaiiiiii! Kow-ha-di-di-di-di!', and usually accompanies the pulling out of the sickness (ibid.:108).

The *kowhedili* shriek is ear-splitting both for the healers and the patient; and they experience it simultaneously. We observe again that acute pain infliction forms an integral part of the treatment, and to a certain extent the climax of the treatment. The question I ask is: how can such pain infliction be therapeutic? What do the disparate experiences of *de qi* in Chinese acupuncture, a nettle massage among the Gnau, and the *kowhedili* shriek in !Kung healing séances have in common?

Acute pain and presence

The article called 'Presence' gives a hint, although its author, Robert Desjarlais (1996), does not speak of acute pain in his description of a shamanic ritual and its effects on a woman who suffers from soul loss. Desjarlais explores which aspects of the shamanic ritual make it into a treatment that is effective. He points to odours, colours, drum and gong, which are supposed to bring back the soul of the woman, and thereby lift her out of her apathetic state. Other anthropologists may have analysed the words the shaman sang, but Desjarlais is primarily interested in the patient's 'embodied experience'. The aesthetics of the ritual attracts the attentiveness of the woman, which, as Desjarlais puts it, is a 'sensory attentiveness':

> For healing to be effective, [the shaman] Meme must alter the sensory grounds of a spiritless body. How does he do so? Our findings suggest that a less cerebral model than those noted above can account for Yolmo spirit-callings: Meme tries to change how a person feels by altering the sensory stimuli around that person. His cacophony of music, taste, sight, touch, and wild, tactile images activates the senses and the imagination. This activation can 'wake up' a person, prompt new sensibilities, and so reform the cognitive and perceptual faculties that, in large part, make up a person (1996:160).

Thomas Csordas (1993), who also takes a phenomenological approach to healing, comes to a similar result in his study of spiritual healing and alternative medicine. In his terms, the basis of alternative medicine's efficacy can be found in so-called 'somatic modes of attention'. Alternative medicine is often directed at eliciting such embodied attentiveness, an attentiveness that involves the person as whole, and does not appeal to the will and the intellect only.

Desjarlais and Csordas provide an answer for explaining the above observations of acute pain infliction during therapy: acute pain evokes 'presence' and alerts one's 'sensory attentiveness'. Elaine Scarry's often cited phrase comes to mind: 'The most crucial fact about pain is its presentness' (Scarry 1985:9).

When Scarry speaks of 'presentness', she refers to the presence of pain in the individual who experiences it. This essay, however, stresses that acute pain causes a sense of presence not only in the one in pain but also in those in his or her immediate vicinity. Scarry, who studied the pain of torture victims, and medical anthropologists, who worked with chronic pain patients, have emphasized that pain is hard to put into words and that chronic pain alienates the person from the environment, to the effect that 'After a While No One Believes You' (Jackson 1992). The point made in this last mentioned essay is that this does not apply to acute pain. In contrast to chronic pain, acute pain is easily, rapidly, and extremely efficiently communicated from one to the other. No words are needed.

In the therapeutic process, the presence caused by acute pain infliction can be understood as an alertness that opens up the patient to a potentially positive input from the social environment, and possibly, it is this directly felt social connectedness that is therapeutic. This becomes particularly obvious as one widens the focus of analysis, for not only the patient but also everyone else in close vicinity is instantly affected by this pain event, in particular the therapist. A shriek of shock, one's contraction of the face, or a sudden bodily collapse have an instant effect on whoever is nearby. Friend or foe will instantly turn to the person in pain, with great attentiveness.

In the moment of an acute pain event it is as though the boundaries between the I and the you are broken down, for both you and I are completely overwhelmed by the pain event. The small finger is caught in the door: suddenly it is the small finger that is in the centre of the world, both for the one in pain as well as for those in his or her immediate vicinity. Acute pain is thus a state of being where the habitual centre of the ego is shaken and displaced – into the small finger, for instance – it decentres and thereby opens up the person beyond the habitual boundaries and limitations (Hsu 1993/94:70-1). Acute pain is acute for both the person in pain and those surrounding him or her, and it thus generates synchronicity, a situation in which all participants involved are acutely aware of only one single event and turn their full attention to it.

Acute pain and the embodied experience of sociality

The argument put forth here is that acute pain infliction can represent a crucial phase in the therapeutic process, not least because an individual's sensory experience of acute pain is eminently social. This argument builds on two premises. The first is that acute pain can be differentiated from chronic pain (see below); the second that acute pain experiences are not only essential for the biological survival of the individual, but also for building up and reinforcing social cohesion between individuals. Although the anthropological literature has not emphasized the latter much, pain is intrinsic to life cycle events, and the latter are known to enhance social bonding within a group. The acute pain event can thus be viewed as a trigger for an embodied experience of sociality and may for this reason be central both to rites of passage and the above therapeutic practices.

The common distinction between acute and chronic pain is a biomedical one (Sternbach 1984), yet it is also an experiential one (see below). From a biologist's viewpoint, acute pain has the function of promoting survival, this in stark contrast to chronic pain which has no biological function at all. Acute pain is usually thought of as a 'warning signal' of impending tissue damage though it also signals a need-state for rest and reconvalescence of already damaged tissue; 'pain as warning signal' and 'pain for stillness' both enhance survival. People with congenital insensitivity to pain therefore generally have a considerably shortened life expectancy (Melzack and Wall 1996:3-7).

An anthropologist, however, is guided by socially structured temporalities and will differentiate acute from chronic pain accordingly (for a detailed anthropological definition of acute versus chronic pain, see below). Acute pain not only has a biological survival function for the individual, but, as argued here, it also has an eminently social potential for enhancing a sense of togetherness between individuals and for making real social relatedness. In other words, the sensory experience of acute pain is essential to community building. It is the cross-culturally observed disposition of human beings to respond instantly to an acute pain event that makes possible the intense experience of commonality, even if only for a brief moment.

It may not be insignificant that acute pain is a concomitant aspect of several life cycle events, birth and death most prominently. In those cases, the labour pain of the mother giving birth and the grief of those who are bereft are primarily in our awareness, although the newborn child, who cries upon entry into the world, and the dying person anticipating death may also experience pain. The life cycle event of marriage is usually marked by strong emotions of love and great joy, even though it often involves pain of separation, for instance, of the bride leaving her family; and in Muslim contexts, the defloration rite can be very painful for the bride and sometimes apparently also the groom. Likewise, the life cycle event of becoming adult in many societies is marked by joy, once the initiates return from seclusion into the village. Yet this process of becoming adult may also consist of a period of intentional pain infliction on the initiates.

Pierre Clastres (1973) asked why the initiation rites he studied were marked by enormous pain infliction, and in an essay – that comes close to poetics – he links the society's laws to the script, the script to the body, the body to torture, torture to memory, and memory to the laws of society. The article suggests that the laws of society are by means of pain inscribed in the individual's body.

Put more prosaically, one wonders whether Clastres implied that pain infliction enhances the learning process and facilitates cognitive acceptance of new ideas. The proverb 'once bitten, twice shy', as many others, would suggest that pain is didactic. Indeed, this seems an idea deeply entrenched in Judaeo-Christian thought, and has been subject to much literary exploration in philosophy and theology (for example Wriedt 1988).[2] The etymology of the word pain is poena, punishment. Is it god's punishment that teaches one how to alter one's ways of life? Job comes to mind... it is a Judaeo-Christian belief that god is known only through the experience of suffering, be it the suffering he inflicts on Job (and humankind) or his own suffering at the cross. Accordingly, it may be no more than a culture-specific myth that suffering purifies, is spiritually enlightening, and deepens a person. Proverbs suggesting that pain is didactic may reflect a Judaeo-Christian conviction rather than a social or biological fact.

Correlations between pain and learning are not as straightforward as the above proverbs would suggest. Experiments in ethology have shown that doves learn more quickly if, rather than being punished when failing a task (for example by being hit with painful electro-shocks), their behaviour is positively reinforced when they fulfil the required task successfully (for example by being given extra grains). It is thus uncertain whether punishment is always didactic and whether pain infliction actually enhances learning. Clastres' 'inscription of the laws of society on individual bodies' is therefore best considered a learning process achieved other than through the pain of punishment.

In this context, Seremetakis' research comes to mind. Although she speaks of funerals, her observation with regard to collectively felt grief may help explain why pain is inflicted on the groups of young men and women who undergo initiation rites. She states: 'It [pain] is a concept that synthesizes bodily and psychic experience; despite its profound individual ramifications, pain, particularly in Greek society, mobilizes trans-individual systems of communication, meaning, and value (Seremetakis 1998:151).'

In other words, the group experience of individually felt acute pain triggers the group experience as one body, experienced as such emotionally and physically. Boundaries between individuals break down, and a state of trans-individual fluidity is experienced. This state may well affect an individual's cognitive and affective faculties, an experience that due to its intensity may have long-lasting transformative effects.

Clastres and Seremetakis both emphasize the trans-individual fluidity between individuals who themselves are in pain. This essay goes a step further based on the observation that human beings generally are affected by another person's acute pain, even if involuntarily (some may avoid the person in pain for this very reason). The essay points out that the pain event captivates the attentiveness of both the one experiencing pain and the other who, as human being, is instantaneously affected by another's acute pain. One could speak of 'instinctive' or 'innate' predispositions to do so, but such ill-defined concepts would lead into a minefield of controversy. The fieldwork methods of the social anthropologist merely allow the observation that an acute pain event usually tends to be at the centre of the attention of all persons present.

To summarise, instead of taking recourse to the biomedical concept of 'counter-irritation' for explaining why acute pain infliction can be therapeutic, this essay likens the pain experience evoked by certain treatment methods to the trans-individual experience of acute pain in life cycle events. Rather than viewing Chinese acupuncture treatment (or Gnau nettle massage) as an example that involves an individual's pain event only, the essay suggests that the distinctive pain event caused by needling (and also nettle massaging) affects at least two persons, as does the *kowhedili* shriek in the !Kung healing dance. Accordingly, these treatment events should be viewed as social events that involve, much like life cycle events, a trans-individual or communal experience of presence, alertness, synchronicity.

To say that pain in life cycle events is 'communally' experienced need not mean that everyone present was affected equally by pain. Pain in a life cycle event may affect participants to different degrees in different ways (just as it does in a healing séance). Sometimes, one person may feel and express pain more intensely than everyone else. During fieldwork in Kunming, for instance, at a funeral held by the parents who had lost their only child, the silence of grief in the crowd was beginning to become unbearable when the best friend of the bereaved father, a much respected adult man in his late forties, started to wail in a deep heart-rendering voice. This one individual's pain expressed and shaped the pain event for everyone present.

Certainly life cycle events are often also accompanied by strong emotions, while sessions at the acupuncturist's may not be as emotionally laden. Yet, it would be wrong to believe that medical treatment occurs in an emotional vacuum. The combination of a heightened emotionality and acutely felt pain allow for an all-encompassing embodied experience; a physically and emotionally felt 'sensory attentiveness' may well be integral to any effective social bonding. The acute pain event in the healing process, as well as in the ritual staged for coming to terms with a new life situation, may enhance one's sense of trust both in oneself and in the other, precisely through such all-encompassing emotionally felt and physically experienced forms of sociality.

This understanding of acute pain, which in Seremetakis' words, 'mobilizes trans-individual systems of communication, meaning, and value' (1998:151) emphasizes that the intensity of the individually felt acute pain breaks down habitual boundaries, carries individuals away from their habitual focus on themselves, and makes possible the experience of an intense feeling of commonality. However, it directly contradicts Scarry's frequently quoted and well-known statement: 'To have great pain is to have certainty, to hear that another has pain is to have doubt' (1985:7).

Admittedly, Scarry's statement is taken out of context here, and no doubt, Scarry is right to say this of heavily traumatised torture victims who were exposed to repeated and chronic pain inflictions in the torture chamber and struggle with their rehabilitation into 'normal' life, after having been pushed to the limits of their existence. The juxtaposition of the contradictory quotes by Seremetakis and Scarry on 'pain' raises the question, however, as to whether it is justified to use the one word 'pain' to refer to a wide variety of different 'pain' experiences.

Pain and pain

Above, I contrasted the pain experience of a torture victim with that of wailing kin over the death of a beloved. The former, Scarry says, alienates the individual from the group, the latter, Seremetakis maintains, mobilizes trans-individual systems of communication. There is one word, 'pain', for these very different life experiences. Are we speaking of the same phenomenon? Indeed, the term 'pain' essentialises most varied phenomena of lived experience:

> Sunburn, an insect bite, ... surgical operations, beating children for educational purposes, having eaten too much, rape, ... hearing a dentist's drill, ... fire walking, lumbago. ... flagellation in order to reach states of altered consciousness, et cetera. (Hadolt 2000:20).

One wonders what these different experiences have in common. In Unani Tibb, there are several terms that delimit a wide range of pain experiences (Pugh 1991). They are in translation the cold contractive 'catching' pain or the hot contractive 'pinching' and 'gripping' pain that is typical of stomach aches. Stomach aches can also be 'piercing', as can be painful feelings in chest and throat; all three can also be said to be 'burning'. The skin in pain feels 'stinging' or 'pricking', the head 'splitting' or 'bursting', and limbs and bones, if in pain, feel 'breaking'. Unspecified pain can furthermore be 'throbbing' or 'shooting'/'radiating'. In biomedicine, the McGill questionnaire lists over seventy adjectives for describing pain, from 'splitting', 'flickering', 'throbbing', 'stabbing', 'sharp', to 'dull', 'sore', and 'itchy' (Melzack and Wall 1996:40). If the insiders' words for describing pain are so varied, how can an outside observer use just one single word 'pain' as though it referred to one experiential datum?

An English acupuncturist comes to mind, who vehemently responded to my suggestion that in acupuncture treatment *suan*, *ma*, and *zhang* designate experiences of acute pain (London, November 2004). 'No', she exclaimed, 'the pricking that the needle inflicts on the patient is not pain!' Indeed, the word for 'pain' in Chinese is *tong*, not *suan*, *ma* or *zhang*. In modern Chinese, the term *tong* has a similar semantic field as pain in English – it often designates primarily physical pain and can also refer to primarily emotional pain – although it has a different etymology (that is *tong* is not cognate to punishment etymologically). Having said this, needling can also hurt in the sense of *tong*, and if it does so, the acupuncturist is considered unskilled.

So, after all, is *suan*, *ma* or *zhang* a quality of acute pain, and how does it differ from *tong*? It is notoriously difficult to talk about sensory experiences for how can I know that you feel like I do when I, or you, say I feel pain or pleasure. In order to overcome the difficulty of communicating one's sensory experiences to one another, one takes recourse to similes (Scarry 1985:15, quotes V.C. Medvei). Rather than describing the experience itself, one invokes a certain situation and says it feels 'as if' this and that were happening. The assumption is that people in similar situations have similar sensory experiences. However, considering the complexity of pain experiences, this assumption is actually rather ill founded.

After repeated experiences of being needled, I learnt to distinguish between *tong* and *suan*, *ma*, *zhang*, although in my experience the boundaries between these feelings could be very fluid. Instances of *tong* clearly were unpleasant, it hurt 'as if' skin tissue were damaged, while instances of *suan*, *ma*, and *zhang*, even if initially experienced as an unpleasant pricking, could also be experienced as a welcome sort of stimulation once one was accustomed to this sort of 'pain'. Accordingly, rather than speaking of pain, Sagli (2003:215) calls *de qi* an 'unfamiliar body sensation'.

However, to call *de qi* a 'sensation' is problematic, for *tong* and *suan*, *ma*, *zhang* are complex forms of 'perception' rather than 'sensations'. These sensory experiences are not reflex reactions but both physiologically and culturally modulated 'perceptions'. When I described *tong*-pain above with a simile I made the assumption that 'skin tissue damage' was a very distinctive feeling among all humans, but 'skin tissue damage' is actually an experience that presupposes concepts like 'skin tissue' and is accordingly a socially and culturally shaped perception. To be sure, the terms *tong* and *suan*, *ma*, *zhang* refer to specific forms of 'perception'.

That one's experience of pain is a 'perception' rather than a 'reflex' or 'sensation' has been convincingly demonstrated through sociological studies of pain, which centred on its culturally specific expression.[3] A classic is Mark Zborowski's (1952) on 'Cultural Components in Responses to Pain' caused by herniated discs and spinal lesions. It was a carefully thought through study that involved open-ended interviews with 103 respondents, and also accounted for intra-group variation. However, as has been rightly remarked (Kleinman et al. 1992:2): 'We blush to read these descriptions today'. The study not only elaborates cultural stereotypes from the study of male veterans, but also states unashamedly that (I quote Kleinman et al. 1992:2): 'Yankees are continent; Jews and Italians are expressive; Jews are more concerned with the future significance of their pain; Italians, focused on the present, are simply relieved that the pain has gone away.' Zborowski's study and many that followed, which centred on the cultural factors in the response to pain, were important despite their reinforcement of cultural stereotypes, because they led to the general acceptance that pain is not a 'reflex' or 'sensation' but a complex 'perception' with a more or less strong emotional component. It is shaped by culture, gender, age, status, et cetera, apart from personal disposition.

The differences of pain intensity and quality, of its modulation through simultaneous cognitive processes and emotional experiences, of cultural meanings, age and gender, social status and personal disposition, cannot be overlooked. These differences may be so important that the use of the one word 'pain' may not do justice to the diversity of the lived experiences. The radical solution would be to do away with the concept of 'pain' altogether, because it essentialises the diversity of painful sensory experiences in social life. However, for the purposes of making sense of the therapeutic quality of *de qi* in Chinese acupuncture, one need not be as radical as this, and in what follows, I propose to differentiate merely between an anthropologically defined 'acute' versus 'chronic' pain.

Culturally constructed temporalities of acute and chronic pain

Considering the diversity of pain experiences, it comes as no surprise that the anthropological literature does not address pain as such but rather, social practices and medical problems marked by specific pain experiences: initiation rites; torture and war trauma;[4] and chronic pain in medicalised societies. This is not to say that other themes have not been discussed, such as masculinity gained through painful gym experiences (Frykman 1998) or pain experiences among intravenous needle sharers (Connors 1994), and others.

Anthropologists generally consider pain infliction in initiation rites 'meaningful pain'. Clastres (1973), as already mentioned, highlights its disciplinary function of inscribing the laws of society on individual male bodies. In her discussion of a female initiation rite, pharaonic circumcision, Janice Boddy stresses a remarkably similar aspect of acute pain infliction:

> Through this operation and other procedures involving pain or trauma, appropriate feminine dispositions are being inculcated in young girls, dispositions, which following Bourdieu (1977:15), are inscribed in their bodies not only physically, but also cognitively and emotionally, in the form of mental inclinations, 'schemes of perception and thought' (1989:57).

Boddy and Clastres both emphasize how in these initiation rites the cognitive and emotional is physically inscribed in bodies; both would shy away from the notion of 'physical pain'. Boddy then goes a step further by contextualising the culture-specific form of acute pain infliction in a field of symbolic attributions. She explains how in Hofriyat heat and pain, known by the same word, *harr*, come to be understood as intrinsically feminine qualities; it is both the women's internally felt pain and heat, and their association with the fluids water and blood, that makes them fertile and feminine. Women should be pure, their skin smooth, white, and without hairs, and by closing off their genital opening, they should preserve moisture. It is the enclosed moist female body, characterised by *harr*, that has generative and transformative powers.

Having said this, culture-specific meanings associated with the practices of female circumcision are ambivalent and ambiguous. They change and can even become meaningless to some (Gruenbaum 1996), particularly in transnational contexts (Johansen 2002). Therefore, rather than calling the ritually inflicted pain 'meaningful pain', I suggest assessing it in light of its culturally given temporality. The temporality that marks initiation rites is typically structured and ever since Van Gennep (1909) considered to have three phases. Acute pain is usually contained within the liminal phase. I suggest calling it 'acute pain' because it occurs in a given temporal structure with a clearly demarcated beginning and end.

The definition of 'acute pain' as pain experienced in culturally demarcated temporalities that delineate the beginning and end of the experience differs from the biomedical definitions of acute and chronic pain. For the biomedical profession, as Kleinman et al. (1992) put it, somewhat polemically, acute pain is real, but chronic pain not. The reality of acute pain can usually be related to tissue damage, albeit to varying degrees. It typically has sympathico-adrenal manifestations:

> Gastrointestinal responses are characterised by an inhibition of motility ... Glucogen is released from the liver into the bloodstream as an energy source. Respiratory changes characterised by increased alveolar ventilation and oxygen consumption, and occasionally increased respiration rate may be associated with the hyperventilation. Muscular responses include both gross hypermotility and increased muscle tension in the area of painful stimulation... Cardiovascular responses are more complex and varied, but usually there is a marked elevation of both systolic and diastolic pressures... there is also an increase in pulse rate... Pupillary dilations, palmar and plantar sweating and escape behaviour and vocalisations are also easily-observable responses (Sternbach 1984:174).

Since these physiological aspects of the pain experience are always modulated by emotion and cognition, biomedical doctors too shy away from the concept of 'physical pain' (Craig 1984, Weisenberg 1984).

Biomedical doctors are well aware that 'chronic pain' is a completely arbitrary convention; sub-acute or ongoing acute pain gets reclassified as chronic pain after six months (Sternbach 1984). Not only is there no function for chronic pain, it often cannot be directly correlated with tissue damage and, while chronic pain does change and transform the person and his or her physiology, the physiological features generally are not those that mark an acute pain episode.

In accordance with the biomedical definitions of acute and chronic pain, one could say that initiation rites inflict acute pain experiences; the duration may be of seconds, minutes, hours, days, and weeks, but hardly of months and years. However, rather than referring to absolute time entities (of more or less six months), it seems more useful to coin these terms in the light of culturally defined temporalities. Accordingly, 'acute pain' is experienced in culturally clearly demarcated temporal structures and 'chronic pain' is defined by a culturally unstructured temporality.

Morris (1990) emphasizes that chronic pain is peculiarly unregulated and Kleinman (1988) illustrates with moving personal histories how it leads to withdrawal and isolation. Chronic pain is unreal for the other, while it is so terribly present and all-encompassing for the sufferer, and this impossibility of the other to empathise with the sufferer enlarges the latter's pain experience. Time becomes distorted, the subjectively suffered pain cannot be socially validated, inner and outer time seem out of sync, the sufferer lives in a temporality isolated from social time (Good 1992). Chronic pain debilitates and alienates, it has a peculiarly changeable nature, and while it is distressing in its milder appearances, it is excruciating at its worst (DelVecchio Good 1992). The sufferer then experiences, as one does in acute pain, that mind-body and subject-object dualisms break down, because pain is simultaneously bodily experience and mental-emotional experience, which resists objectification (Jackson 1994). These accounts all report on temporally unstructured and peculiarly changeable pain experiences. They are best comprehended in terms of the above coined anthropological concept of 'chronic pain' that by definition is marked by a culturally unstructured temporality.

Temporally structured acute pain in ritual and unregulated chronic pain in medicalised societies

Chronic pain belongs among the most frequent reasons for disablement in the United States and the European Union (Kleinman et al. 1992).[5] No doubt, 'chronic pain', like 'PTSD' (Young 1995), is one of these cultural constructs of societies in the northern hemisphere that due to globalisation processes are reified also in other cultural settings. However, regardless of whether they are cultural constructs or not, and whether they are indefinable due to their diversity or not, the lived experience of the peculiarly changeable sort of pain known as 'chronic pain' is real. Medical anthropologists have amply documented this.

Ivan Illich (1976) describes the 'killing of pain' as one of the prime features of what he dubs 'medicalised society'. He traces the marketing of the first medicine called 'pain killer' to 1853 – to be succeeded by aspirin in 1899, which, despite the more recent popularity of valium and cocaine, remains the main painkiller to date (Morris 1990). According to Illich:

> Progress in civilization became synonymous with the reduction of the sum total of suffering. From then on, politics was taken to be an activity not so much for maximizing happiness as for minimizing suffering. ... In this context it now seems rational to flee pain rather than to face it, even at the cost of giving up intense aliveness. It seems reasonable to eliminate pain, even at the cost of losing independence. ... With rising levels of induced insensitivity to pain, the capacity to experience the simple joys and pleasures of life has equally declined. Increasingly stronger stimuli are needed to provide people in an anaesthetic society with any sense of being alive. Drugs, violence and horror remain the only stimuli that can still elicit an experience of self (1976:106).

Medicalised society is marked by the intention to minimise pain at the cost of recognising, as Illich says, 'in the capacity for suffering a possible symptom of health' (ibid.). Incidentally, life cycle rituals have also been drastically reduced in scale and frequency in medicalised societies. For instance, the social management of pain in birthing is minimised by anaesthetics or caesareans, and the mere thought of painful initiation rites is abhorrent. The corpses of the dead are deported to hospital and hung on to dehumanising revitalisation machines instead of being mourned over at the bedside in an intensely felt, temporally structured acute pain episode. Likewise, lavish wedding ceremonies are on the decline, where the pain of separation from the one family and the anxiety accompanying entry into the other, is eased by being together in an exalted social gathering.

In medicalised societies acute pain is not openly displayed. Great efforts are made to suppress it whenever it surfaces – with the compartmentalisation of suffering into institutions that make death and protracted illness invisible to daily life and with pain killers that reinforce the imperative of individual autonomy. However, pain manifests itself in the silently increasing chronic pain syndromes. Interestingly, this overt versus covert expression of pain parallels that of the power of government. As power is no longer displayed in a spectacle of inflicting gruesome pain in punishment, but has become invisible (Foucault 1975), acute pain episodes are rarely played out in temporally structured life cycle events. Yet people increasingly suffer from peculiarly unregulated temporally unstructured chronic pain syndromes. Chronic pain syndromes, which result in the complete isolation of the individual, are bound to reinforce the currently observed fragmentation of medicalised societies. By contrast, acute pain events in life cycle rituals make possible the embodied experience of social cohesion, which indirectly may strengthen the health of all participants, as may the above described therapeutic measure of *de qi* in Chinese acupuncture.

E-mail: elisabeth.hsu@anthropology.oxford.ac.uk

Notes

* This article elaborates on an idea sketched out in German in 1993/94. I thank Gilbert Lewis for recommendations on pain literature, Katherine Morris and David Parkin for valuable comments on an earlier draft, and the editors of this special issue and of Etnofoor for pertinent editorial advice.

Qi is the 'stuff that makes things happen' or 'the stuff in which things happen'. It is rendered in translation as 'breath', 'air', 'vapour', or 'energy' (Sivin 1987:47).

2 See also authors cited in Illich (1976: chapter 6), Scarry (1985), Morris (1990), Rey (1995).
3 And more recently also on gender-specific ones (for example Bendelow 2000).
4 The experiences of torture and trauma, which Scarry (1985) conceptualises as 'physical pain', and their effect on the unmaking and making of culture, are too complex an issue to be discussed in this essay.
5 See for example *http://www.efic.org/ewap_part2.htm*, accessed September 2005.

References

Bendelow, G.
    2000 *Pain and Gender.* Essex: Pearson Education.

Boddy, J.
    1989 *Wombs and Alien Spirits: Women, Men, and the Zar Cult in Northern Sudan.* Madison: University of Wisconsin Press.

Bourdieu, P.
    1977 *Outline of a Theory of Practice.* Cambridge: Cambridge University Press.

Clastres, P.
    1973 De la torture dans les sociétés primitives. *L'Homme* 13(3):114-120.

Connors, M. M.
    1994 Stories of Pain and the Problem of AIDS Prevention: Injection Drug Withdrawal and its Effect on Risk Behavior. *Medical Anthropology Quarterly* 8(1): 47-68.

Craig, K. D.
    1984 Emotional Aspects of Pain. In: P. D. Wall and R. Melzack (Eds.), *Textbook of Pain.* Edinburgh: Churchill Livingstone. Pp. 153-161.

Csordas, T. J. (Ed.)
    1993 Somatic Modes of Attention. *Cultural Anthropology* 8:135-156.
    1994 *Embodiment and Experience: the Existential Ground of Culture and Self:* Cambridge University Press.

DelVecchio Good, M. J.
    1992 Work as a Heaven from Pain. In: M. J. DelVecchio Good et al. (Eds.), *Pain as Human Experience: an Anthropological Perspective.* Berkeley: University of California Press. Pp. 49-76.

Desjarlais, R.
    1996 Presence. In: C. Laderman and M. Roseman (Eds.), *The Performance of Healing.* London: Routledge. Pp. 143-164.

Foucault, M.
    1975 *Discipline and Punish: the Birth of the Prison.* London: Peregrine Books.

Frykman, J.
    1998 On the Hardening of Men. In: J. Frykman, N. Seremetakis and S. Ewert (Eds.), *Identities in Pain.* Lund: Nordic Academic Press. Pp. 126-150.

Good, B. J.
    1992 A Body in Pain: the Making of a World of Chronic Pain. In: M. J. DelVecchio Good et al. (Eds.), *Pain as Human Experience: an Anthropological Perspective.* Berkeley: University of California Press. Pp. 29-48.

Gruenbaum, E.
    1996 Cultural Debate on Female Circumcision: the Sudanese are Arguing This One Out for Themselves. *Medical Anthropology Quarterly* 10(4):445-475.

Hadolt, B.
    2000 The Making and Unmaking of the World: Considerations on Medical Anthropologists' Recent Contributions to the Anthropology of Pain. *Viennese Ethnomedicine Newsletter* 11(2):18-24.

Hsu, E.
    1993/94 Schmerz, Individuum und Gemeinschaft. *Ethnologica Helvetica* 17/18:65-74.
    1995 The Manikin in Man: Cultural Crossing and Creativity. In: G. Aijmer (Ed.), *Syncretism and the Commerce of Symbols.* Göteborg: The Institute for Advanced Studies in Social Anthropology. Pp.156-204.

1996 Innovations in Acumoxa: Acupuncture Analgesia, Scalp Acupuncture and Ear Acupuncture in the PRC. *Social Science and Medicine* 42(3):421-430.
1999 *The Transmission of Chinese Medicine*. Cambridge: Cambridge University Press.
Forthcoming Learning to be an Acupuncturist, and Not Becoming One. In: K. Maynard (Ed.), *Medical Identities*. Oxford: Berghahn.

Illich, I.
1976 *Medical Nemesis: the Expropriation of Health*. London: Calder and Boyars.

Jackson, J. E.
1992 "After a While No One Believes You": Real and Unreal Pain. In: M. J. DelVecchio Good et al. (Eds.), *Pain as Human Experience: an Anthropological Perspective*. Berkeley: University of California Press. Pp. 138-168.
1994 Chronic Pain and the Tension between the Body as Subject and Object. In: T. J. Csordas (Ed.), *Embodiment and Experience: the Existential Ground of Culture and Self*. Cambridge: Cambridge University Press. Pp. 201-228.

Johansen, R. E. B.
2002 Pain as a Counterpoint to Culture: toward an Analysis of Pain Associated with Infibulation among Somali Immigrants in Norway. *Medical Anthropology Quarterly* 16(3):312-340.

Katz, R.
1982 *Boiling Energy: Community Healing among the Kalahari Kung*. Cambridge, Mass.: Harvard University Press.

Kleinman, A.
1988 *The Illness Narratives: Suffering, Healing, and the Human Condition*. New York: Basic Books.

Kleinman, A. et al.
1992 Pain as Human Experience: an Introduction. In: M. J. DelVecchio Good et al. (Eds.), *Pain as Human Experience: an Anthropological Perspective*. Berkeley: University of California Press. Pp. 1-28.

Lewis, G.
1999 *A Failure of Treatment*. Oxford: Oxford University Press.

Lo, V.
2001 Influence of Nurturing Life Culture on the Development of Western Han Acumoxa Therapy. In: E. Hsu (Ed.), *Innovation in Chinese Medicine*. Cambridge: Cambridge University Press. Pp. 19-50.

Lu Shoukang et al. (Ed.)
1987 *Zhenci shoufa yibai zhong* (One Hundred Techniques of Acupuncture). Beijing: Zhongguo yiyao keji chubanshe.

Melzack, R. and P. Wall
1996 [1982] *The Challenge of Pain*. London: Penguin Books.

Morris, D. B.
1990 *The Culture of Pain*. Berkeley: University of California Press.

Pomeranz, B.
1996 Scientific Research into Acupuncture for the Relief of Pain. *Journal of Alternative and Complementary Medicine* 2(1):53-60.

Pugh, J. P.
1991 Semantics of Pain in Indian Culture and Medicine. *Culture, Medicine and Psychiatry* 15:19-43.

Qiu Maoliang and Zhang Shanchen
    1985   *Zhenjiuxue* (The Study of Acupuncture and Moxibustion). Shanghai: Shanghai keji chubanshe.

Ren Yingqiu (Ed.)
    1986   *Huangdi neijing zhangju suoyin* (Concordance to the Yellow Emperor's Inner Canon). Beijing: Renmin weisheng chubanshe.

Rey, R.
    1995   *The History of Pain.* Cambridge, Mass.: Harvard University Press.

Rosenblatt, D.
    1997   Anti-Social Skin: Structure, Resistance, and 'Modern Primitive' Adornment in the United States. *Cultural Anthropology* 12(3):287-334.

Sagli, G.
    2003   *Acupuncture Recontextualized: the Reception of Chinese Medical Concepts among Practitioners of Acupuncture in Norway.* Oslo: Unipub AS.

Scarry, E.
    1985   *The Body in Pain. The Making and Unmaking of the World.* Oxford: Oxford University Press.

Seremetakis, N. C.
    1998   Durations of Pain: a Genealogy of Pain. In: J. Frykman et al. (Eds.), *Identities in Pain.* Lund: Nordic Academic Press. Pp. 151-168.

Sivin, N.
    1987   *Traditional Medicine in Contemporary China.* Ann Arbor: Centre for Chinese Studies, University of Michigan.

Sternbach, R. A.
    1983   Acute Versus Chronic Pain. In: P. D. Wall and R. Melzack (Eds.), *Textbook of Pain.* Edinburgh: Churchill Livingstone. Pp. 173-177.

Van Gennep, A.
    1909   *Les rites de passage.* Paris: Nourry.

Weisenberg, M.
    1984   Cognitive Aspects of Pain. In: P. D. Wall and R. Melzack (Eds.) *Textbook of Pain.* Edinburgh: Churchill Livingstone. Pp. 162-72.

Wriedt, M.
    1988   Solidarität mit den Leidenden – Schmerz als Thema der Theologie. Ein historischer Überblick. In: K. Griefeld et al. (Hrsg.), *Schmerz: Interdisziplinäre Perspektiven. Curare Sonderband* 6:153-171.

Young, A.
    1995   *Harmony of Illusions: Inventing Post-Traumatic Stress Disorder.* Princeton: Princeton University Press.

Zborowski, M.
    1952   Cultural Components in Responses to Pain. *Journal of Social Issues* 8(4):16-30.

Zhang, R.
    1989   *Zhongguo zhenci mazui fazhanshi* (The History of the Development of Acupuncture Analgesia in China). Shanghai: kejishu wenxian chubanshe.

Japanese Fragrance Descriptives and Gender Constructions
Preliminary Steps towards an Anthropology of Olfaction

Brian Moeran, Copenhagen Business School

ABSTRACT   We start with a paradox. On the one hand, academic literature asserts that the sense of smell varies in different social and cultural contexts, and that every social group has its own distinct olfactory culture. On the other hand, global advertising campaigns for perfumes suggest that fragrance is a universal form of semiotic communication. Are there, or are there not, specific olfactory cultures? This paper examines some of the evidence from Japan. Many languages have virtually no vocabulary to describe odours, except in terms of other senses of sight, sound, touch and taste, so that fragrance is communicated primarily through similes and metaphors. The paper describes how fragrance descriptives are used in Japanese journalism, marketing and related literature, before examining ways in which they help create and maintain gender constructions of various kinds. It then outlines specific aspects of Japanese olfactory culture, and suggests a methodology for the study of the anthropology of olfaction.

Introduction

The theoretical discourses devoted to smell reflect a maze of fascinating taboos and mysterious attractions. They also include all kinds of anatomical speculation about why the nose is the shape it is in relation to the rest of the face (Morris 2004:61-63), as well as detailed discussion of the part it plays in the nature of smell (Watson 2000). And yet olfactory experience is not just difficult to define; it remains 'in the limbo of cognition' (Rouby et al. 2002:1). It was only in the early 1990s that Richard Axel and Linda Buck began to publish their Nobel Prize-winning research on odorant receptors and the organization of the olfactory system (Buck and Axel 1991).[1] Among their findings was the fact that, even though human beings have only one third the number of odorant receptors as mice (350 as opposed to 1,000), they can still recognize and form memories of 10,000 different odours.

Smell is many things: boundary marker, status symbol, distance-maintainer, impression management technique, danger signal, and sign of protest. Smell mediates social action; yet it is the least valued, and least researched (Synnott 1991), of all the senses (especially, perhaps, by anthropologists) – possibly because, by its 'radical interiority', it threatens 'the abstract and impersonal regime' that characterizes social order in contemporary societies (Classen, Howes and Synnott 1994:4-5).

How do we know what odours, fragrances and scents 'mean'?[2] Is smell a universal form of semiotic communication, or does it vary in different social and cultural contexts? Global advertising campaigns suggest the former – at least visually (headlines may, though not necessarily, be adapted to local languages). Anthropological literature suggests the latter. Can we talk of specific 'olfactory cultures'? If so, in what do they consist? And how do these affect the creation, appraisal and use of fragrances in such different countries as Japan, France and the USA?

Every society appears to have its own hierarchy of senses, or sensory order. This ranking differs from one society to the next, and between different social groups within the same society, as well as from one historical period to another. Odours are used to mark social categories of race, class, gender, and age, as well as to make symbolic distinctions relating to purity, pollution, sexuality, and so on (Classen, Howes and Synnott 1994). Advertising plays to these social and symbolic categories and so reinforces different societies' moral constructions of reality.

Although the anthropology or sociology of olfaction (I assume no difference) tends to focus on cultural differences, it also allows for universals. For example, available historical and sociological literature suggests that there exists a fundamental hypothesis in almost all societies: that what smells good is good, and that what smells bad is bad (Classen 1992), so that particular odours, whether real or alleged, may be used to indicate the moral purity or impurity of particular individuals and groups within the social order (Largey and Watson 1972:1221). The issue arising from this hypothesis is twofold: firstly, what smells 'good' or 'bad' in one society or group of people may not necessarily smell the same for others – either in other societies, or among other groups of people living in the same society; and secondly, 'good' and 'bad' need to be defined before we proceed to analyse odours further. In short, to paraphrase Hamlet: 'there is nothing foul nor fragrant, but thinking makes it so' (Synnott 1991). We need to find out *why* Japanese, French, or Americans, for example, regard one thing as 'fragrant' and another as 'foul', and what the *social repercussions* of such classifications might be.[3] What linguistic and visual metaphors are used, and what do they tell us about the societies and cultures in which they are used?

These are some of the broader questions that I wish to address in forthcoming research and fieldwork. For the purposes of this essay, however, I will look at two, not unrelated, issues highlighted by journalism, marketing and related literature: first, the use of descriptives in the marketing of fragrances in Japan: and second, the way in which these descriptives classify men and women in Japan. I will then summarise the discussion in the context of the anthropology of olfaction and its research methodology.

Japanese olfactory culture

Histories of fragrance in European languages tend to start off with Mesopotamian and Egyptian civilizations, discuss examples of the use of perfumes in the Old and New Testaments of the Bible, and then move on to Greece, Etruria, the Roman and Byzantine empires. They then take in the Renaissance, before discussing the development of the modern perfume industry in France.

But what of a non-Western society like Japan? Japanese olfactory culture does not go back nearly as far as that of Sumeria, Egypt, ancient Greece, or even China, but it is still substantial. One of the country's earliest chronicles, the *Nihon Shoki*, records that in 562 AD, a large piece of driftwood was washed up on the shore of Awaji Island on the Inland Sea near Osaka. Local villagers discovered on burning it that the wood gave off a remarkable and pleasing odour, so they sent the remainder to the Imperial Court as tribute (Miyazawa and Werner 2001:19-20).

The main force for the development of an olfactory culture, however, was the introduction to Japan in 662 A.D. of Buddhism, which made frequent use of incense in its rituals.[4] This was incorporated into the everyday practices of the Heian court aristocracy, and by the 10th century the latter had developed an extremely detailed and elaborate set of rules regarding clothing, colours and related scents (Morris 1969:202-17). These emerge most clearly in the famous novel *Genji Monogatari* (*The Tale of Genji*) written by Murasaki Shikibu, who constructed almost the entire work around the concept of odour. Besides its olfactory structure, the novel contains numerous scenes in which smell is crucial to social interaction and plot development. The hero, Hikaru Genji, is renowned for his beauty, which is described as 'scent' (*nioi*; in modern day Japanese 'odour' or 'smell') (and there is a contrast here between the two senses of sight [in that Hikaru means *Light*] and smell). Like many other Heian courtiers, he is much admired for the skill with which he mixes incenses and fragrances. Moreover, his two sons are called Kaoru (Lord Fragrance) and Nio (Prince Scent). As Ivan Morris (1969:157) says:

> Nothing more symbolizes the ideals of this period, and contrasts it with the subsequent age of military heroes, than the fact that two of Murasaki's most respected male characters should be named 'Lord Fragrance' and 'Prince Scent.'

The blending of incense, often used to add scent to clothing, was seen to be an art, and the methods used by each individual were carefully guarded secrets (as they have been until recently in the contemporary fragrance industry). The fragrance worn by a gentleman was deemed to be almost as important as the clothes he wore.[5] Connoisseurs were able to tell who was passing their enclosed rooms by his or her odour. In this respect, incense burning enabled people of a certain class to share a common experience and olfactory unity with others in that class (cf. Largey and Watson 1972:1031).

But a fictional description of olfactory usage in 10th century Japanese court society, while revealing many of the classic social distinctions enabled by odour found in other societies (for instance, that the elite smell 'better' than the lower classes), does not necessarily represent faithfully the place of smell in everyday life among contemporary Japanese. However, evidence suggests that one of the primary 'webs of significance' (Geertz 1973:5) spun to form modern Japanese culture is olfactory (Katz 1996:11), and that 'group intimacy and alignments are at least partially established by olfactory stimuli' (Largey and Watson 1972:1027). From the elaborated tradition of *kōdō* incense ceremony or 'way of fragrance', to vending machines offering teenage girls' used underwear for sale to discriminating noses, by way of programmed air conditioning systems that send different scents through buildings in various sequences at different times of the day (Hasegawa 1993:158), many people in Japan

Figure 1: "After her farewell. Once she'd gone, her fragrance remained – a fragrance like a white breeze" (*Sayōnara, no ato de. Kanojo ga satte, kaori ga nokotta. Shiroi kaze no yō na kaori desu*)
(Kanebo, *Impress*, 1994)

make conscious use of smell in their everyday lives as they manipulate odour settings and olfactory identity.

For example, Japanese often remark on the various fragrances marking different seasons (like the set-phrase *umegaka* [spring plum blossom] or *kunpū* [fragrant summer breeze]), and use the generic term 'smell' (*nioi*) to describe the atmosphere they experience as particular to a foreign country (tourist brochures regularly comment on this).[6] They distinguish themselves from non-Japanese both by odour (Westerners have often in the past been said to 'smack of butter' [*butter-kusai*]) and by the shape of their noses (Caucasians have 'high noses' [*hana ga takai*]). Their own noses also act as markers of identity. Like some other peoples in east and south east Asia, they point to their noses when referring to themselves.[7] They also have a broad range of smell-related descriptives used in everyday conversation: *dorokusai*, meaning unrefined (lit. 'stinking of mud'); *kane no nioi ga suru* (lit. 'smacks of money'); and *kanryōshū ga tsuyoi* (lit. 'smelling strongly of the bureaucrat). They still practise and appreciate the art of the 'lingering fragrance' (*nokori-ga*) – either from an incense stick burned before the arrival of guests at a tea ceremony, or from the understated *sillage* of a woman's fragrance in the street (Figure 1). Generally, modern Japanese are very sensitive to scents, fragrances, and odours of one sort or another.

A relatively recent study carried out by the research arm of Japan's second largest advertising agency reveals a number of points of interest with regard to how smell is perceived in contemporary Japanese society (Hakuhōdō Seikatsu Sōgō Kenkyūjo [HILL] 1994). Based on a survey of 2,000 respondents equally distributed between the two sexes and six age groups, this study suggests that, in general, Japanese are quite perceptive sensually. Smell was ranked highest or lowest among the five senses in terms of respondents overall 'sensitivity', and women in Japan – like women in many other parts of the world (cf. Dubois and Rouby 2002:48) – were found to be particularly sensitive to smell.[8] For men, on the other hand, smell ranked lower in sense perception than sight, hearing or taste (HILL 1994:60).

Taking four different criteria into account (degrees of importance [*jūyōdo*], expressiveness [*hyōgendo*], pleasure [*kairakudo*], and impression [*inshōdo*]), the survey also revealed that sight was the sense that a very large majority of respondents did not want to lose, and smell just one percent.[9] At the other extreme, smell was the sense that people were most prepared to lose if they had to.

When asked which of the senses was easiest to express through language, respondents ranked sight first and smell, by a long way, last. Only ten of the 2,000 people interviewed thought that smell was the most effective sense with which to express their feelings. Perhaps surprisingly, given the direct connection between smell and the limbic system which filters recollection and memory, smell ranked extremely low in relation to memory recall (HILL 1994:56-57).[10]

What is noticeable about these four tests of sense perception is that sight and smell always come out as opposed extremes. The HILL study also revealed that, in general, Japanese prefer either 'faint' (*honoka*) fragrances or no fragrance at all (cf. Katz 1996:13)[11] – a preference which ties in with the concept of *nokori-ga* lingering fragrance mentioned above. As the Director of HILL confirmed in an interview some years later:

Figure 2: "If your clothes had a nose, it would surely be crooked" (*fuku ni hana ga attara, kitto magatte'ru*). (American Drug Corporation, *Kimmy*, 1993)

Japanese have been concerned to get rid of smell, rather than add it in the way that Westerners do… There was a period earlier when Japanese added things to stop smells – as in lavatories, for example – but nowadays the idea is to produce things that do not smell in the first place. Cosmetics are a good example of this, of course, and Shiseido has been working on non-perfumed products, like the *Lucido* range, which now sell rather well. So there is a distinction in Japan between 'extinguishing smell' (*nioi o kesu*) and 'adding smell' (*nioi o tsukeru*).

But there are occasions when Japanese purposely make smells. Like *yakitoriya* barbecued chicken places, for example. If you go round the Yamanote line in Tokyo, you get special food smells marking different areas of the city – the smell of *yakitori* means you've reached Shinbashi, the smell of curry hits you in Kanda. But this is unusual, I think. For the most part, hotels and places like that are trying to get rid of the smells of people. By using floral fragrances and so on…

I think lifestyle can affect people's sense of smell, too. Compact living styles in close quarters encourage either milder forms of smell or the removal of all smell. The Japanese experience would seem to be spreading now to Taiwan in an intriguing extension of globalisation.[12]

This distinction between 'adding' and 'extinguishing', or masking, odour – between odorizing and deodorizing – is undoubtedly problematic, as my informant recognizes, since both are basic practices in the establishment and maintenance of a socially accepted olfactory identity – in Japan, as in the rest of the world.[13] Although a cursory glance at supermarket shelves in Japan reveals a wide range of products marketed specifically to housewives worried about untoward smells in their clothing (Figure 2), kitchens, bathrooms, hallways and other parts of their homes, it is equally clear that a lot of different outdoor stalls, shops and restaurants purposely create food smells (barbecued chicken, for example, or supermarket bread sections) to attract customers. At the same time, the art of perfumery itself consists of creating fragrances that aim both to mask unpleasant body smells and to bring out more pleasant odours. This is the function of including in a perfume 'refreshing' herbal and flowery ingredients, on the one hand, and more 'sultry' odours of myrrh, benzoe, labdanum, ambergris, musk and civet, on the other (Jellinek 1997:3-7). Every olfactory culture, therefore, undoubtedly combines these two opposing principles, and it is the differing emphases put on bringing out or masking odours, as well as the particular scents used in this process, that may be said to distinguish one culture from another. According to this line of argument, therefore, we may hypothesise that Japanese olfactory culture is indeed to be found at the deodorizing, rather than odorizing, end of the olfactory continuum.

The fragrance industry

The fragrance industry exemplifies that fact that smell is both an emanation of material culture and part of the empire of the senses, 'more *like* a concept than it is like a "thing" in the usual sense' (Gell 1977:28). As Holley (2002:16) puts it: 'The art of concocting perfumes can be seen as a specifically human activity that leads a biological mechanism out of its natural domain of expression in order to make it serve a cultural purpose'. From this latter point of view, 'perfumery is the art of creating pleasurable and meaningful odour experiences' (Calkin and Jellinek 1994:x). The fragrance market as a whole is divided into: soaps and detergents (in which scents are not intrinsic but are added in an obvious way); cosmetics and toiletries (including fragrances, which are by definition scented); and other products like air fresheners, polishes, foods, car interiors and sports shoes, which have no obvious or functionally intrinsic odour, but which are designed to convey an unconscious scent experience). The market is more or less equally divided between flavours and fragrances.[14]

Fragrances, perfumes and deodorants are part of a global beauty business that has been estimated to be worth $160 billion a year in total and to be growing at an annual rate of seven percent – more than twice the rate of the developed world's GDP. The global market for perfumes and fragrances alone is estimated at $15 billion, of which the Japanese market is worth about $4.5 billion.[15] Between one fifth and one quarter of overall revenues is spent on advertising and promotion. A good fragrance launch usually brings in an income of $30 million during the first quarter of sales.[16] Smell is a serious business.

Fragrances are the profitable part of the business done by the *haute couture* houses, and are thus closely connected to fashion images in general. Indeed, they provide consumers with an entry point to high fashion. Future wearers of a Chanel 'little black dress', an Armani suit, or an Yves Saint Laurent evening gown start by wearing *Coco*, *Mania* or *Rive Gauche*. (They then move on to fashion accessories: belts, eyewear, handbags, shoes, and so on.) Fragrances are among the most affordable item in the fashion industry and each fashion house produces (or licenses under its name) a *series* of perfumes, each of which is targeted at different groups of consumers: *Youth Dew*, *Estée*, *White Linen*, *Beautiful*, *Knowing*, *Spellbound*, *Tuscany per donna*, and *Pleasures*, for example, by Estée Lauder, or *Eternity*, *Obsession*, *Escape*, *Truth*, *Contradiction*, *CK Be* and *CK One*, by (Unilever for) Calvin Klein. Individual fragrances should therefore be seen as part of a single product range, on the one hand, and as positioned against a range of competing brands (Chanel, Givenchy, Christian Dior, Shiseido and so on), on the other. Precisely because of these sets of oppositions, there may be shifts in marketing strategies over time to take account of new entries in the fragrance market. In this respect, the marketing of fragrances (as of all other goods) follows the principles laid down by De Saussure (1983:114) in his analysis of syntagmatic and paradigmatic (associative) relations in language, where he argued that 'the value of any given word is determined by what other words there are in that particular area of the vocabulary'.

New fragrances used to be created rather irregularly. For example, Christian Dior Perfumes initiated its product range with *Miss Dior* in 1947. This was followed by new fragrances approximately every ten years: *Diorissimo* in 1956, *Eau Savage* in 1966, and *Dioressence* in 1979. From the mid-1980s, however, there was a distinct increase in tempo as new fragrances were introduced every three years: *Poison* (1985), *Fahrenheit* (1988), *Dune* (1991), *Tendre Poison* (1994), *Dolce Vita* (1996), *j'adore* (2000), *Lily* (2001) and *Addict* (2004). Similar trajectories of new fragrance products can be found for Chanel, Estée Lauder, L'Oréal and other major fragrance brands.

Two factors appear to underlie this tendency. One was the commercialization of

Figure 3: Perfume blotter strip (front and back) for Britney Spears fragrance, marketed in Japan, April 2005. (Wakaba, *Curious*, 2005)

gas chromatography, which led to a breakdown of secrecy in the perfumery profession and to an intensification of competition in the fragrance industry as a whole (Calkin and Jellinek 1994:vii-viii). Another has been a breakdown in brand loyalty among consumers. Marketing data from Japan suggest that fragrance users closely follow emerging trends and fashions. They will try several new fragrances simultaneously and use those that they like in rotation, depending on feeling and TPO (time place occasion), during the first six to twelve months after launch, before moving on to newer products. This tendency towards short-term use of fragrances has led to the introduction of smaller 15ml and 20ml spray-type bottles.[17]

This rapid turnover of new fragrances may be seen as part of the incorporation of the fragrance industry into the fashion system that now characterises creative industries in general. Both trends, and the concept of time itself, have become basic and essential components of fragrance production and consumption. Moreover, like other creative industries, the fragrance industry makes use of celebrities to link otherwise separate fields of organisations, markets and networks in the entertainment industries. By naming perfume brands after fashion designers (Giorgio Armani, Nina Ricci, Coco Chanel, Hanae Mori, and so on), models (Inès de la Fressange, Naomi Campbell), film stars (Grace Kelley, Isabella Rossellini, Liz Taylor, Alain Delon), singers (Britney Spears, Jennifer Lopez, Celine Dion, Beyonce, Luciano Pavarotti) (Figure 3), artists (Salvador Dali, Andy Warhol), sports heroes (Michael Jordan, Gabriela Sabatini), and 'personalities' (Paris Hilton) (Figure 4), the fragrance industry integrates itself into a *name economy* (Moeran 2003).

Like the fashion industry with which it is so closely allied, the fragrance industry appears to be extremely fragmented. For example, there are at present approximately

Figure 4: Point of sales leaflet for Paris Hilton fragrance, marketed in Japan, April 2005. (Wakaba, *Paris Hilton Sheer*, 2005)

1,480 perfumes, fragrances, and colognes on sale in retail outlets in the United States (cf. The Fragrance Foundation 2001), while Perfume World lists a grand total of 7,501 products worldwide.[18] At the same time, though, there is a growing concentration of the ever-increasing number of brands under the control of particular fragrance manufacturers. Besides its own 23 perfume brands, for example, Estée Lauder Companies manufactures and markets the Aramis, Clinique, Prescriptives, Bobbi Brown Professional Cosmetics and Donna Karan Cosmetics ranges. Similarly, L'Oréal USA subsumes all perfumes made under the name of Lancôme and Ralph Lauren, as well as those of a variety of European designers like Giorgio Armani, Jean Cacharel, and Guy Laroche.

Classifying perfumes

If Japan is marked by a olfactory culture that is based more on 'odourlessness' than 'odour', we may wonder how fragrance companies advertise their products in Japan and how Japanese themselves react to modern – primarily Western – perfumes and the use thereof. In the early 1990s, it was remarked that the Japanese fragrance market constituted a mere three percent of the total cosmetics market, as compared with 30 percent in Europe (Wilk 1993: 52). This falls in line with common perceptions by Japanese themselves that they do not smell when compared with Caucasians or blacks and therefore, by implication, that they do not need to odorize their bodies.[19] The later HILL study affirmed that there is an overall resistance to the use of perfumes in Japanese society (a resistance echoed in marketing data that show a gradual decline in perfume sales in Japan over the past decade),[20] and that only one in twelve respondents said that they used fragrances and colognes more or less every day (HILL 1994:169).[21]

One survey reports that women generally buy fragrances in department stores or when travelling abroad; that they make their selection on the basis of magazine advertising and/or store testers; that they wear fragrances when they are going out or because they feel like it, either as a fashion or personal statement, or in connection with their mood. Only a small minority wear fragrance to appeal to men (Marie Claire Japon 1996). Consumers have generally preferred light, clean and fresh products and equated imported fragrances in their minds with (French) elegance (Wilk 1993:53).

Fragrances and perfumes *are* actively produced and marketed in Japan[22] and how they are described in advertising, promotional and other literature should tell us something about Japanese perceptions and classifications of smell.[23] Generally speaking, odours of all kinds are highly elusive and often cannot be directly named. Many languages have virtually no vocabulary to describe them, except in terms of the *other senses* of sight, sound, touch and taste – which may be why Sperber (1975:115-116) has suggested that there is no taxonomy of smells and that the only way to classify them, therefore, is by referring to their causes (in other words, to the smell of fresh green leaves, fish, plum blossoms, tobacco, sweat, and so on). As it is, fragrances are communicated primarily through metonymy and metaphor.[24]

Consequently smell comes to be viewed as 'a primitive, archaic, *needed* sense, one more important to sensory pleasure than to knowledge' (Le Guérer 2002:4). This emphasis on smell's hedonistic aspects is clearly apparent in the vast majority of Western-language advertising, promotional literature and general writings devoted to the marketing of perfumes and fragrances: from 'Create your dream' (Cerruti *Image*), to 'Men will melt' (Elizabeth Arden, *Provocative Woman*), by way of 'Absolutely delicious' (Carolina Herrera, *Carolina*). It is more muted in Japanese advertising, where we find phrases like: 'All women are angels' (*subete no josei wa tenshi de aru*) (Shiseido, *Angelique*); 'Recollection of serenity' (Christian Dior, *Dune*); and 'The night becomes opaque... Mounting tenderness' (*yo wa urumi... yasashisa wa takamaru*) (Caron, *Nocturnes*) (Figure 5).[25]

Most contemporary Japanese descriptives rely on Western perfumery's discourse of fragrance. The latter, however, is notoriously inconsistent. For example, in one of her papers, Linda Buck (Buck *et al.* 1999) uses a broad range of words to describe the smells formed by different odorant receptor combinations (for example, sweet, herbal, rancid, goat-like, repulsive, waxy, nut-like, rose and so on), even though stereochemical theory reduces the range of smells to seven primary odours (camphoraceous, musky, floral, pepperminty, ethereal, pungent and putrid) (Dahl 1976:119; Lévi-Strauss 1981:691). Most books about perfume (for example, The Fragrance Foundation 2001) rely to a greater or less extent on the classification outlined by the Technical Department of the *Société Française des Parfumeurs* (1990). These are citrus (often called 'fruity' in English), floral, fern, chypre, woody, amber (often referred

Figure 5: *Yo wa urumi… yasashisa wa takamaru.* (Parfums Caron, *Nocturnes*, 1995)

to as 'oriental'), and leather.[26] These different classes are then described as having characteristic odours – like 'dry' notes for woody family, or 'sweet', 'powdery', and 'animalic' notes for the oriental family. But even these become confused, as when the leather family is also seen to be characterised by 'dry' notes (Pavia 1995:69). Japanese marketers, for their part, tend to keep matters simpler by adhering to four main families. These are floral (amounting to 70 percent of the perfume, and 60 percent of the total fragrance market in Japan),[27] green,[28] chypre,[29] and oriental.[30]

In theory, these fragrance groups are blended in such a way that a perfume exudes different smells on the skin over time, as the alcohol and other ingredients evaporate. This development of a fragrance is classified in terms of 'notes' – 'top notes' for the immediate effect upon application, 'middle notes' (or 'heart notes') for a second set of smells that emerges after the initial burst and represents a perfume's 'heart', and 'base notes', 'dry down', or 'dry out' (in Japanese 'last') for the long-term fragrance effect after several hours.[31] We should recognize, however, that development only truly takes place when natural materials are used in creating a scent. Synthetic materials, which now form a very large percentage of modern perfumes' ingredients, do not of themselves develop, so that what changes take place are primarily due to the wearer, rather than the worn.[32]

As intimated above, finding consistency in Japanese (as in European) language fragrance-related writing is extremely difficult – thereby upholding David's (2002) note that smells are talked about as properties of objects experienced by people, and not as 'objects' or entities in themselves located in time and space. As a result, descriptions of smell are strongly influenced by emotional and subjective factors (Chastrette 2002:101). A popular book devoted to describing perfumes in general (mainly designed to stimulate the Japanese market, I suspect) limits its initial classification to three groups of smells, but then subdivides these into various sub-types: floral (subdivided into green, fruity, fresh, floral, aldehyde and sweet sub-types), oriental (amber and spicy sub-types), and chypre (fruity, floral, fresh and green sub-types) (Fukuji 1992).

The same book proceeds to rank individual perfumes on a five star scale on what are clearly two opposed pairs of categories: *sweetness* and *tanginess* or *spiciness (karasa)*, on the one hand, and *freshness* and *sexiness*, on the other (Figure 6). This kind of classification brings to mind distinctions made in the appreciation of wine (cf. Lehrer 1983), although the *balance* sought in the latter is replaced in perfume by *development* as – ideally, at least – the three layers of notes unfold on the skin.

A perfume dictionary (Arai 1996) distributes fragrances among 20 different types, based on image rather than ingredient. These may be broadly grouped under the headings of: seasonal nature (living floral; watery; summer); life stages (baby; mother's; madame; bridal); emotions (new sexy; love; happiness; relaxation); TPO (formal; career; night); gender distinctions (men's fragrance; unisex); and perfume *per se* (classic; precious; for beginners). It goes on to classify individual perfumes on a series of two-dimensional scales, overwhelmingly pervaded by combinations of freshness (*sawayakasa*) and sweetness (*amasa*) (in line with the fact that almost three quarters of the perfumes marketed in Japan are floral based). This classification gives rise to the following combinations in what might be described as a 'moral construction' of

Figure 6: Guerlain's *Samsara* as an example of an Oriental Amber(y) perfume, with five star rating for sexiness. (From *Kōsui*, Fukuji 1992)

the Japanese sense of self (Synnott 1991):[33]
- *Sweetness* and -freshness, -sexiness (*sekushīsa*), -softness (*yawarakasa*), -spiciness (*supaisīsa*), -sweetness, -tanginess (*karasa*);
- *Freshness* and -coolness (*kūrusa*), -sexiness, -softness, -spiciness, -tanginess;
- *Gorgeousness* (*gōjyasusa*) and -softness;
- *Sexiness* and -freshness, -spiciness, and -sweetness;
- *Sharpness* (*shāpusa*) and -freshness, and -sexiness;
- *Spiciness* and -freshness, and -sweetness;
- *Warmth* (*atatakasa*) and -sweetness.

Classifying the classifiers

Where does this preliminary outline of the Japanese classification of fragrance leave us?

Firstly, as has been more generally noted, Japanese words describing smell often depend on the other four senses of taste, touch, sight and sound, rather than on smell *per se*. At the same time, however, Japanese does have a handful more of such strictly olfactory terms than many other languages described in the literature (they are marked by an asterisk below). Sense by sense, the following classification of terms can be constructed:[34]

1. Touch
- Texture: *yawarakai* (soft), *soft*, *katai* (hard), *konappoi* (powdery), *maroyaka* (rounded), *surudoi* (sharp), *sasu yō na* (sharp, prick)
- Weight: *karoyaka*, *karui* (light), *omoi* (heavy)
- Strength: *rich*, *odayaka* (gentle), *yowai* (weak), *chikarazuyoi* (strong)
- Temperature: *atatakai* (warm), *tsumetai* (cold), *cool*
- Humidity: *dry*, *kawaita* (dry), *shimetta* (damp)
- Tactile (onomatopoeia): *beta beta* (clammy), *sara sara* (dry)

2. Taste
- Taste: *amai* (sweet), *suppai* (sour), **sui(i)* (sour [dialect]),[35] *nigai* (bitter), *karai* (spicy), *shibui* (astringent)

3. Smell
- Fragrance: **kaguwashii*, **kōbashii*, **fukuiku(taru)* (fragrant)
- Odour: **kusai* (stink), **namagusai* (raw)
- Olfactory (onomatopoeia): **kun kun* (sniff sniff), **pun pun* (pungent), **pun to* (aroma, stink), **baga baga*, **banga banga* (stink [dialect]), **tsun to* (pungent)

4. Sight
- Appearance: *floral* (*rose*, *jasmine*, etc.), object + **-kusai* (smack of; stink, of sweat [*ase-kusai*], tobacco [*tabako-kusai*], Japanese *sake* [*sake-kusai*] etc.), **aokusai* (smell of fresh green leaves)
- Clarity: *akarui* (bright), *azayaka* (vivid), *kurai* (dark), *mizumizushii* (watery), *tōmei* (transparent)
- Shape: *maroyaka* (rounded), *surudoi* (sharp) (see Texture above)
- Colour: *okufukai* (profound [refers to both hue and depth])

5. Sound
- Musical: *note*, *harmony*, *chōwa* (harmony)
- Aural: *kaori o kiku* (listen to a fragrance)[36]

We should note here that Japanese only partly follows the general principle that 'a particular sense can be qualified by terms from senses deemed more basic, but can itself be used to qualify senses deemed more specialised' (Classen 1993:55). In other words, touch – deemed to be the most 'basic' sense because of its physical immediacy (Takahashi 2005:611) – provides terms for taste, smell, sight and sound, whereas (the comparatively distant sense of) sound ideally should not provide descriptives for any of the other senses. The fact that terms used to describe taste double as olfactory terms in Japanese fragrance descriptives is, therefore, unexceptional. However, the fact that Japanese olfactory terms are qualified by visual, and to a lesser extent aural, terms *is* exceptional. What is particularly interesting is that in Japanese one 'listens' to a fragrance, while the Chinese character (*in*) adopted most commonly to express the idea of smell (*nioi*) in Japanese in fact means 'sound' (Takahashi 2005:608).

Secondly, descriptives of particular fragrances often result from the name, speciality or style of a particular fashion house, designer, or celebrity. Thus, *KL* is described as a 'Karl Lagerfeld-like modern, semi-oriental' fragrance, hinting at the folding fan that is that designer's public trademark. *Fendi* is described as 'a chypre group fragrance to be worn with a rich fur coat', and so alludes to the fashion house's history as a furrier. *Passion* has a 'gorgeous (*hanayaka*) fragrance redolent of Liz (Taylor's) numerous passionate love affairs'.

Similarly, descriptives also relate to a perfume's name, although the ingredients and descriptives here form a chicken-and-egg relation that merely serves to brand the perfume. Thus, *Christalle* has a 'transparent fragrance', while *Knowing* has a 'fragrance appropriate for a woman of intelligence who knows herself, who knows elegance, and who knows the real thing'. In similar vein, *Vent Vert* is 'light and fresh like its name'. Occasionally, ingredients are given a 'Japanese twist', as in the following description of *Sacré* by Caron: 'a stern fragrance redolent of eastern mystery, as implied in its name "a sacred thing"'.

Thirdly, there appears to be no hard and fast rule linking fragrance descriptives exclusively to a perfume's classification and main ingredient. For example, *romantic* and *classy* (*kihin aru*) are used of both floral and chypre types, while other common adjectives like *fresh* (*sawayaka*), *passionate* (*jōnetsuteki*) and *mysterious* (*shimpiteki*) are used across the ingredient board. An exception may be *sweet* which seems to apply only to the floral notes. The same may be true of *mysterious*, applied to chypre, and *eastern* (*tōyōteki*), to oriental, perfume notes, although occurrences were too few for any hypothesis to be reliable. In general, fragrance descriptives define odours – and thus the women who apply them to parts of their bodies – in numerous different ways that are more often than not simultaneously *evaluative* or 'hedonic' (Chastrette 2002:108; Dubois and Ruby 2002:55-62) (thereby echoing Lehrer's findings with regard to wine vocabulary).[37]

Fourthly, these evaluative words used for fragrances are in general very similar to those used to describe fashion clothing (cf. Moeran 2004). Examples include *azayaka, elegant, gorgeous, hanayaka, karoyaka, kawaii, koseiteki, otona no, romantic, senren sareta, yūga*, and so on. The dominant fragrance descriptives, however, revolve around two – possibly redundant – pairs of opposites: freshness (*sawayaka*), and elegance (*kihin no aru*), on the one hand, and passion (*jōnetsuteki*) and beauty (*utsukushii*), on the other. These in part parallel, in part contrast with, the emphasis on femininity, elegance, classical taste, charm, and so on found in the language of fashion. Fragrance descriptives are in particular marked by elements of sensuality, mystery and passion not found in the latter discourse.

Fifthly, while both Japanese and English loan words are used to describe smells of different kinds, the most commonly used words are Japanese, not loan words. This contrasts markedly with the language of fashion, and suggests that the sense of smell and its communication is somehow still specifically 'Japanese', rather than 'Western' (in spite of the fact that the majority of perfumes marketed in Japan are European and American in origin). Commonly used descriptives in order of frequency across fragrance families were: *sawayaka* (fresh); *kihin no aru* (elegant, refined); *utsukushii* (beautiful) and *jōnetsuteki* (passionate); *shimpiteki* (mysterious), *amai* (sweet) and *romantic*; *dokusōteki* (original, creative), *hanayaka* (gorgeous), *jōhin* (high class), *kannōteki* (sensual) and *yūga* (graceful, elegant, urbane).

But how do Japanese women themselves react to the language of fragrance marketing? Inquiries among a dozen fellow employees at the National Museum of Ethnology, where I am currently employed as visiting researcher, reveal that that there is, in fact, a lot of agreement about the difference between, for example, *shimpiteki* and *mysterious*. The former they see as positive in meaning and imbued with an element of 'nobility' or 'divinity' (*tōtoi*) – primarily because the word makes use of the Chinese character for 'god' (*shin*) – which *mysterious* does not necessarily have. The latter can be somewhat 'suspicious' (*ayashii*) and – as the word implies in English – a bit of a 'puzzle' (*nazo ga aru, nazome*). It does not always have a good meaning and can be misconstrued (*chotto warui fū ni omou ka mo shirenai*), so that it has a bit of a 'dangerous feeling' about it (*chotto kiken na kanji*).

Informants were less clear about the difference between 'Japanese' (*nihonteki*) and 'eastern' (*tōyōteki*) fragrance. Many of them felt that 'eastern' meant 'not Western' (*seiyō ja nai*), or something that 'avoided the West' (*seiyō o nozoku*), but could not be more specific about its attributes. They had no trouble in agreeing about the meaning of 'Japanese', however. A 'Japanese' scent could be summarised in the phrase *o-kō*, 'artistic' incense that often makes use of aloes and sandal wood, so that a 'Japanese' fragrance does not include flowers, and does not force itself on you too much (*shuchō shisugite iru mono ja nai*). Rather, it is 'reserved' (*hikaeme*), 'graceful' (*okuyukashii*), 'tasteful' (*omomuki*) and 'refined' (*kihin*). In this respect, 'Japanese' odours might be seen to reflect a kind of purity of Japanese culture.

It is vis-à-vis this last semantic set that 'femininity' (*onna rashisa*) was also viewed. Although informants recognized that the word changed all the time in meaning, from one generation to the next, and that it could easily slip into a seductive (*iroppoi*) sexiness and so become very 'vulgar' (*gehin*), if an offensive element (*iyarashii bubun*) was added to it, they were virtually unanimous in thinking that 'femininity' should ideally be 'graceful' (*okuyukashii*). Thus, 'femininity' and 'Japaneseness' become identical.

Gender constructions

As noted, many of the fragrance descriptives used in the journalism and marketing literature provide evaluations of how women should be or appear in the modern world. Classen (1992:142ff.) has noted that in most male-centred societies particular odours are ascribed to women, and that these differ according to a particular society's cultural preoccupations. This '*odor di femina*' includes the odours of the skin, hair, genital region and mouth, and leads to all kinds of classifications of women in Western-language literature. Blondes, for example, are supposed to exhibit 'a very delicate amber colour', chestnut brown haired women 'a sort of violet colour', and brunettes 'an odour of ebony wood' (Bloch 1934:52-53). More generally, a tripartite classification is made of women as sluts or prostitutes; maidens, wives, or mothers; and seductresses. This classification has a corresponding olfactory symbolism.

> In *The Odour of the Other* women are found to be divided into three different olfactory and symbolic types in western tradition: fragrant for exemplars of ideal womanhood, foul for socially unacceptable women such as prostitutes and witches, and spicy for alluring but dangerous *femmes fatales* (Classen 1993:9-10).

Unlike some European languages, in which a direct connection exists between bad smell and slovenly women (for example, putrid and *puta* or prostitute), Japanese does not, so far as I know, make any such symbolic association.[38] In European and American societies, the discourse of modern perfumes would seem to make a clear distinction between the 'maiden' and the 'seductress'. This may be seen most readily in the naming of products. The 'maiden' is symbolized in particular by perfumes associated with a floral bouquet (for example, *Angel (Innocent), Miss Dior, Venus*) and by their associations (*Amour Amour, J'Adore, Youth Dew*). The seductress appears in *Animale, Flirt, Libertine, Panthère*,[39] and *Sirene,* with associated desires like *Allure, Desire, Envy, Fetish, L'Interdit, Magie Noire, Passion, Rapture,* and *Tabu* – perfumes which usually rely on exotic floral and spicy oriental notes.[40] Some perfume houses manufacture and market both types: *Eternity* and *Obsession* (Calvin Klein Cosmetics); *Baby Doll* and *Opium* (Yves Saint Laurent Parfums); *Amarige* and *Fleur d'Interdit* (Parfums Givenchy).

As Classen (1992:143) notes, maidens are generally – universally – associated with fragrance (in this context, read floral notes),[41] while 'seductresses are associated with heavily sweet and spicy odours; the sweetness of the scent signifying their beauty and attraction, and the spiciness and heaviness, their exotic status and overwhelming powers of fascination'. Certainly, such characterizations would appear to hold in English-language books describing individual perfumes, where phrases like 'sexual explicitness', 'unbridled suggestiveness', 'persistent sensuality', 'tropical charmer', 'sheer tigress', and so on are used (cf. Oakes 1996).

Japanese words, however, are less sexually explicit. Of perfumes graded five stars in terms of sexiness in *Kōsui*, for example, only a very few imitate English language descriptions and even these are, by comparison, quite mild. For example, *Parfum d'Hermès* is for 'passionate feelings', *Saso* for 'the developed, adult woman', and *Armani* 'for a woman of atmosphere'. *Obsession* is 'a fragrance that makes tigers out of men', while *Luciano Soprani* is 'a fragrance for the adult woman who would stimulate men' (Fukuji 1992). The remainder are described in generally mild terms (as in *Cabotine* for the 'innocent woman' [*mujaki na onna*]), where the fragrance of a perfume – and thus the character of the woman wearing it – is usually limited to such simplicities as *sexy* and two variations on *mystery* (*shimpiteki* and *mysterious*). This is not to suggest that the woman who wears a perfume like *Opium* or *Obsession* is a pure 'maiden'; rather that the contemporary Japanese version of a 'seductress' is a much milder version than that found in the West – primarily because most Japanese women are not, as yet, ready to make the move from 'maiden' to raunchy 'seductress'.

But what of men and their fragrances? Traditionally, it is the dry, spicy, woody category that has dominated the male end of the fragrance market, so that there is an immediate contrast between women's fragrances defined by sweetness (*amakuchi*), based primarily on flowers and fruit, and giving rise to a 'femininity' (*onnarashisa*);

and men's fragrances, defined by spiciness (*karakuchi*), based primarily on spices and green chypre, and giving rise to a 'masculinity' (*otokorashisa*). In each case, the common descriptive is 'fresh' (*sawayaka na*) which would seem to express both sexes in their 'natural' state.[42]

But descriptions of men's fragrances suggest that this traditional distinction is not so cut and dried and that, contrary to what Classen suggests, men are also coming to be categorised in different ways (Classen, Howes and Synnott 1994:191). For a start, there are now numerous men's floral scents in which sweetness becomes a defining character in Japan. From these emerges the image of a 'gentle man' (*yasashii otoko*) who is *chic*, *elegant*, *modern*, and *urban*. This type of man contrasts with the more traditional tones conveyed by tangy, woody and spicy colognes: *dry*, *pure*, *simple*, and *transparent* – the more or less odourless, 'natural man' (*shizen na otoko*). At the same time, thanks to the introduction of brands like *Opium Pour Homme* and *Obsession For Men*, a third type of man – the 'dandy' – is coming to be defined in Japanese writings which focus on the 'tangy' and 'mysterious' sexiness he needs to cope with the 'one rank up, mature woman.'

Towards a sociology of olfaction

This paper has presented some very preliminary observations about the place of odours in Japanese society and the marketing of fragrances there, in an attempt to introduce some new material into what are becoming somewhat repetitive discussions in the sociology of olfaction (a word to be preferred to the more limiting and static sociology of odours?). As part of this endeavour, ideally I should now ask what effect differences in culture and lifestyle have upon the perception and generation of odours in Japan, as a means of opening up avenues to facilitate the exploration of social and cultural relations underpinning Japanese olfactory culture.

Preliminary findings have suggested, firstly, that Japanese olfactory culture may be defined as one in which odours are extinguished rather than added, and that it may in this way be differentiated from European and American olfactory cultures. This hypothesis, though interesting, will almost certainly need to be refined, given that Japanese *do* add scents to a wide range of fast moving consumer goods, building materials, air conditioning, and so on. As part of this process of refinement, I have suggested that in all societies (as in all products) odours are both masked and added, and that it may be possible to map different societies' olfactory cultures according to how much they odorize and deodorize the social world around them.

Secondly, the Japanese vocabulary of smell appears, initially at least, to be as undeveloped as smell vocabularies in other languages, in the sense that it describes an odour in relation to other objects ('this fragrance smells like a baby just come out of the bath' [*chōdo o-furo kara agatta akachan no kaori shite iru kōsui*]), or with words that are related to senses other than smell (*refreshing* [*sawayaka*], *heavy* [*omoi*], and so on). However, Japanese seems to go against the rule that words for sight and colour are not generally used for smell. It also has a comparatively large (though still very small) number of terms used exclusively for olfaction. At the same time, 'pure' Japanese words and phrases (such as *sweet-scented* [*kanbashii*] and *invigorating* [*sugasugashii*], but also including long-used Chinese compounds) seem to be preferred to more recently imported Western language loanwords (*charming*, *sexy* and so on). This linguistic preference supports, perhaps, the idea that smell has been historically, and still is, a fundamental aspect in the structuring of Japanese people's relations to the social and material world about them.[43]

Thirdly, the discourse of fragrance in Japan follows a near universal pattern in distinguishing between two types of woman – the 'maiden' and the 'seductress' – but the latter is phrased more in terms of 'mysteriousness' than of 'seduction' or 'eroticism'. At the same time, it has created a tripartite classification of *men* – provisionally called the 'Gentle Man', the 'Natural Man', and the 'Dandy' – which hitherto has not been noted in anthropological discussions of the male sex. In this respect, market research conducted in Europe during the late 1980s, suggests a similar tripartite division in men's aesthetic preferences. First, there is the 'cultivated gentleman' who is described as an 'elegant and yet unobtrusive personality who is oriented towards traditional values'. His fragrance should be 'classic', 'elegant', and 'harmonious'. Then there is the 'dynamic optimist', described as 'active' and with a desire for 'stimulation and accomplishment'. He wants his fragrance to be 'fresh', 'modern', and 'stimulating'. Finally, there is the 'emotional individualist' who has a 'sensitive and introverted personality with a tendency towards stimulation'. His ideal fragrance notes should be 'natural', 'sensuous', and yet 'masculine' (Schmidt 1991:152-153).

Lastly, we should realize that research into a sociology of olfaction is important because technology is bringing smell back into our everyday lives. We are all of us very aware of the scent of our after-shaves, soaps, and clothes after being washed with a particular washing powder. We also take more or less conscious note of the flavours of food and drink, as well as of the natural smells and scents of other products with which we come into daily contact. Scents are being used more and more in marketing – as when an item of furniture from Ikea, for example, is impregnated with a special 'freshly cut wood' scent, or the plastic dashboard of a luxury car with a special scent to make consumers aware that they are sitting in a Mercedes, and not in a Ferrari or BMW. Similarly, airline companies have been known to impregnate their tickets with a particular scent, capsules of which they will also sprinkle in their aircraft so that boarding passengers will crush them with their feet and cause an identical scent to pervade the cabin environment. In other words, scents are being used subtly to brand companies, as well as products.

Under such circumstances, the uses of scents are likely to become even more pervasive. Already, some people are talking about how the development of broad band technology in cell phones, for example, will enable users to transmit odours as well as visual images to those with whom they are communicating. It is being suggested, too, that it will not be too long before the cinematic experience will include odour in its visual repertoire (something already practised in some theatre performances, as well as in theme park experiences). In other words, as we see a man cooking a delicious meal in a film like *Eat Drink, Man Woman*, so will we be able to simultaneously smell that food. Similarly with other (possibly less pleasant) smells: like the exhaust fumes from the car driven furiously by the hero, the perfume worn by the heroine to seduce her man, and the vomit that seems to be *de rigueur* among actors who come across a dead body in the woods.

But how, as anthropologists, are we to go about studying smell, when in all probability we are conducting our research in a society which, unlike that of the Andaman islanders, is not particularly attuned to olfactory experiences and communication? One way, of course, is to focus on a particular group of people: a *kōdō* incense master, for example, and his school of devotees, together with their practices (Cobbi 2004); a community whose inhabitants are primarily employed in the production of perfume (Grasse); or a large corporation specialising in the development of fine fragrances, cosmetics and toiletries, or fabrics and detergents (like IFF, Shiseido, or Procter & Gamble). But such research, while potentially fascinating, would be likely to lead away from olfaction *per se*, as the intrepid fieldworker follows the different economic, political, kinship, and organizational leads that have brought such people together and bind them in on-going, long-term social relationships. It would, of course, in this way integrate the olfactory with other socio-cultural forms of communication (as well as contribute to research on global commodity chains), but it would also result in but a partial account of a particular society's olfactory culture.

A second, complementary way of conducting research on the sociology of olfaction, therefore, is to interview a wide variety of people who use smell professionally in their everyday lives (cf. Candau 2000), and ideally observe them in their olfactory environments. These would include perfumers, chemists, and incense blenders, on the one hand, and sewerage treatment and garbage disposal engineers, on the other – as well as wine, whiskey, beer, *sake* and tea tasters; manufacturers of shampoos, soaps, and toiletries; bee keepers, herbalists, florists; blind and anosmic people; doctors, surgeons, nurses, *kanpōyaku* chemists, aroma therapists, masseurs and masseuses; chefs, cooks, and food tasters; workers in slaughter houses, fermented food and cheese factories; firemen; interior designers of buildings, houses, and cars; and so on and so forth. By finding out how such specialists *articulate* (Latour 2004:209) their olfactory experiences, competences and knowledge, and how they register and deal with the layers of differences that exist between and within different specializations, one can begin to put together the myriad pieces of information that make up the puzzle of a society's olfactory culture.

E-mail: bdm.ikl@cbs.dk

Notes

1 Axel and Buck were awarded the Nobel Prize in Physiology or Medicine on October 4, 2004, two weeks after I gave a first draft of this paper at the European Association of Social Anthropologists' biannual conference in Vienna.
2 I will here use 'smell' and 'odour' (both *nioi* in Japanese) as generic terms to describe all kinds of olfactory sensations, both natural and artificial, without regard to their positive or negative connotations. 'Fragrance' will be used to refer to different kinds of perfumes (*parfum, eau de parfum, eau de toilette, eau de Cologne*) (*kōsui* in Japanese), and 'scent' (*kaori*) to odours that are added to products (like soaps and toiletries) which would otherwise be

unscented. This strikes me as more useful than Synnott's (1991) distinction between 'natural', 'manufactured' and 'symbolic' odours which, by his own admittance, tend to overlap.
3 For research purposes, Japan has been selected for study because of the recorded importance of smell in its cultural history and because it represents a non-Western olfactory tradition in an advanced industrialized society. France has been selected because of its importance in recent Western (specifically European) cultural history, and because the southern region of Grasse is the production centre of many of the world's fragrances and perfumes. The United States is chosen because it produces a large number of, primarily synthetic, fragrances and because it boasts the greatest consumption, and most varied numbers of brands, of fragrances and perfumes.
4 The burning of incense is common to many religions, including Christianity. We might note that the origin of the word 'perfume' in English is to be found in the Latin *fumum* (smoke) or *fumere* (burn), and *per* (right through or thoroughly). By burning incense, people enabled their prayers to be transported to the heavens for contemplation by the gods (Pybus 1999:3).
5 The same was true of medieval European courts (cf. Classen, Howes and Synnott 1994).
6 On smell in tourism more generally, see, for example, Dann and Jacobsen (2003).
7 Indeed, the Chinese character for *self* was originally a drawing of a nose (the currently used character for nose has a sound element added to the original) (Kato 1953:261-2).
8 Gibbons (1986:328) suggests that this may be because women 'pay more attention to odours – cooking, sniffing meat for freshness, using spices and perfumes'. Although these may be contributing factors (based on their gender inequality?), it is more likely that women's sense of smell is related to their hormone cycles and physical well-being (cf. Fox n.d.:11-12).
9 Immanuel Kant also thought smell the most dispensable of the senses (in Howes 2002:67).
10 Sperber (1975:117) relates the evocative power of smells to the absence of a semantic field in which to express them. If, as I shall later suggest, the Japanese language performs comparatively well in expressing odours, it may explain the HILL survey anomaly.
11 Cf. American perfumers' comments that 'Japanese fragrances are delicate, fine, not blunt or obvious as they tend to be in the U.S.' (Boyd 1986:358).
12 Interview with Hidehiko Sekizawa, October 29, 2002. It is interesting in this respect that the Japanese cultural studies scholar, Koichi Iwabuchi (2002), has chosen the metaphor of 'culturally odourless' to describe the marketing of Japanese popular culture in Asia.
13 Odorozing and deodorizing would appear, too, to underlie both primary positive (fragrant and neutral smelling, or inodorate) and negative (foul, dangerously fragrant, and inodorate) olfactory characteristics ascribed to 'the other' in many different societies (Classen 1992:158).
14 Leffingwell and Associates, 1999-2002 Flavor & Fragrance Industry Leaders, http://www.leffingwell.com/top_10.htm
15 Advertising agency marketing data, 2002.
16 'Atomising a generation', *New Statesman & Society*, 9 August, 1995.
17 Advertising agency marketing data, 2002. This is a chicken-and-egg manufacturing-consumption cycle, of course, so that it is hard to tell whether consumers are basically fickle and so force manufacturers to come up with a new fragrance, or whether manufacturers keep producing new fragrances in order to prevent consumers from developing loyalty to a – possibly competing – brand.
18 http://www.perfumeworld.net/ehomeframe.htm.
19 One early study notes that blacks used to use a lot of perfume to 'avoid the odour-stigma of being ill-smelling' (Dollard 1957:383). A Japanese woman informant has suggested that if she wore a strongly fragrant perfume at work, she would open herself up to accusations by

her colleagues of 'sexual harassment'. This echoes an early British law that permitted men to divorce their wives on the ground of having been seduced by the enticing perfumes and cosmetics they wore.
20 Advertising agency marketing data, 2000.
21 It transpired that a large majority of this group consisted of men in their 30s. For the most part, fragrance users are in their teens and 20s (Advertising agency marketing data, 2000).
22 They are also marketed internationally. In June 1992, Shiseido launched its first international fragrance, *Fémininité de Bois*, which was made in Gien, France. Shiseido's $18 million investment was at the time equal to the company's annual sales of all its products in France (Wilk 1993:54).
23 One traditional classification of smell, dating back to at least the 10th century, is *Rokkoku gomi*. This phrase stands for the 'six countries' of origin (*kyara* [Java or the Malay Peninsula], *rakoku* [Thailand], *manaban* [India, Marabal region], *manaka* [Malacca], *sumotara* [Sumatra] and *sasora* [India, Sassore]): and the 'five bouquets' (spicy hot [*shin*], sweet [*kan*], bitter [*ku*], sour [*san*], and salty *kan*]) (cf. Gatten 1977:47).
24 The uses of metonymy and metaphor that make up the fragrance marketing rhetoric can ideally be expanded with infinite variety. However, as we shall see, they tend to be marked by cliché and redundance (Boutaud 2002:130).
25 Various kinds of classifications are used to define the particular characteristic of a fragrance, which in the perfumery industry is itself defined by the proportion of oil essentials it contains and resulting staying power. Thus a perfume contains 15-30 percent of natural oil essences and lasts for five to seven hours, whereas an *eau de parfum* (10-25 percent) lasts for up to five, and an *eau de toilette* (5-10 percent) just three to four, hours.
26 On the basis of this and other classifications, staff working at the Neurosciences & Systèmes Sensoriels at the Université Claude Bernard Lyon 1, in France, have regrouped odour descriptives into 36 categories (including 'odourless') (http://olfac.univ-lyon1.fr/documentation/olfaction/descripteur/d-regrp.htm).
27 For example, *Chanel No 5*, Lancôme's *Miracle*, and Clinique's *Happy*.
28 For example, Shiseido's *Chant de Coeur* and Miyake Issey's *L'Eau d'Issey*.
29 For example, *Miss Dior* and *Cabochard*.
30 For example, Chanel's *Coco* and Shiseido's *Angelique*. Advertising agency marketing data, 2000.
31 Credit for this method of describing the development of a fragrances – which my research suggests is not necessarily adhered to by practising perfumers – is usually given to William Poucher (1923) who, in the 1920s, measured the evaporation rates of perfume ingredients and classified them on a scale of one to 100, with faster evaporating ingredients ranked closer to the 'top' of the scale. The English perfumer, S. Piesse, first related specific odours to notes on a music scale in 1865 (Pybus 1999:18).
32 In this context, we might note, though not necessarily agree with, the argument put forward by Gell (1977:30-31) that people do *not* wear perfume in order to communicate something about themselves. Rather, it is the symbolic *act* of putting on a fragrance which is important. In this respect, perfume is seen as occupying a space between thing and idea, of the world but not in it. As such, it is closely allied with transcendence and the wearing of perfume becomes a magical act.
33 Cf. the English vocabulary of 'words of sense' described by Classen (1993:60-76).
34 I have here included ongoing fieldwork data based on interviews in Japan to augment the written material on which the discussion has so far been based.
35 Informants say that *sui(i)* is derived from *suppai* (sour), but is not used at all of food or taste, but only of smell.

36 For the sake of brevity, I will omit fragrance descriptives that fall into such socio-cultural categories as age, class, personality, time and space.
37 Preliminary written material research produced 52 different fragrance descriptives, ranging from *new* (*atarashii*) and *exotic*, to *beautiful* and *mysterious* (*shimpiteki*).
38 Indeed, the *Genji Monogatari* suggests that both positive 'fragrance' (*kaori*) and – the now sometimes negatively perceived – 'smell' (*nioi*) were used in the masculine, rather than feminine, symbolic realm.
39 Classen (1992:144) notes that one Elizabethan English clergyman compared sexual sorceresses to panthers, which were believed in ancient times to attract other animals by the sweetness of their breath. The House of Cartier is virtually synonymous with the reclining panther as its logo. The woman who wears this scent is described in one book as an 'ultrasophisticated huntress... a strong, sensual creature... poised and elegant, but not over 50' (Oakes 1996:215).
40 This type of olfactory classification is reinforced by a classification of nature which moves from 'tamed' (cultivated flowers and ferns) to 'untamed' (wild plants and animals) (cf. Classen 1992:147).
41 Iwan Bloch (1934:183) discusses Shunammitism, or 'that very ancient belief in the therapeutic and macrobiotic effect of the scent of young people upon older ones, especially when different sexes are concerned', and proceeds to give numerous examples of kings and ordinary mortals who tried to prolong their lives by having them inhale the scent of virgins who slept by their side.
42 When we recall that femininity, elegance and charm were the themes highlighted by American perfume advertisements in the 1950s (cf. Classen, Howes and Synnott 1994:189), we might prefer to think that Japan is in a process of 'catching up' and that, in 20 years' time, Japanese women will wear as obviously 'seductive' fragrances as their American counterparts do today.
43 There appears to be some continuity between contemporary Japanese and Heian Court aesthetics in terms of elegance, gorgeousness, sensuality and attraction (cf. Gatten 1977:44-46).

References

Arai, T.
    1996   *Kōsui Jiten.* (*Perfume Dictionary*). Tokyo: Fujin Gahōsha.
Bloch, I.
    1934   *Odoratus Sexualis: A Scientific and Literary Study of Sexual Scents and Erotic Perfumes.* New York: Panurge.
Boutaud, J.J.
    2002   Image et Tropisme du Parfum: Sémiotique et Communication de l'Image Olfactive. In: J. Candau, M-C. Grasse, and A. Holley (Eds.), *Fragrances du Désir et Plaisir.* Marseille: Éditions Jeanne Laffitte. Pp. 129-138.
Buck, L. and R. Axel
    1991   A Novel Multigene Family May Encode Odorant Receptors: A Molecular Basis for Odor Recognition. *Cell* 65(1):175-187.
Buck, L. *et al.*
    1999   Combinatorial Receptor Codes for Odors. *Cell* 96(5):713-723.

Calkin, R. and Jellinek, J. S.
    1994 *Perfumery: Practice and Principles*. New York: Wiley-Interscience.

Candau, J.
    2000 *Mémoire at Expériences Olfactives: Anthropologie d'un Savoir-faire Sensorial*. Paris: Presses Universitaires de France.

Chastrette, M.
    2002 Classification of Odors and Structure-Odor Relationships. In: C. Rouby *et al.* (Eds.), *Olfaction, Taste, and Cognition*. Cambridge: Cambridge University Press. Pp. 100-116.

Classen, C.
    1992 The Odor of the Other: Olfactory Symbolism and Cultural Categories. *Ethos* 20(2):133-166.
    1993 *Worlds of Sense: Exploring the Senses in History and across Cultures*. London and New York: Routledge.

Classen, C., Howes, D., and A. Synnott
    1994 *Aroma. The Cultural History of Smell*. London and New York: Routledge.

Cobbi, J.
    2004 Éducation Olfactive au Japon. In: J. Cobbi and R. Dulau (Eds.), *Sentir: Pour une Anthropologie des Odeurs*. Paris: L'Harmattan. Pp. 93-106.

Commission Technique de la Société Française des Parfumeurs
    1990 *La Classification de Parfums*. Paris: Comité Français du Parfum.

Dahl, R.
    1976 *Switch Bitch*. Harmondsworth: Penguin.

Dann, G. and J. K. Jacobsen
    2003 Tourism Smellscapes. *Tourism Geographies* 5(1):3-25.

David, S.
    2002 Linguistic Expressions for Odor in French. In: C. Rouby *et al.* (Eds.), *Olfaction, Taste, and Cognition*. Cambridge: Cambridge University Press. Pp. 82-99.

Dollard, J.
    1957 *Caste and Class in a Southern Town*. New York: Doubleday.

Dubois, D. and C. Rouby
    2002 Names and Categories for Odors: The Veridical Label. In C. Rouby *et al.* (Eds.), *Olfaction, Taste, and Cognition*. Cambridge: Cambridge University Press. Pp. 47-66.

Fox, K.
    n.d. The Smell Report. Overview of Facts and Findings. Unpublished manuscript. Oxford: Social Issues Research Centre.

Fragrance Foundation, The
    2001 *The Fragrance Foundation Reference Guide*. 21st Edition. New York: The Fragrance Foundation.

Fukuji, Y.
    1992 *Kōsui. (Perfume)*. Tokyo: Fujin Gahōsha.

Gatten, A.
    1977 A Wisp of Smoke: Scent and Character in the Tale of Genji. *Monumenta Nipponica* 32(1):35-48.

Geertz, C.
    1973 *The Interpretation of Cultures*. New York: Basic Books.

Gell, A.
  1977 Magic, Perfume, Dream... In: I.M. Lewis (Ed.), *Symbols and Sentiments: Cross-Cultural Studies in Symbolism*. London: Academic Press. Pp. 25-38.
Gibbons, B.
  1986 The Intimate Sense of Smell. *National Geographic* 170(3):324-361.
Hakuhōdō Seikatsu Sōgō Kenkyūjo [HILL]
  1994 *'Gokan' no Jidai: Me, Mimi, Hana, Aji, Shoku no Shōhi Shakaigaku. (The Age of the Five Senses: A Consumption Sociology of the Eye, Ear, Nose, Taste and Touch)*. Tokyo: President-sha.
Hasegawa, T.
  1993 Kūchō to Kaori. In: *Kōdō Nyūmon (Introduction to the Incense Ceremony)*. Tokyo: Tankōsha. Pp. 158-159.
Holley, A.
  2002 Cognitive Aspects of Olfaction in Perfumer Practice. In: C. Rouby *et al.* (Eds.), *Olfaction, Taste, and Cognition*. Cambridge: Cambridge University Press. Pp. 16-26.
Howes, D.
  2002 Nose-wise. Olfactory Metaphors in Mind. In: C. Rouby *et al.* (Eds.) *Olfaction, Taste, and Cognition*. Cambridge: Cambridge University Press. Pp. 67-81.
Iwabuchi, K.
  2002 *Recentering Globalization: Popular Culture and Japanese Transnationalism*. Durham and London: Duke University Press.
Jellinek, P.
  1997 *The Psychological Basis of Perfumery*. Edited and translated by S. Jellinek. London: Blackie Academic and Professional.
Kato, J.
  1953 Chinese Characters [II]. *Monumenta Nipponica* 9(1-2):258-276.
Katz, J.
  1996 *Koh-Doh: The Japanese Way of Fragrance*. MA Thesis, Department of Anthropology, Copenhagen University.
Largey, G. and D. Watson
  1972 The Sociology of Odors. *The American Journal of Sociology* 77(6):1021-1034.
Latour, B.
  2004 How to Talk about the Body? The Normative Dimension of Science Studies. *Body & Society* 10(2-3):205-229.
Le Guérer, A.
  2002 Olfaction and Cognition: A Philosophical and Psychoanalytic View. In: C. Rouby *et al.* (Eds.), *Olfaction, Taste, and Cognition*. Cambridge: Cambridge University Press. Pp. 3-15.
Lehrer, A.
  1983 *Wine and Conversation*. Bloomington: Indiana University Press.
Lévi-Strauss, C.
  1981 *The Naked Man: Introduction to a Science of Mythology: 4*. London: Jonathan Cape.
Marie Claire Japon
  1996 *A Reader's Survey on Fragrance*. December 1996. Tokyo: Chuokoron-sha.
Miyazawa, M. and S. Werner
  2001 *Kaori no Hikaku Bunka-shi (A Comparative Cultural History of Fragrance)*. Tokyo: Hokuju Shuppan.

Moeran, B.
   2003   Celebrities and the Name Economy. *Research in Economic Anthropology* 22:291-321.
   2004   A Japanese Discourse of Fashion and Taste. *Fashion Theory* 8(1):35-62.

Morris, D.
   2004   *The Naked Woman: A Study of the Female Body*. London: Jonathan Cape.

Morris, I.
   1969   *The World of the Shining Prince*. Harmondsworth: Peregrine.

Oakes, J.
   1996   *The Book of Perfumes*. Sydney: Harper-Collins.

Pavia, F.
   1995   *The World of Perfume*. New York: Knickerbockers Press.

Poucher, W.
   1923   *Perfumes and Cosmetics*. London: Chapman and Hall.

Pybus, D.
   1999   The History of Aroma Chemistry and Perfume. In: D. Pybus and C. Sell (Eds.), *The Chemistry of Fragrances*. Cambridge: The Royal Society of Chemistry. Pp. 3-23.

Rouby, C. et al. (Eds.)
   2002   *Olfaction, Taste, and Cognition*. Cambridge: Cambridge University Press.

Saussure, F. de
   1983   *Course in General Linguistics*. Translated and annotated by Roy Harris. London: Duckworth.

Schmidt, H.O.
   1991   The 'New Man' and His Fragrance: A Psychology-Oriented Analysis of Target Groups Among Male Fragrance Users in Europe'. In: The European Society for Opinion and Marketing Research (Ed.), *Fine Fragrances and Fragrances in Consumer Products*. Amsterdam: ESOMAR. Pp. 149-155.

Sperber, D.
   1975   *Rethinking Symbolism*. Translated by A. Morton. Cambridge: Cambridge University Press and Paris: Hermann.

Synnott, A.
   1991   A Sociology of Smell. *Canadian Review of Sociology and Anthropology* 28(1):437-459.

Takahashi, Y.
   2005   Nioi no Hyōgen (Expressions of Smell). In: M. Yatagai et al., *Kaori no Hyakka Jiten (Fragrance Encyclopedia)*. Tokyo: Maruzen. Pp. 608-613.

Watson, L.
   2000   *Jacobson's Organ*. New York: Norton.

Wilk, R.J.
   1993   Fragrance in Japan: Kirei is Beautiful. In: The European Society for Opinion and Marketing Research (Ed.), *Consumer Research in the Fragrance Business*. Amsterdam: ESOMAR. Pp. 51-55.

Signs and Sight in Southern Uganda

Representing Perception in Ordinary Conversation

Ben Orlove, University of California
Merit Kabugo, Makarere University

ABSTRACT   Conversations in Luganda, a widely-spoken language in the East African nation of Uganda, frequently include discussions and evaluations of signs — readily observable phenomena that are understood to predict events that will soon take place. A corpus of material on this topic is examined, consisting of twenty signs and of four conversations in which these signs are discussed. Certain links are noted between specific sensory modes and these signs. The cultural significance of these sensory modes supports the cultural understanding that these signs are publicly available, rather than being restricted to certain individuals or conditions. It also supports the active discussion, rather than passive acceptance, of claims that individuals make to observing and interpreting signs. In this way, the cultural dimensions of sensory modes influence human perception and experience, and also support the public sphere of debates about the significance of events and about courses of action.

Introduction

In this paper, we explore the topic of the ethnography of the senses through the examination of a body of material that is structured culturally and linguistically. This body of material, drawn from field work that we have conducted in Uganda, centers on a set of beliefs that certain sensory perceptions (mostly, but not exclusively, of external objects) are indications that specific events will take place in the near future. We examine the beliefs themselves, and also review a set of conversations in which individuals discuss particular instances of such perceptions.

Though many anthropologists might classify this body of material as 'traditional knowledge' or 'folk belief' or 'cosmology', and center their analysis of it on cognition and epistemology, we argue that this material offers novel and interesting insights into the realms of sensation and perception as well. More specifically, we present the ways in which these specific cultural premises and forms can influence human sensation and perception. We note that this material contrasts with some of the other essays in this volume, which focus on the direct analysis of sensory experience. We suggest that these more direct analyses can be complemented by work like our own, that studies culturally codified systems of thinking and talking about sensory experience.

More concretely, we examine several aspects of a means that speakers of Luganda, a major language in Uganda, use to describe, present and draw on sense perceptions. This means is the *akabonero* (plural, *obubonero*), a word derived from the verb *kubona*, to see. Ugandans who are bilingual in Luganda and English often translate *akabonero* as 'sign.' Following this practice, we sometimes use the English word 'sign' in this paper to refer to it. To explore these points, we open with a discussion of the classification of sensory modes in Luganda, and then continue with an examination of some representative *obubonero* and a few conversations, in which they are discussed. We close with some reflections and conclusions.

Sensory modes in Luganda

Though sensory modes are, in some ways, part of the biological substrate of our species, shared by all human groups, there is great variation in the understandings of these modes — and therefore in the experience and the use of these modes — in different cultures and, as Jay (1993) shows in his magisterial study of vision in modern French thought, in different historical periods as well. To examine these differences, one can turn to a consideration of some simple features of language. One can list the verbs that are used in a specific language to describe the act of perception that links the perceiver and the object, and study the patterns of usage of these verbs. One can also examine the ways in which speakers of a language draw upon sensory modes as source domains for metaphors that describe less immediate forms of perception and knowledge. These features are connected to aspects of ordinary conversation in which speakers seek to persuade others of their beliefs and of the value of proposed courses of action.

Luganda, the most widely spoken Bantu language in Uganda, offers an interesting and instructive case of these relations. We open with a comparison of the verbs of sense in English and Luganda. English-speakers share a common-sense understanding that able-bodied humans are endowed with five senses, sight, hearing, taste, smell and touch; to these senses correspond the verbs to see, to hear, to taste, to smell and to feel. They are nearly always listed with seeing first and hearing second, though the others are not ordered as consistently. These words all apply to objects external to the body and the self of the observer, and the first two senses are ones that apply to objects at some distance from the body. Psychologists note at least two other senses, oriented internally rather than externally, the sense of balance or equilibrium, and *proprioception*, the awareness of the position of the body and its parts in space; some claim that hunger and thirst are senses as well. When these additional senses are discussed by most English-speakers, they are usually treated as a kind of feeling: 'I feel dizzy.'

In Luganda, the actions of perceiving that correspond to the English 'to see' are divided between two verbs, *kulaba* and *kubona*. The basic difference between them is in the nature of the objects of perception. The former, *kulaba*, is used for permanent and stable entities such as land, human beings, tables, books and the like. The latter verb, *kubona*, is used for objects that appear and disappear. There are a number of common objects in the sky for which it is used, such as the moon and planets, and also shooting stars, which are called 'comets' in Ugandan English. This verb can also be used for fire, fog and other objects that are not always present and tangible.

There are a number of occasions in which either verb could be used, depending on the particular circumstances. Thus, *kubona* could be used to emphasize the length of absence that preceded the reappearance of a physically stable entity for which *kulaba* could otherwise be used. *Kulaba* would ordinarily be used to refer to seeing a friend or relative who lives near the speaker, but *kubona* will be used to refer to a friend or a relative who suddenly appears after a long absence. There are some creatures, such as ants, which appear seasonally after being absent a long time, to which the verb *kubona* applies. Even a product that suddenly comes on the market in large stocks after being unavailable for some time will be described with *kubona*. In effect, the word is used in reference to things which are seen suddenly and which are also expected to disappear after some time.

By contrast, *kulaba* could be used to emphasize the long duration of a condition that is in its nature temporary. *Kulaba* is also used in cases where one encounters serious trouble, suffering, pain, etc. For example, to render in Luganda, 'In Iraq, there is a lot of suffering' one would say *mu Iraq, waliyo okulaba ennaku kungi*. In this example, 'suffering' is *okulaba ennaku*, literally meaning 'seeing suffering'. In other words, in Luganda, bad experiences are 'seen'. In fact, to say 'I'm sorry' or to express shared feelings of sympathy, one says *ng'olabye,* literally meaning 'you have seen'. *Kulaba is* used for even brief or transitory negative experiences, perhaps to emphasize the speaker's recognition of their harshness; *kubona* can be used for positive experiences, such as happiness, pleasure or good fortune, that come after a long period and that may not remain very long. From *kubona,* the word *akabonero* (plural *obubonero*) is derived, to which we will return later.

The Luganda verbs *kuloza* and *kuwunyiriza* correspond fairly closely to the English 'to taste' and 'to smell'.[1] The verbs for hearing and touch are different, though. The Luganda verb *kuwulira* covers the semantic space of hearing in English, and also includes what could be called feeling-with-the-whole-body or feeling-at-a-distance: feeling that the sun is warm, or that a wind is cold.[2] The verb *kukwatako* refers to touching objects, especially with the hand, but also with other parts of the body. Touching with the hand is a core referent, since the verb derives from the stem *kwata* (touch/hold), with the suffix *-ko*, which means 'on'. The experiences of balance and proprioception are covered by *kuwulira*, which suggests that the feeling-with-the-whole-body is part of the meaning.

We note that *kuwulira* can serve as a general verb 'to sense,' much like the English verb 'to feel'. The core sense of the English verb 'to feel' lies near touch, while the core of *kuwulira* lies near hearing.[3] It is interesting to note that neither English nor Luganda use sight as the sense that is metonymically extended to other senses, even though it is the most valued sense in both cultures. We speculate that sight may be linked with the agency of the person who senses, since sight is so connected to looking, and to directing one's gaze and attention to the object that is seen. Feeling and *kuwulira* emphasize more the capacity of the human body to register impressions, whether willed — through the purposive touching in English and the deliberate listening in Luganda — or not.

An introduction to *obubonero* or signs

We now turn to *obubonero*, derived from the verb *kubona*. This paper explores the sensory, linguistic and social aspects of *obubonero*. One of us (Merit Kabugo) spoke with a number of other native speakers of Luganda and collected a set of twenty *obubonero* from a variety of semantic domains. Though this list, included here as Table 1, is not exhaustive, it seems representative.

We note that the *obubonero* that we collected are examples of only one meaning of the word. It is of course difficult and somewhat arbitrary to assign a specific number of independent meanings to any given word, even if this practice has been enshrined by centuries of lexicographers; two senses of a word that one person might think of as separate meanings might be treated as a single category by another. Nonetheless, the word seems a fairly unproblematic instance of polysemy. The word *akabonero* has a broad series of referents, just as the English word 'sign' does. A sign on a post that bears the name of the street is an *akabonero* of that name. The word comes close as well to some uses of the English word 'symbol': political parties have *obubonero*, such as a hand, used in rallies and posters. A wedding ring is an *akabonero* of marriage. The word can be used to refer to symptoms of illnesses. The Luganda translation of the New Testament, dating to the closing years of the nineteenth century, uses the word to refer to the 'signs' that Jesus and his disciples discuss in the Gospels.[4] Children in primary schools who are being taught to read and write learn that punctuation marks such as the comma and period are *obubonero*.

The twenty *obubonero* that we collected have a different meaning. They are signs that forecast some future event or condition; in a few instances, they indicate a present event or condition, such as pregnancy, illness or danger, which would not otherwise come to be known for some time.

We note that all twenty *obubonero* have a characteristic form. They link an object that is perceived, a specific attribute of the object, and a perceiver. The perceiver already understands the significance of this attribute of this object; it indicates a certain outcome, either for an individual or a set of individuals. Let me give some illustrations. It is generally held that seeing red ants swarming around the house, especially in the courtyard, means that a member of the extended family in the compound is going to die in about a week. Likewise, experiencing a sudden itching in the palms means that the individual is going to receive money in the next few days.

We note that the Luganda-speakers who provided us with these examples omitted certain other instances of signs that seem much closer to this sense. They restricted themselves to signs of future events, even though it is possible to speak of an *akabonero* of an event in the recent past, with a meaning close to the English word 'clue'. For example, if a courtyard has not been swept, it is a sign that nobody in the compound has been at home. In a similar vein, if there are scratches at a door, it is a sign that someone tried to break in. However, the informants did not provide such examples. They also restricted themselves to signs that are not linked by simple mechanical or physical causality to their outcomes. For example, if one hears the lowing of cattle, one could say, in semantically correct Luganda, that it is an *akabonero* that a herd is passing, and, similarly, if one sees many plants sprouting, it is a sign that a field

Table 1. Twenty cases of signs

	sign	sensory mode (Luganda)	sensory mode (English)	attribute
1	cooked rice	*kuwunyiriza*	smell	smelling in the forest
2	earth	*kuwunyiriza*	smell	smell after the rains
3	bean	*kuwunyiriza*	smell	smell of rotting bean seeds
4	red ants	*kulaba*	sight	swarming around house or courtyard
5	shooting star	*kubona*	sight	zooming through the sky
6	woman or dog	*kulaba*	sight	meeting any as the first thing in the morning, on road or at door
7	plantain	*kubona*	sight	peeled finger standing upright in cooking pot
8	ringworm spot	*kulaba*	sight	on body of a youngest child
9	dust-devils	*kubona*	sight	on the ground during the day
10	owl	*kuwulira*	hearing	hooting at night
11	fox	*kuwulira*	hearing	crying at night
12	shrieking noise	*kuwulira*	hearing	continuous noise in the ear
13	bird (Abyssinian hornbill)	*kuwulira*	hearing	call (gulu mpa nkuba, 'Heaven, send rain')
14	general fatigue	*kuwulira*	feeling	general body weakness
15	sunshine	*kuwulira*	feeling	a sudden brief hard biting scorching sun
16	chill	*kuwulira*	feeling	a sudden brief chill
17	itching	*kuwulira*	feeling	sudden itching of the palms
18	stickiness and sweatiness	*kuwulira*	feeling	feeling of body upon waking up in the morning
19	wind	*kulaba*	seeing	moving dust, leaves, etc. shifting direction
20	bitterness	*kuloza*	taste	bitter taste in the mouth

will produce a good harvest. However, our informants did not provide any examples of such patently obvious signs; rather, they gave only ones that would require some additional knowledge. We recognize the long legacy of discussions of causality in studies of African culture by many writers, and we will touch lightly on these issues in the conclusions. We note as well that there is a specific word in Luganda for 'omen,' *bisiraani*. Some, but not all, *obubonero* can be classified as omens, often depending on the circumstances under which they are observed and discussed.

An examination of a set of twenty signs

We include a list of the twenty signs in table 1. We collected some of these by observation of ordinary conversations. Once we recognized the importance of the term *akabonero*, we asked native Luganda-speakers, at group meetings and in informal

entity to which sign applies	consequence	interval
people nearby	a snake is in the midst	there and then
entire village or neighborhood	a destructive rain ahead	usually after a few days
person who detects smell	you will catch malaria	usually after a few days
extended family in the compound	a member in the house is going to die	in about a weeks time
person who sees the star	seer will acquire wealth	indefinite
person who sees the woman or dog	seer will have bad luck that day	that very day
household associated with kitchen	a visitor at the meal	that very meal
the child's mother	child's mother is pregnant	that very time
entire village or neighborhood	rains will come	in the next two weeks
household or compound	a close person will die	the next few days
neighborhood	someone in the village will die	the next few days
person who hears	the person will fall sick	the next few days
entire village or neighborhood	rains will come	in the next two weeks
person who feels	a close person will die	the next few days
area around person who feels the heat	it is going to rain	in the next few minutes
person who feels and those nearby	danger is ahead	in the next few minutes
person who feels	the person will receive money	in the next few days
entire village or neighborhood	rains will come	in the next two weeks
entire village or neighborhood	rains will come	in the next two weeks
person who tastes	the person will catch malaria	in the next few days

one-on-one conversations, to provide us with examples. Many examples were repeated frequently. This form of elicitation is well-established in field linguistics (Duranti 1997:98). We note that this list includes a number of examples that are particularly well-known and familiar, and were offered to us repeatedly. They are often among the first to be cited in discussions of signs, such as the sign of a woman or a dog (meeting a woman or a dog before meeting a man when departing the compound or house in the morning as a sign of bad luck that day), and the sign of plantain (seeing a peeled plantain stand upright when it is thrown into a cooking pot as a sign that a visitor will arrive at the meal). The very familiarity of these instances indicates a certain level of self-consciousness of these signs, since it shows that many Luganda-speakers have already discussed them with others.

We note a number of characteristics that these twenty signs have in common. Firstly, all of them refer directly to a sensory perception. They do not refer to intuitions or hunches. They come to people when they are fully awake, rather than when they are asleep, or in a state of trance or intoxication. In addition, these sensory perceptions come to individuals without their being willed, chosen, sought or invoked. They simply occur, usually in the routine course of daily life. Moreover, these signs are not ordinarily susceptible to human intervention; one would not, for example, scatter ants in an area to make people think that someone will die.[5]

We note that these signs include most, but not all, the senses. As table 1 indicates, the list contains examples that are based on five of the six senses described by Luganda-speakers. The one that is not included is *kukwatako*, to feel by touching. There are instances of *kuwulira*, feeling-with-the-whole-body, including generalized senses of hot, cold and fatigue[6] (These signs also happen to include all five senses listed by English-speakers). Moreover, all twenty signs are associated with one, and only one, sensory mode. There are no instances of both seeing and hearing something, for example.

Another characteristic of these signs is that they all refer to a one, and only one, object of the experience: the call of a fox, a feeling of a chill, a taste of a bitter substance. These objects are all natural rather than supernatural, though the names of two signs, both associated with rain, have some overt supernatural significance. One of the signs that are observed during the dry season to note the coming of rains is the call of the Abyssinian hornbill, *Bucorvus abyssinicus*. It is said to cry *gulu mpa nkuba* ('Heaven, send rain') and God is believed to attend to it. Another sign of the oncoming rains is the presence of dust-devils, small whirlwinds that raise dust from the dry grounds; these are called *akazimu* or 'wind-ghosts,' a term that refers to the ancestors who accompany the first rains as they come to the lands of their descendants. The word *zimu* refers to the spirits of deceased individuals. As the English term 'dust-devil' suggests, though, these names may be what are termed frozen metaphors, ones that ordinarily do not evoke associations for the speaker and hearer. Moreover, these are natural objects—a bird, dust carried by a wind—rather than supernatural beings.

The projected outcomes can be all classified as positive or negative. 40% (8/20) of the cases are positive, and 60% (12/16) are negative. The outcomes are concentrated in specific semantic domains. Three about illness, four about death, five are about rain, and five about fortune and danger. Moreover, the outcomes all occur within a specific temporal range. All twenty signs refer to the future that follows the moment of perception of the sign. The signs may refer to something that will occur in the future, such as a rainstorm or the arrival of a visitor. In at least one instance, the sign refers to a condition that already exists, but that is not otherwise perceptible by ordinary means. This is the sign of the ringworm spot; the sign shows others that a woman is pregnant before the swelling of her belly makes this evident (we reiterate that the spot is seen on the body of a woman's youngest child, not on the woman herself). The sign of a chill, indicating that a danger lies near ahead, and the sign of bitterness, that a person has malaria, seem similar, since the individual would soon learn of the danger by seeing or hearing it, or of the illness by its usual symptoms. We note that nearly all the signs refer to the near future. 6/20 or 30% of the cases indicating something that will happen in the same day, and 14/20 or 70% indicating something that will happen in no longer than a few days. The breakdown of the timing of the outcome is as follows: immediately, two signs; in a few minutes, three signs; the same day, one sign; in a few days, eight signs; in a week or so, one sign; in two weeks, four signs, all of which have to do with the onset of rain. There is only one instance of a sign forecasting something in the indefinite future.

All twenty signs have a high, though somewhat variable, degree of spatial and social proximity among the sign, the perceiver, and the outcome. Spatially, the sign covers a nearby area. Socially, the sign refers to small social field (individual, seven signs; household, five signs; village, five signs; neighborhood, three signs). Though this social field is small, it is usually larger than a single individual; 13/20 or just under two-thirds of the signs refer to a collectivity rather than just one person. The social field, moreover, is demarcated largely by spatial distance. Though Baganda keep close track of clan membership, the outcomes do not affect members of particular clans exclusively. Nor do they distinguish by gender, age, or religious affiliation, all important social categories. At most, there seems to be a suggestion that the signs might affect permanent or long-term residents of an area, rather than visitors or short-term residents. We note that this spatial and social proximity corresponds generally to the temporal proximity noted above.

A characteristic that struck us as particularly interesting is what we call the public availability of the signs. Most of these signs are readily perceived by all people in a particular place at a particular time. Of these twenty signs, at least fifteen can be publicly sensed: objects that anyone can see, sounds that anyone can hear, scents that anyone can smell, or sensations of heat or cold that anyone in a group would feel.[7] The exceptions are of common perceptions that everyone has experienced at one time or another and they are the ones that potentially could be experienced at the same time by others. These examples are the sign of the bean, in which a person smells a rotting bean; the sign of a shrieking noise, heard in the ear; the sign of general fatigue, a feeling of general body weakness; the sign of itching, felt in the palm of the hand; and the sign of bitterness, tasted in the mouth.

We note an association between these last characteristics. The more publicly available signs, the ones that can be observed by anyone in a household, compound, village or neighborhood, apply to that wider social group. The less publicly sensed signs forecast outcomes for individuals only. However, their temporal characteristics do not differ from those of more publicly sensed signs; they foretell events that will occur in a few days.

The use of *obubonero* in conversation

We wished to study the use of signs in conversations between Luganda-speakers. We recognized the difficulty of recording spontaneous everyday conversations in which signs were discussed; the taping and transcription of many hundreds of hours of conversation in natural field settings would have been laborious and expensive. We therefore chose to use elicitation techniques, more technically known as elicited production tasks, to obtain representative conversations. A wide variety of elicitation techniques are used in linguistic anthropology for many ends. They include interviews, sentence completion tasks, stimulated recall, and production questionnaires (Marchman 1997; Billmyer and Vargehese 2000; Gass and Mackey 2000; Golato 2003). The elicita-

Table 2. Four conversations in which signs are discussed

1. A conversation about a sudden death.
This conversation takes place between two elderly (50+) women. It is early in the morning in the compound of one of them.

A: Neighbor, are you aware that Wamala died?
B: The Wamala we know?
A: Yes, he is dead!
B: Has he been sick?
A: No, the man jokingly [capriciously, surprisingly] died suddenly.
B: Ooh! That is why, recently, I forget when exactly, the owl hooted all night long. Did you hear it too?
A: Yes! We heard it and the fox had cried the previous evening. I told my husband that there was likely to be trouble on the village.
B: I too have been waking up feeling very weak these days, and that is why I had to dig near the house, but then there are red ants all over he place!
A: So, that is it, my dear. Wamala is dead.
B: It is a great pity!

2. A conversation about a pregnant woman.
This conversation takes place between two women. 'A' has a one year old baby which she is walking with along a village path. The baby has a ringworm spot on its face. They meet 'B'.

B: You 'A', why does the baby have this spot! Aren't you in some funny state?
A: What kind of state?
B: Do you mean to say you don't see the spot?
A: Come on, I am not pregnant.

3. A conversation about a poor day at work.
This conversation takes place between a husband and a wife, at home in the evening after the husband has returned from work.

Wife: Welcome back, dear.
Husband: Thank you (flatly with low spirits)
Wife: You look sad. What is the matter?
Husband: I don't know, but generally the day has been a loss. The car broke down. I didn't get clients.
Wife: What is the matter? Whom did you meet on your way in the morning?
Husband: When I was getting to the main road, I came across Muske's dog.
Wife: That is the bad omen you met.

4. A conversation about a snake.
This conversation takes place between two men walking along a path in the bush through a forest.

A: You, do you smell rice? [Literally, do you you sense [*kuwulira*] the smell [*wunya*] of cooked rice?]
B: How? It seems you are just hungry
A: Uh! But I smell [*kuwunya*] cooked rice!
B: I do not smell [literally, sense [*kuwulira*]] it.
A: All right.
B: Eh! Wait a moment, I have also had a sudden chill through my body
A: Quiet, I heard [hear [*kuwulira*]] something moving... eh! There it is... a snake.

tion technique that we selected was a discourse production task. Kabugo asked three instructors at the Institute of African Languages at Makerere University in Uganda to produce representative conversations that included *obubonero*, a task which these individuals readily understood.[8]

We offer brief synopses as follows. In the first conversation, one neighbor tells another of the recent sudden death of someone in the neighborhood. Troubled by this event, they seek to explain his death, which was not preceded by illness. They recall signs that forecasted his death. The second conversation, one woman meets another walking with her toddler. Upon seeing a ringworm spot on the toddler, the first woman hints broadly that the second is pregnant, a claim which the second woman tries to brush off. (We note that a number of *obubonero*, not included in our set of twenty, interpret signs on a child, especially the youngest, as indications of the child's mother's pregnancy and even the sex of her unborn child). We note as well that, despite cultural values that favor fertility, this sign would be seen as unfavorable, since the mother would be understood as not wealthy or careful enough to prevent a case of ringworm in her youngest child and therefore as not ready to have another child. In the third conversation, a man returns home, discouraged from a bad day at the market. His wife, seeking to cheer him up and to explain his misfortune, encourages him to recall a sign that would have forecast this bad day. In the final conversation, two men walk in the forest. The first says that he notices a sign that forecasts the arrival of a snake, a misfortune in this context. The second attempts to cast doubt on the significance of this sign, but is later persuaded when he perceives a second sign that also forecasts the arrival of a snake.

We note a number of characteristics of these conversations.[9] It is striking that *obubonero* are often presented near the beginning of the conversation. In the first three conversations, the *obubonero* come up early in the conversation, when A and B meet and soon find a topic to discuss, whether of mutual interest (a sudden death, a poor day at work) or a topic imposed by one individual (the pregnancy of a woman). In the conversation about a snake, the two speakers had been walking, and presumably conversing, for some time when the *akabonero* appears. This location of signs early in conversations may reflect the fact that several of the conversations (the first three) are connected to greetings. The formalized exchange of greetings is characteristic polite behavior in Luganda conversation. Other evidence shows an association between the use of signs and formal exchanges of greetings, particularly in the discussion of signs about rain and weather, and the health of humans and livestock. We also speculate that proverbs, a generally similar form of common-sense knowledge used in conversation, may be linked to these signs as well.

The perceiver and the object or perception are often, but not always, linked by a verb of perception. Sometimes there is a simple statement of fact. In the conversation about a sudden death, B states 'there are red ants all over the place' rather than 'I saw red ants,' in the conversation about a poor day at work, B says, 'I came across [a] dog' rather than 'I saw a dog,' and in the conversation about a snake, B states 'my body got a chill' rather than 'I felt a chill'.[10]

We note as well that the outcomes are temporally close to the signs and conversations. The conversations about a sudden death and a poor day at work draw on *obubonero* to explain recent events (misfortune in both instances). The conversation about a pregnant woman includes an indication of a current state that will lead to a future outcome. The conversation about a snake forecasts an event to take place, and that event does occur during the conversation.[11] In contrast to this characteristic, found in all conversation, we note a variety of relations of speakers and forecasts. In the conversation about a sudden death, the signs explain a misfortune that occurred to a third party. In the conversation about a pregnant woman, the sign suggests a possible outcome for one of the speakers, which that speaker seeks to deny. In the conversation about a poor day at work, the sign explains a misfortune that occurred to one of the speakers. In the conversation about a snake, the signs indicate a misfortune that occurs to both speakers.

We were interested in the observation that there is some variation in the number of *obubonero* and the agreement of the speakers on the *obubonero*. The conversations about a pregnant woman and a poor day at work include only one sign; the conversation about a snake has two, and the conversation about a sudden death — a particularly troubling topic — has three. We note that in this last conversation, the additional *obubonero* are mentioned as a product of the agreement of the speakers. By contrast, in the conversation about a snake, they are mentioned as an outcome of their disagreement. In the conversation about a sudden death, each speaker presents perceptions that are public (hearing an owl, hearing a fox, seeing red ants). Note that B asks A if she heard the first sign; A agrees that she has, and offers some evidence that she has. The conversation about a snake is interesting in that each speaker has a relatively private sensation (smell, chill), and indeed B explicitly states that he did not experience the first sensation. (This conversation merits further attention, since two verbs, *kuwunyiriza* and *kuwulira*, are used to denote the same perception, smelling rice. A uses the former more positively, and B denies the experience by using the latter. Only after both speakers perceive an *akabonero* does the outcome occur).

When one speaker presents an *akabonero*, the other speaker can actively support the line of interpretation of events that the first speaker is suggesting, or can actively oppose it. These two possibilities, at the most general level, consist of the second speaker either implying, 'yes, your perception of x is significant, since it forecasts the standard outcome' or 'no, your perception of x is just a routine perception of an ordinary object, and does not forecast anything'. These could be called local challenges to the significance.[12] In these conversations at least, the second speaker does not offer global challenges such as 'no, x does not forecast y, but rather z' or 'no, x is never significant and never forecasts anything' or 'no, ordinary objects never work to forecast outcomes'.

Regarding the possibility of support, the other speaker can back up the claim 'I perceived x and therefore y' through active encouragement, suggestion of other relevant signs, and the like. In the conversation about a sudden death, there is a direct effort to locate *obubonero*. When B hears from A that a third person, C, dies, B first establishes that this is indeed the C known to both A and B. B then seeks a naturalistic explanation, that C had been ill, and only after having this possibility rejected turns to locate signs. A and B, both, contribute to locating these signs. Exchanges like this may well be common after deaths occur, especially sudden unexpected ones. The conversation about a bad day at work also shows such direct effort to locate signs. A, noting B's despondency, first asks whether specific events provoked this state, and, finding that they did, suggests looking for an *akabonero* to explain these events. When the sign is located, A uses the word *bisiraani*, omen, to describe it—a strong support of the significance of *obubonero*.

Regarding the possibility of opposition, the claim 'I perceived x and therefore y' can be challenged by denying that the particular perception of x is a perception of a meaningful *akabonero* (but allowing that other perceptions of x might be) or by rejecting indirectly the connection between x and y. The conversations about a pregnant woman and about a snake, as mentioned above, contain some debate about the significance of potential signs. In the former, B drops broad hints that she can detect A's pregnancy by a sign on A's baby. A feigns ignorance of the commonly known significance of the sign, and tries to deflect the discussion away from the sign. It is possible that A is attempting to deny, or conceal, her pregnancy. In the latter, B suggests that A's experienced sensation may not be a genuine *akabonero*, but rather merely an ordinary perception that can be explained by appeal to the ordinary operation of human physiology (that is, that A smells rice because he is hungry, not because he is sensing an *akabonero* that indicates the arrival of a snake). B agrees about the significance of the first sign after noting a second sign, by hearing it. (In this conversation, there is a subtle play of different verbs of sense, with the more general *kuwulira* which, in this case, means 'to feel' or 'to sense' being less emphatic than the more specific *kuwunya* 'to smell').

Following on the previous point, we note that speakers engage actively with claims about the significance of *obubonero* for interpreting events, rather than taking them for granted and assuming that their meaning is certain. We would like to suggest that this engagement demonstrates the operation of cultural assumptions about perception, speech, action and the world. The assumptions run something like this: there is regularity in the everyday world. Human life is usually, but not always, governed by ordinary forces, both visible natural forces and invisible supernatural forces (God, the ancestors, spirits and magical practitioners). These forces operate in ways that can easily be observed and understood by everyone, and they can create good and bad fortune.

Readily available signs assist people in anticipating and explaining these turns of fortune, though these signs, too, are not infallible. On the one hand, people might not notice them, and on the other hand, they might mistakenly assume that an ordinary perception is a sign. The conversation about a sudden death illustrates these assumptions. When B hears of this misfortune, she takes three steps: first to verify that she has heard the information correctly, second to seek a naturalistic explanation of the death (by illness), and third, after the second had failed, to locate signs that foretold the death. A supports this effort through various moves, such as interjections, leading questions, expressions of agreement, and noting parallels between her experiences and B's. We suggest that if their efforts to locate such signs had failed, they would assumed the frightening possibility of a death caused neither by natural causes nor by commonplace supernatural causes but rather by some extraordinary supernatural cause, such as strong witchcraft or supernatural retribution for hidden immoral behavior.

The course of the conversation about a poor day at work is generally similar. On noting B's poor emotional state, A first seeks a general explanation and then, on hearing of misfortune, tries to locate a sign that would have foretold it. B supports these efforts by offering an answer with a concrete detail that completes A's reassuring line of thought. By contrast, the conversation about a pregnant woman shows the strong efforts of A to reject B's suggestion that the ringworm spot on her baby indicates that she is pregnant. In the conversation about the snake, it is less clear why B at first rejects A's claims that a sign warns them of danger. This rejection might stem from some element in their prior conversation, or some aspect of their relationship, or perhaps, to speculate even more widely, that B fears that to speak of misfortune will bring that misfortune, or, alternatively, that B thinks that this talk of signs is old-fashioned and backward.

Discussion

To recapitulate our argument, we note that the word for sign, *akabonero,* derives from the Luganda word *kubona*, one of the two verbs that mean 'to see'. The signs may be seen or detected by other senses; they are usually easily perceived by anyone in the area. They offer an indication of events or conditions, that will take place, or, that are already taking place but would not be otherwise known. People who come upon a sign may just notice it, and perhaps modify or alter their actions, but they often comment on the sign in conversation with others. Indeed, individuals often feel a strong impulse to discuss signs with others close to them, particularly when they think that misfortune is about to occur, or when apparently anomalous misfortune strikes someone. We note that these signs are treated in a variety of ways in conversations.

Our materials lead us to offer some observations about these *obubonero*. Firstly, they draw on three elements, which can be called cultural assumptions. The first assumption is that humans share certain capacities to perceive entities in the world. The second is that certain attributes of certain entities operate as reliable predictors of events and states of other entities, in a way that goes beyond the simple regularity of operation of mechanical and physical causes. The third is that the knowledge of the operation of these predictors is widely shared. In other words, though *obubonero* seem somewhat different from a straightforward mechanical or physical notion of causality, they are part of a common-sense world that operates independent of human action.

To elaborate on this point about cultural assumptions, we note that these *obubonero* bridge what might be seen as the private and individual (and perhaps biological) world of sense-perception and the more public and social (and perhaps cultural) world of discussion of human action. (Moreover, the fact that *obubonero* are widely accepted as a topic of conversation means that individuals who perceive these signs can easily anticipate talking about them, unlike other sense-perceptions that would be less culturally available as topics of conversation). Phrased differently, the social construction of reality is based not only on cultural framings of human subjects and of objects in the world, but, as Csordas (1993) has shown, on the embodiment of human attention, and, more specifically, on the types of sense-perception that link human subjects with these objects. In this case, *obubonero* are not merely about the relations of attributes of certain objects, but also about the capacities of human perceivers. Indeed, these *obubonero* rest strongly on a cultural elaboration of certain characteristics of the human sensory apparatus. In particular, the perceptions in certain sensory modes, such as the ones called sight and hearing in English, allow for a greater distance between the perceiver and the perceived object, and the perceptions themselves are commonly shared by individuals in the same space at the same time. Perceptions in other sensory modes, such as the ones called taste and touch, rest on close contact between the perceiver and the perceived object, and the perceptions themselves are less commonly shared. These dimensions of sense perception are elaborated in this case of signs, since objects that are more publicly sensed connote information about events that will affect a larger group of people.

We note a second point about these signs: Luganda-speakers do not automatically accept and take for granted a claim that an *akabonero* has been perceived. Rather, they sometimes seek out these signs, and at other times challenges claims that a sign has been perceived. This variation may reflect the fact that the significance of true signs is widely shared among Luganda-speakers. It also shows the strong interdependencies that link people. We note as evidence the fact that most signs indicate outcomes for groups, rather than for individuals. We note as well the efforts of speakers in the conversations about a sudden death and about a poor day at work to locate the sources of misfortune that might continue to affect them, and the similar efforts of speakers in the conversations about a pregnant woman and about a snake to reject the possibility of pending misfortune. One would rather have good rather than bad fortune; one would rather be able to anticipate or explain misfortune — through normal causal means or through signs — than to have unexplained misfortune.

Thirdly, we speculate that these *obubonero* could be examined as part of a public sphere of conversation. They imply a strong equality of all speakers, who share the capacity to detect and interpret signs, and to use them to account for anomalous incidents in the recent past and future. The examples that we have seen are all deployed on a small social and spatial scale. The instances of the discussions of pending rainfall are at a somewhat larger scale. It would be interesting to explore how signs are deployed on even larger scales, and to compare these face-to-face conversations about signs to larger speech situations, such as those in churches, which also involve signs, assessment of the future, and which also form part of a public sphere (Breckenridge 1998; Frederiksen 2000; Meyer 2004).

Finally, we return to the theme of the senses with which we opened. These human efforts to comprehend a world prone to contingency, and to respond to those contingencies, rest not only on the understandings of that world, but on the understandings of human perceptions of that world. These understandings of human perception, in turn, have a specific form that is rooted in language. The verb *kabona* — 'to see impermanent things' — gives rise to the word *akabonero* — 'sign'. That word, in turn, gives rise to the conversations in which individuals agree or disagree on the acts of interpretation that allow them to operate in a space between the ordinary domain of mechanical causality and the extraordinary domain of the inexplicable. This intermediate space of common-sense acts of signification is a crucial one.

E-mail: bsorlove@ucdavis.edu
mkabugo@educ.mak.ac.ug

Appendix

Luganda transcriptions of conversations

1. A conversation about a sudden death.
A: Muliraanwa, wategedde. Wamala bwe yafudde?
B: Wamala on owaffe?
A: Yee, munnange yafudde!
B: Abadde mulwadde?
A: Nedda, omusajja yafudde mangu awo bya lusaago.
B: Ooh! Wamma ennaku ezo, oba lunaku ki, ekiwuugulu kyasula kikaaba; oba naawe wakiwulira?
A: Eeh! Twakiwulira ate n'akabe nako kaali kaakabye eggulo limu. Ne ngamba omwama nti ku kyalo kunaabaako omutawaana.
B: Era nange ennaku zino zonna nkeera ndi muyongobevu, era kwe kulima na wano awaka, naye ate nawo wajudde nsanafu.
A: Munnange nno bye byo, Wamala yatufuddeko.
B: Kitalo nnyo!

2. A conversation about a pregnant woman.
B: Owange 'A', omwana ekisente nga kimwetimbye! Tobeemu engeri ggwe?
A: Engeri etya?
B: Kyogamba ggwe ekisente tokiraba?
A: Twala eri naawe, nze siri lubuto.

3. A conversation about a poor day at work.
Wife: Kulikayo ssebo.
Husband: Nvuddeyo (flatly with low spirit)
Wife: Nga toli musanyufu, kiki?
Husband: Simanyi, naye olunaku lwonna lunfudde, emmotoka efudde, abaguzi tebazze.
Wife: Kiki, wasanze ani ku makya ng'ogenda?
Husband: Bwe nabadde ntuuka ku kkubo ne nsanga akabwa ka Musoke.
Wife: Bye ebyo bye wasanze.

4. A conversation about a snake.
A: Ggwe, owulira omuceere oguwunya?
B: Gutya? Twala eri naawe, ndowooza njala y'ekuluma.
A: Uh! Nze nga mpunyirwa omuceere omufumbe!
B: Nze siguwulira.
A: Kale ggwe.
B: Eh! Naye lindako! Nange omubiri gunesisiwadde omulundi gumu!
A: Sirika, mpulidde ekitambula... eh! Guugwo... omusota.

Notes

1 It is interesting to note that English and Luganda have similar overlaps of verbs related to the sense of smell. In English, the verb 'to smell' can refer to the purposive act of sniffing an object to detect its odor, to the act of perceiving that odor of that object, and to the odor-emitting property of the object itself. The Luganda verb *kuwunya* refers to the act of inhaling and also to the odor-emitting property of the object itself. Adding the suffix –*iriza* 'to do something repeatedly' gives the verb *kuwunyiriza*, which refers to the purposive act of sniffing an object to detect its odor and also to the act of perceiving that odor of that object.
2 In her discussion of cultural framing of the senses in Ghana, Geurts (2002:8) describes another case in which hearing is extended to feeling, to sensation and to other modes of experience.
3 Adding the suffix –*iriza* 'to do something repeatedly' to *kuwulira* gives the verb *kuwuliriza*, 'to listen'.
4 *Tubulire, ebyo biribeerawo ddi? Era kabonero ki akaliraga okujja kwo, n'enkomerero y'ensi?* - (Matayo 24:3). '[And as he sat upon the Mount of Olives, the disciples came unto him privately, saying]. Tell us, when shall these things be? and what [shall be] the sign of thy coming, and of the end of the world?'
5 The closest case to such intervention that we have heard was told to us by a speaker of Lusoga, a language closely related to Luganda and spoken in the area immediately the east of Baganda. Describing his childhood in a rural area, he told us that his father would sometimes send him out of the compound early in the morning, and tell him to stay nearby. This way, when the father left the compound in the morning, the first person whom he would see would be his son, a male, rather than a less auspicious woman or a dog. He told this story as a bit of a joke, and suggested that his father was not entirely sure that this ruse would be efficacious.
6 It is interesting to note that the case of itching, localized in the palms, is covered by kuwulira rather than by kukwatako, which seems to be restricted to active touching and grasping. We are still not sure whether these two are distinguished by the distance of the subject and the object, the direct action of the subject in perceiving the object, or the localization of the sensation within the subject's body.
7 Panopolous (2003) offers an interesting discussion of the contexts in which sound is deemed to have greater public availability than sight in a Greek village.
8 The four resulting conversations are contained in table 2; the conversation about a sudden death is based most directly on recent memory, and the other three draw on field experience of the instructors. Though these cannot be taken to be spontaneous conversations, they are nonetheless of use. The people who developed them are all native speakers of Luganda, and, moreover, they have considerable experience in developing Luganda language conversations for a variety of purposes, including pedagogical materials for use in public education and instructional material for health, agriculture and other extension programs by government agencies and NGO's. These materials had gone through testing and review with native speakers of local background, so it may be assumed that the individuals who produced these conversations are skilled at this task.
9 One characteristic, the fact that the conversations that we include here involve only two speakers, may not be very representative. The conversation about a pregnant woman is the only one to include a third person, an infant who does not speak or vocalize in any way. We have observed larger groups that discuss signs in our ethnographic and sociolinguistic research on other topics. For example, farmers gather in villages to discuss the signs that indicate the timing of the onset of rainy seasons, sometimes forming groups of several dozen. However, we have no such conversations in our sample of four.

10 In the conversation about a snake, *Nange omubiri gunesisiwadde omulundi gumu!* The word *omubiri* means 'body', *kwesisiwala* is 'get a chill' and *omulundi gumu* is 'sudden'.
11 This last case shows the difficulty of establishing a clear boundary between present and future events. The snake was already nearby at the time of the conversation, though it did not appear until well into the conversation.
12 Povinelli (1993) offers a thoughtful discussion of these local challenges to significance in a very different setting, in an Aboriginal community in Australia, where the sensory modes of perception, the links of signs to outcomes, and the distribution of outcomes to social groups and categories all vary significantly from this Ugandan case, but where the possible significance of signs is also an important topic of conversation.

References

Breckenridge, K.
    1998 "We Must Speak for Ourselves": The Rise and Fall of a Public Sphere on the South African Gold Mines, 1920 to 1931. *Comparative Studies in Society and History* 40(1):71-108.
Billmyer, K. and M. Varghese
    2000 Investigating Instrument-Based Pragmatic Variability: Effects of Enhancing Discourse Completion Tests. *Applied Linguistics* 21(4):517-552.
Csordas, T. J.
    1993 Somatic Modes of Attention. *Cultural Anthropology* 8(2):135-156.
Duranti, A
    1997 *Linguistic Anthropology*. Cambridge: Cambridge University Press.
Frederiksen, B.F.
    2000 Popular Culture, Gender Relations and the Democratization of Everyday Life in Kenya. *Journal of Southern African Studies* 26(2):209-222.
Gass, S. M. and A.Mackey
    2000 *Stimulated Recall Methodology in Second Language Research*. New Jersey: Lawrence Erlbaum Associates, Inc.
Geurts, K. L.
    2002 On Rocks, Walks, and Talks in West Africa: Cultural Categories and an Anthropology of the Senses. *Ethos* 30(3):1-22.
Golato, A.
    2003 Studying Compliment Responses: A Comparison of DCTs and Recordings of Naturally Occurring Talk. *Applied Linguistics* 24(1):90-121.
Jay, M.
    1993 *Downcast Eyes: The Denigration of Vision in Twentieth-Century French Thought*. Berkeley: University of California Press.
Marchman, V. A.
    1997 Children's Productivity in the English Past Tense: The Role of Frequency, Phonology, and Neighborhood Structure. *Cognitive Science* 21(3):283-303.
Meyer, B.
    2004 Christianity in Africa: From African Independent to Pentecostal-Charismatic Churches. *Annual Review of Anthropology* 33:447-474.

Panopoulos, P.
   2003   Animal Bells as Symbols: Sound and Hearing in a Greek Island Village. *Journal of the Royal Anthropological Institute* 9:639-656.

Povinelli, E.
   1993   "Might Be Something": The Language of Indeterminacy in Australian Aboriginal Land Use. *Man* 28:679-704.

Afterword: Sense, Sentiment, and Sociality

Donald Brenneis, University of California, Santa Cruz

A few weeks after I had returned from extended fieldwork in Fiji to Cambridge, Massachusetts, where I was beginning to write my doctoral dissertation, I realized that, as the evening approached, I would recurrently feel a sense of real loss. I discarded the interpretations that this could be attributed to moving from the tropics to mid-winter Massachusetts or to the major project looming before me. I came to understand, rather, that what triggered these passing moments of regret was a sound or, more properly, its absence. During my months in Fiji, the advent of evening was almost always signaled by the resonant sound of the dried stems of the *yaqona* plant (*Piper methysticum*, also known as *kava*) being pounded in mortars made from old artillery shell casings. Infused in water and shared with neighbors and visiting friends, *yaqona* defined evenings of relaxed sociability and talk in Bhatgaon, the Indo-Fijian village where I worked. Such *yaqona*-drinking events were, for the ethnographer, the prime moments of ethnographic research as well as amiable interaction. Absent the sound of *yaqona*-pounding – and absent the moments of intense sociality it prefigured and captured – those early winter evenings were empty indeed.

I revisit these passing moments of loss experienced to highlight several themes permeating the essays in this issue. The first point has to do with the remarkable and complex relationship between sensory experience and memory. In this instance, the deep clang of *yaqona*-pounding, while quite resonant in the moment, indeed, echoing across the rice and cane fields of Bhatgaon, was nonetheless ephemeral, as is most sensory experience. At the same time, it proved a remarkably durable acoustic experience, one that could, whether through recurrent hearing or through its absence when unconsciously anticipated, catalyze strong if at times inarticulable memories. A second theme has to do with the situated character of sensory experience. Smells, sights, touches, tastes, and sounds are not abstract but in many ways abstracted from experience. They inhere in particular events and are, both in the moment and in memory, linked to the multiple sensory and social dimensions of those events. Such complex connections across the senses *in situ*, whether strictly synesthetic or more generally associative, constitute a third recurring theme. Fourth, the sociality of sensory experience and of the broader memories that it can conjure is often critical. Whether through instances of intense interaction and common identity or those of marked disgust and social differentiation, the senses figure powerfully in social life. Finally, the language upon which we frequently rely for relating sensory experience is that of feeling, of the emotions. Sense and sentiment are deeply linked, often difficult to articulate verbally, embedded in webs of association and memory, and not easily translatable. They are often quite meaningful, but in ways that do not lend themselves to a strictly semantic analysis.

I share Regina Bendix's enthusiasm for the empirical richness of each of these essays and for the very promising intellectual trajectories that they jointly and severally suggest. I also share her insistence that our conversations here be understood not as arguing for 'the senses' as yet another, separate domain for anthropological inquiry but rather as pointing towards provocative entry points for rethinking some core questions in social and cultural analysis: the interplay of the broadly human and the culturally specific, the almost subliminal cultural practices through which similarity and difference are negotiated, and the complex linkages among place, memory, and social identity, to name a few.

One way of pointing to the revelatory potential of taking the senses seriously for a broader social anthropology is a brief exploration of a somewhat resonant literature, that concerned with the anthropology of emotion. 'The emotions' share certain analytical problems and possibilities with 'the senses,' among them the complex interplay of assumedly natural and cultural dimensions; what could be more 'natural,' after all, than how – or what – we feel? In both domains there are deep analytical tensions between what are often taken to be individual, personal experiences and the deeply social events and consequences within which they are entangled. And, as noted above, emotion and sense often share a common vocabulary, one that links affect with the effects of sensory phenomena.

A core question in anthropological investigations of emotion has been that of the extent to which emotions are somehow a natural, often physiological response to certain kinds of environmental stimuli, whether social or otherwise. On the other, ethnographic evidence makes it clear that there are dramatic differences in the vocabularies for, narratives about, and metaphorical extensions of different emotional states when viewed cross-culturally. Discussions in the literature all too often turned on the inherently irresolvable question of whether emotions were natural or cultural. The late Robert Levy (1984) suggested an invaluable analytical distinction between those emotions that are 'hypercognized' within particular cultural contexts, that is, that are salient, elaborated (verbally and in other ways), and of ongoing interests, and those that are 'hypocognized,' that is, neglected, of little interest to members of the community, and often left unlabelled. This distinction brackets the naturalness issue, suggesting as it does a complex interplay between the two, especially at the level of representation, whether local or ethnographic. Language is central here. Lexicon, metaphor, and such nonverbal but nonetheless consequential practices as tone of voice and speech rhythm may all play important roles in such elaboration. While Levy's original focus was on the variable salience of various emotions within particular cultures, his approach also opens up a much broader field for ethnographic exploration, as in Besnier's (1995) subtle demonstration that emotions that may be hypocognized in some media or performance genres may be quite marked in others. Letters home from Nukulaelae individuals working abroad are emotionally very expressive, a quality rarely evident in face-to-face conversation and other oral practices at home in Nukulaelae. Thinking of the senses along these lines, that is, as, on the one hand, culturally elaborated or, on the other, mostly effaced, might well prove similarly productive. Some of these essays focus on less ostensibly mediated dimensions of sensory experience, as in some aspects of the fox hunting so eloquently captured by Marvin, while others attend more to highly elaborated, conversationally and ritually salient ways of sensing, ranging from the gustatory connoisseurship evident in Walmsley's account of taste in Esmeraldas and the complex vocabulary for and narratives concerning 'signs' among Luganda speakers.

A second crucial theme in the anthropology of emotion has to do with the locus of its experience. In contrast to the common Western European idea that the locus of emotion lies within individual persons, in much of the Pacific, 'emotion words...[are] statements about the relationship between a person and an event' (Lutz 1982: 113). As Fred Myers (1979) and others have demonstrated, local theories of emotion often are marked by a crucial relational dimension. Indeed, 'feelings' often provide a social rather than an individual idiom, a way of commenting more about oneself in relation to others rather than about oneself alone. In Bhatgaon, the culturally most salient emotions were ones that could only be engendered and experienced through particular forms of stylized interaction, whether as intensive playfulness or respectful amity (Brenneis 1987). The parallels to sense are striking. The sociality of smell, for example, is central to Young's discussion of the smell of green among Pitjantjatjara people. Both the shared perception of greenness – and the rain and plenty it indexes – and its deliberate replication in plant-infused ointments that make fellow smelling – and through that fellow feeling – possible point to the social relations inherent in Pitjantjatjara understandings of scent. Similarly, in Hsu's analysis, the acute pain of therapeutic acupuncture derives its curative power in large part from its intensely interactive character, while part of the pleasure hunting affords Marvin's consultants lies in the intensification of their relationship with nature, in essence, in a kind of cross-species sociality.

A third theme common to the emotion literature and sensory anthropology has to do with time and memory. While both emotional and sensory experiences may well be quite transient, they also have a remarkable capacity for providing the stimulus for and stuff of remembering, retelling, and otherwise making events memorable. Culturally hypercognized types of emotion combine the power of immediacy with the communicative and mnemonic resources that can enable their subsequent recapture. Having the language, both literally and metaphorically, with which to recount such significant experiences and to chart their consequences through past narrative and future scenarios makes possible the deployment of emotion as a crucial rhetorical practice as it supports moral claims, suggests undesirable outcomes, and otherwise shapes ongoing social relations. Again, these essays resonate. Sight provides, for Luganda speakers, a recurrent nexus for remembering cautionary tales and projecting their implications into the future; the smells of local produce and cooking capture for many Ecuadorians particular constellations of place and time, linking memory and senses of self and belonging or difference.

A final relevant dimension of anthropological work on emotions has to do with their close relationship to notions of self and of personhood. Here two recent special issues of *Ethos*, the journal of the Society for Psychological Anthropology, suggest particularly useful interpretive strategies. First, a series of papers (Desjarlais and O'Nell 2000) addresses the underlying question of how subjectivity and subject position are intertwined. The papers argue that talk and communicative practice, at once the stuff of quotidian social life and a range of rarely straightforward but nearly omnipresent resources for shaping, revealing, representing and transforming selves, provide an invaluable juncture between positionality and the personal. Most relevant here is the analytical point that some of the most important forms of communication concerning self and emotion do not carry stable, explicit semantic meanings. They rather point to or index (Silverstein 1974) a range of possible associations and implications, alerting one's audience to the fact that more is intended than is said and guiding rather than wholly constraining audience understandings. Such interpretive open-endedness can increase listeners' investment in and identification with one's performance. Kenneth Burke has argued that such identification is a key rhetorical goal, and that speakers and writers work to move their interlocutors towards a sense of 'consubstantiality' with the subjects of their performance (1950:19-27). It seems that such consubstantiality also figures signally in these essays, whether in terms of shared sensations, for example, savoring the tastes of Esmeraldas, or of literally making oneself smell the same as one's countrywomen through scented ointments.

A second special issue focused on 'positioning and subjectivity' (Holland and Leander 2004). A central question in these essays is that of duration, that is, of how individual interactions and experiences can, over time, acquire a sense of permanence and stability: how does one move from a range of encounters to a having a particular kind of subjectivity? Holland and Leander work very effectively from a practice theory perspective, noting that the essays included 'strive, from different angles, to describe the *relationships* [italics in original] between available positions, individual subjectivities, and specific episodes of (positioning) practice' (2004:131). In my comments on the symposium that led to that special issue, I offered the notion of 'lamination' as a possibly useful metaphor for pursuing such questions. To be a bit more specific, many musical instruments are constructed not simply by casting or carving a single piece of material. The casings for drums, for example, are often made by laminating multiple pieces of wood, joining and shaping them together under pressure. Cymbals, similarly, are, at least in the worlds of Western jazz, classical, and popular musics, not made from a single sheet of metal but, rather, from a heavy wire wound round and round, from the central point outwards. This winding affords a complex sound, resonance, and material strength that cannot be provided by an instrument pressed from a single sheet of metal. Percussionists have further noted that such, in this instance horizontal, layering and lamination makes it possible for the cymbal's timbre to develop over time, becoming brighter and more complex over time. As Holland and Leander suggest, the notion of lamination may well be 'good for thinking about the production of the sorts of hybrid social/psychological entities predicted by social practice theory' (2004:131). Lamination may also be good for thinking about the long and consequential afterlives of some kinds of sensory experience, pointing as it does to the textured overlay of recurrent, foregrounded, and culturally salient phenomena.

Before turning to the individual papers, I want briefly to note that these essays make a strong case that the senses might most productively be approached not as individual modalities, as, for example, smell alone, but as part of larger sensory complexes in which taste and smell, sound and sight, touch and balance are powerfully linked. Claiming an analytical space for senses other than sight, a central theme in many of the works Bendix cites in her introduction (cf. Feld and Brenneis 2004), has led to a productive rethinking of questions of ethnographic apprehension, documentation, representation, and argument. Bringing sound, smell, taste, touch, balance, and the propriocentric separately into consequential account has helped us make an invaluable step forward. These essays, however, argue that, while local theories might privilege one sense or another, a more conjunctural and synergistic if not wholly synesthetic exploration of the senses is in order. They demonstrate the value of rethinking the units of our sensory participation in the world and of how they are linked and laminated. The exact nature or multiple possible natures of these intersensory relationships is an open question. In a recent *Etnofoor* article, for example, Jojada Verrips (2002) has suggested that touch is the underlying sense, with hearing, for instance, being ultimately a kind of haptic assault on our eardrums (cf. Holden 2005). Perhaps this is indeed the case, perhaps not, but Verrips' piece is very helpful for heuristically pointing to the benefits of such a broadly holistic approach to the senses.

Garry Marvin's essay provides, among other things, an elegant demonstration of the virtues of the EASA workshop forum, as it is clearly both a rich and thought-provoking paper in its own right and a promissory note for what should be an extraordinary larger project. At its heart is a compelling descriptive account of fox hunting as experienced. In it Marvin wrestles to very good effect with the challenge of providing a direct, relatively unmediated representation of the sensations of moving across the landscape in pursuit of a fox. Several features of his essay are particularly significant. First is his recognition that the meaning of hunting is inseparable from its immediacy, and that its immediacy is very difficult to reduce to or represent verbally. Not only are all the senses employed by hunters, and matched against those of their prey, but the hunters themselves are generally in rapid motion across a potentially daunting landscape. And it is not solely movement after the fox; it also is, to Marvin's view, also movement towards the animal, reducing distance and foregrounding a sense of connection and involvement. The hunters not only use their senses to guide their actions; they also take part in shaping the sensory nature of the event, especially acoustically. Marvin addresses the key aesthetic question, 'What are the pleasures of hunting?,' quite directly, arguing that being in and moving through the landscape, placing oneself 'fully... in the event' are central. Marvin's foregrounding of the hunt as event and his compelling account of its multisensory immediacy are persuasive in themselves and, further, model a particularly revealing strategy for sensory ethnography.

Katrin Lund's insightful examination of the 'pedestrian geographies' of hill walkers in Scotland brings balance, motion, touch, and sight together in another multisensory ethnography of moving through landscape. Her core notion of the 'touching eye' suggests the experiential interdependence of grounded contact and expansive viewing characteristic of climbing; it further cuts any notion of vision as an isolated, distanced capacity crisply down to size. As in Marvin's essay, movement, balance, and the ongoing shaping of a sense (actually multiple senses) of where one is figure critically. Some of the sensory experiences at the core of hill walking require being in motion, however laborious; other experiences demand moments of repose and reflection.

Emily Walmsley's quite elegant essay also traces particular sensory geographies, in this instance relying primarily on taste and smell to map racial and social topography in Ecuador. Her evocative example of a bus trip across the Ecuadoran landscape, a passage that encompasses the earthy smell of highland potatoes and the brilliance of tropical fruit, beautifully demonstrates the linkage of sensory experience not only with events but with location, or what David Howes terms 'emplacement' (Howes 2005). The heart of her paper focuses on the possibilities for regional and racial identity afforded by cooking in Esmeralda, whether at home or in the context of street fairs. Local cuisine is clearly a topic of highly elaborated and, to use Levy's term, hypercognized commentary. Not only are particularly accomplished and distinctive cooks recognized, so too are tasteful eaters who consistently display – and discuss – a kind of performative connoisseurship. Emplacement is not merely, however, a matter of where you are, but of who you are. Race, ethnicity, and social identity are strongly marked through food preferences, whether as cook or diner, and analogies between the character of the cuisine and those who delight in it are common.

Diane Young's account of the 'smell of green-ness' lays out with great clarity a particularly elaborated intersensory domain for Pitjantjatjara people. At its core is a strong association between the visible green of fresh vegetation emerging after rain in the Western Desert of Australia and the particular odor released by such rains, a smell that she artfully describes as 'eucalyptus with a top note of dust and shit.' Eucalyptus oil is the dominant smell of newly moistened desert, but Pitjantjatjara people consider a variety of plants as 'really green,' among them wild tobacco and *Irmangka-irmangka* ('bush medicine number one'). *Irmangka-irmangka* is cooked with fat to make an ointment with multiple medical uses; it also figures centrally in major women's ceremonies, when all rub it into their exposed skin, stressing the powerful sociality of shared smell. Young frames her detailed consideration of the social life of green-smelling substances with a broader characterization of the Pitjantjatjara association of the color green with a particular range of smells as a powerful instance of cultural synesthesia.

Sociality of a different sort lies at the heart of Elizabeth Hsu's provocative article, which focuses upon the role of pain in therapeutic (as opposed to analgesic) acupuncture. Acute pain, momentary yet literally piercing, is central to *de qi*, 'getting the *qi*,' a moment of intense connection not only between the acupuncturist's needles and the patient's body but also between the patient and the practitioner. In contrast to standard Western explanations of acupuncture working through counter-irritation, Hsu suggests that the efficacy of acute pain in such treatments derives from the intense social connectedness it enacts, however momentarily. Hsu also considers the temporal dimension of sensory experience with real imagination and insight, contrasting Western medical understandings of chronic pain – and its relatively high incidence in the United States and the EU – with therapeutic regimes in which acute pain figures significantly, and within which chronic pain appears far less common.

Brian Moeran's essay provides a comprehensive and engaging preliminary mapping of the language and culture of scent in Japan. Moeran here draws upon a classical ethnographic strategy, using the vocabulary associated with olfaction, in the language of marketing and of experts as well as in everyday Japanese, as a starting point for detailed analysis. He is concerned with a quite hypercognized sensory domain here, especially when turning, as he does with particular insight, to the professionals involved in developing and selling new perfumes. It also becomes clear that, from both expert and vernacular perspectives, scent is inseparable from other sensory domains, especially visual appearance and taste. Of all the contributors, Moeran most explicitly addresses the tension between universal and culturally specific aspects of sensory experience. His fascinating discussion of the marketing dimension of olfactory language adds considerably to the complexity to his suggestive analysis. As with Marvin's piece, this article represents an early stage in what should be a remarkably rich project.

Finally, Merit Kabugo and Ben Orlove similarly map a particularly salient lexical domain, that of *obubonero* or 'signs,' among Luganda speakers in Uganda. Etymologically this term is linked to one of the verbs used to refer to sight. Significantly the root verb connotes seeing things that suddenly appear (and disappear) rather than the routinely visible. While vision figures centrally, such signs can be heard or perceived through other senses as well. Several dimensions of such signs are particularly interesting. The first has to do with temporality. Such signs can serve either as indicators of some future event or as revelations of some current, contemporary phenomena that are otherwise not publicly known; *obubonero* can be both predictive and revelatory. Second, Luganda speakers do not mechanically assign particular meanings to such signs. The signs rather provide the stimulus for etiological and explanatory discussions, serving as a germ for discussion; the sociality of such discussions is important in itself. Kabugo and Orlove also elaborate on Luganda theories of the capacities of and limitations of humans as perceivers, and of what features make otherwise insensible phenomena graspable. The discussions represented in this article display a fascinating mix of intentionality and play, at times taking on a humorous yet highly moralistic flavor, at times wrestling seriously with potentially catastrophic outcomes.

These essays present deeply contextualized cases of sensory experience, linking senses to each other and to event, sentiment, emplacement, identity, and the ongoing shaping of social life. In doing so, they make a strong joint case for the importance of taking the senses seriously, not in isolation but as integral elements of culture and interaction. They also demonstrate, often with real evocative and analytical power, ways in which such complex and multidimensional work might most effectively be pursued.

E-mail: brenneis@ucsc.edu

References

Besnier, Niko
    1995 *Literacy, Emotion, and Authority: Reading and Writing on a Polynesian Atoll.* Cambridge and New York: Cambridge University Press.

Brenneis, Donald
    1987 Performing Passions: Aesthetics and Politics in an Occasionally Egalitarian Community. *American Ethnologist* 14: 236-250.

Burke, Kenneth
    1950 *A Rhetoric of Motives.* Berkeley: University of California Press.

Desjarlais, Robert, and Theresa O'Nell (Eds.)
    2000 The Pragmatic Turn in Psychological Anthropology. Special issue of *Ethos* 27 (4).

Feld, Steven, and Donald Brenneis
    2004 Doing Anthropology in Sound: Steven Feld in Conversation with Donald Brenneis. *American Ethnologist* 31 (4): 461-474.

Holden, Stephen
    2005 How Sound Feels to Musician who Lost her Hearing (Film review of *Touch the Sound*). *New York Times*, September 7, 2005.

Holland, Dorothy, and Kevin Leander
    2004 Ethnographic Studies of Positioning and Subjectivity: an Introduction. *Ethos* 32 (2): 127-132.

Howes, David
    2005 Introduction. In: David Howes (Ed.), *Empire of the Senses: The Sensual Culture Reader.* Oxford and New York: Berg.

Ingold, Tim
    2000 *The Perception of the Environment: Essays on Livelihood, Dwelling, and Skill.* London: Routledge.

Levy, Robert
    1984 Emotion, Knowing, and Culture. In: Richard Shweder and Robert LeVine (Eds.), *Culture Theory: Essays on Mind, Self, and Emotion.* New York: Cambridge University Press. Pp. 214-237.

Lutz, Catherine A.
    1982 The Domain of Emotion Words on Ifaluk. *American Ethnologist* 9: 113-128.

Myers, Fred R.
    1979 Emotions and the Self: A Theory of Personhood and Political Order among Pintupi Aborigines. *Ethos* 7: 343-370.

Silverstein, Michael
    1974 Shifters, Linguistic Categories, and Cultural Description. In: Keith Basso and Henry Selby (Eds.), *Meaning in Anthropology.* Albuquerque: University of New Mexico Press, Pp. 11-55.

Verrips, Jojada
    2002 'Haptic Screens' and Our 'Corporeal Eye'. *Etnofoor* XV (1/2): 21-46.

advertisement

UITGEVERIJ HET SPINHUIS

NIEUWE TITELS
(verkrijgbaar in elke boekhandel en rechtstreeks bij de uitgeverij)

📖 Leen Sterckx & Carolien Bouw
Liefde op maat
Partnerkeuze van Turkse en Marokkaanse jongeren
ISBN 90-5589-250-5, 159 pp., euro 17,50

📖 Mieke Komen & Krista Schram
Etniciteit en uitgaan
ISBN 90-5589-255-6, 128 pp., euro 17,50

📖 Janneke Verheijen
De 'nieuwkijkers' van El Remate
Vrouwen en soaps in de Guatemalteekse jungle
ISBN 90-5589-249-1, 160 pp., euro 14,50

📖 Els van Dongen & Sylvie Fainzang (eds)
Lying and Illness
Power and performance
ISBN 90-5589-245-9, 200 pp., euro 35,00

📖 Carla Risseeuw, Kamala Ganesh, Maithreyi Krisnaraj & Rajni Palriwala
Welfare, care & intimacy
Gendered negotiations of the public and the private in the Netherlands
ISBN 90-5589-239-4, 224 pp., euro 35,00

📖 Herman Ketting
Leven, werk en rebellie aan boord van Oost-Indiëvaarders (1595-1650)
*ISBN 90-5589-258-0, 384 pp., rijk geïll., nu in **paperback-editie**, euro 24,50*

Announcement Etnofoor

Whatever happened to older heroes ... in Dutch Anthropology? In the 1990s a changing of the guards took place in Dutch anthropology. Professors who played leading roles in the rapid development of anthropology as an academic discipline, especially during the 70's and 80's, went into retirement and were succeeded by a new generation of scholars. The forthcoming issue of Etnofoor will offer a series of interviews with some of these leading anthropologists who shaped anthropology in the Netherlands. How do they evaluate their work in the past, what are the projects they are currently involved in, and what are their perspectives on the future of our discipline.

The following back issues of *Etnofoor* are available:

II(1)	Het Weer	(€ 2,25)
II(2)	Geluk	(€ 2,25)
IV(1)	Eten	(€ 4,50)
IV(2)	Dromen	(€ 4,50)
V(1/2)	Het Kwaad	(€ 9,00)
VI(1)	Herinneren en Vergeten	(€ 4,50)
VI(2)	Het Wilde Westen	(€ 4,50)
VII(1)	Endo-Ethnography	(€ 4,50)
VII(2)	Seksualiteit	(€ 4,50)
VIII(1)	De Betoverde Wereld	(€ 4,50)
VIII(2)	Religion and Modernity	(€ 4,50)
IX(1)	Words and Things	(€ 4,50)
IX(2)	Anthropology as...	(€ 4,50)
X(1/2)	Muziek & Dans	(€ 10,00)
XI(1)	Verzamelen	(€ 6,00)
XI(2)	Gossip, Rumor, Slander!	(€ 6,00)
XII(1)	Kids & Culture	(€ 6,00)
XII(2)	Personality Cults	(€ 6,00)
XIII(1)	Catastrophe	(€ 9,00)
XIII(2)	Money	(€ 9,00)
XIV(1)	Suburbia	(€ 9,00)
XIV(2)	Masquerades	(€ 9,00)
XV(1/2)	Screens	(€ 18,00)
XVI(1)	Kinship	(€ 9,00)
XVI(2)	Fashions & Hypes	(€ 9,00)
XVII(1/2)	Authenticity	(€ 18,00)
XVIII(1)	Senses	(€ 9,00)

Back issues and single issues can be ordered as follows: transfer the required amount of money to postal giro account no. 4753313, Irene Stengs inz. Etnofoor, Amsterdam, Netherlands, and mention the issue(s) you would like to receive. A subscription to *Etnofoor* (two issues per volume) is € 20,00 (students and unemployed: € 15,00; institutes and libraries: € 40,00). Transfer the subscription rate to the above-mentioned account and mention the volume with which your subscription should start.

**AUTOCHTONEN, BURGERS
EN VREEMDELINGEN:
KWESTIES VAN IN- EN UITSLUITING**

Landelijk congres

Georganiseerd door
Antropologen Beroepsvereniging
In samenwerking met Nederlands Openluchtmuseum

Thema
Globalisering, In- en Uitsluiting

Organisatie
De Antropologen Beroepsvereniging (ABV)
en het Nederlands Openluchtmuseum

Datum
3 en 4 november 2005

Locatie
Openluchtmuseum Arnhem

Panels
Nederlandstalig of Engelstalig

Leden: € 40; Niet-leden: € 60;
Student-leden: € 30; Studenten: € 50

Voor het volledige programma zie www.antropologen.nl

Etnofoor
Anthropological Journal

Authenticity
Beyond Essentialism and Deconstruction
Bd. XVII/1,2/2004, 2005, 248 S., 25,00 €, br., ISBN 3-8258-8754-5, ISSN 0921-5158

Anthropological Journal on European Cultures
founded by Christian Giordano & Ina-Maria Greverus
Editorial Board:
Jorge Freitas Branco (Lisbon),
Henk Driessen (Nijmegen),
Ina-Maria Greverus (Frankfurt),
Karl Kaser (Graz),
Elisabeth Katschnig-Fasch (Graz),
Gabriela Kiliánová (Bratislava),
Sharon Macdonald (Sheffield),
George Marcus (Houston),
Regina Römhild (Frankfurt),
Gisela Welz (Frankfurt),
Helena Wulff (Stockholm)

Karl Kaser;
Elisabeth Katschnig-Fasch (Eds.)
Gender and Nation in South Eastern Europe
Bd. 14, Herbst 2005, ca. 256 S., ca. 29,90 €, br., ISBN 3-8258-8802-9

Comparative Anthropological Studies in Society, Cosmology and Politics
ed. by
Prof. Dr. Josephus D. M. Platenkamp (University of Münster/Germany) and
Prof. Dr. Bruce Kapferer (University of Bergen/Norway)

John Christian Knudsen
Capricious Worlds
Vietnamese Life Journeys
Bd. 2, Herbst 2005, ca. 304 S., ca. 24,90 €, br., ISBN 3-8258-8108-3

Beiträge zur Afrikaforschung
hrsg. vom Institut für Afrika-Studien der Universität Bayreuth

Peter Probst; Gerd Spittler (eds.)
Between Resistance and Expansion
Explorations of Local Vitality in Africa
Bd. 18, 2004, 480 S., 29,90 €, br., ISBN 3-8258-6980-6

Gordon R. Woodman;
Ulrike Wanitzek;
Harald Sippel (Eds.)
Local Land Law and Globalization
A comparative study of peri-urban areas in Benin, Ghana and Tanzania
Bd. 21, 2004, 392 S., 29,90 €, br., ISBN 3-8258-7843-0

LIT Verlag Münster – Berlin – Hamburg – London – Wien
Grevener Str./Fresnostr. 2 48159 Münster
Tel.: 0251 – 62 032 22 – Fax: 0251 – 23 19 72
e-Mail: vertrieb@lit-verlag.de – http://www.lit-verlag.de

History and Theory of Anthropology / Geschichte und Theorie der Ethnologie
edited by / hrsg. von Prof. Dr. Klaus-Peter Köpping (University of Heidelberg)

Klaus-Peter Köpping
Adolf Bastian and the Psychic Unity of Mankind
The Foundations of Anthropology in Nineteenth Century Germany
Bd. 1, 2005, 296 S., 20,90 €, br., ISBN 3-8258-3989-3

Novara
Beiträge zur Pazifik-Forschung/Contributions to Research on the Pacific
hrsg. von Hermann Mückler für die Österreichisch-Südpazifische Gesellschaft (OSPG)

Andrew E. Robson
Prelude to Empire
Consuls, Missionary Kingdoms, and the Pre-Colonial South Seas Seen Through the Life of William Thomas Pritchard
Bd. 3, 2004, 208 S., 19,90 €, br., ISBN 3-8258-6999-7

Halle Studies in the Anthropology of Eurasia
General Editors: Chris Hann, Richard Rottenburg, Burkhard Schnepel and Shingo Shimada

Joachim Otto Habeck
What it Means to be a Herdsman
The Practice and Image of Reindeer Husbandry among the Komi of Northern Russia
Bd. 5, 2005, 296 S., 29,90 €, br., ISBN 3-8258-8045-1

Chris Hann; Mihály Sárkány; Peter Skalník (Eds.)
Socialist Era Anthropology in Eastern and Central Europe
Studying Peoples in the People's Democracies Socialist Era Anthropology in East-Central Europe
Contributors:
Chris Hann, Tamás Hofer, Wolfgang Jacobeit, Zbigniew Jasiewicz, Josef Kandert, Gabriela Kiliánová, Martina Krause, Klára Kuti, Petr Lozoviuk, Ute Mohrmann, Dagmar Neuland-Kitzerow, Karoline Noack, Juraj Podoba, Aleksander Posern-Zielinski, Mihály Sárkány, Peter Skalník, Olga Skalníková, Zofia Sokolewicz, Dietrich Treide, Ulrich van der Heyden, Bea Vidacs
Bd. 8, 2005, 392 S., 29,90 €, br., ISBN 3-8258-8048-6

Modernity and Belonging
edited by Peter Geschiere and Birgit Meyer
(University of Amsterdam)

James Kiernan (Ed.)
The Power of the Occult in Modern Africa
Continuity and Innovation in the Renewal of African Cosmologies
Bd. 4, Herbst 2005, ca. 256 S., ca. 29,90 €, br., ISBN 3-8258-8761-8

LIT Verlag Münster – Berlin – Hamburg – London – Wien
Grevener Str./Fresnostr. 2 48159 Münster
Tel.: 0251 – 62 032 22 – Fax: 0251 – 23 19 72
e-Mail: vertrieb@lit-verlag.de – http://www.lit-verlag.de

Ibrahim Mouiche
Autorités traditionnelles et démocratisation au Cameroun
Entre centralité de l'Etat et logiques de terroir
Bd. 5, Herbst 2005, ca. 288 S., ca. 29,90 €, br., ISBN 3-8258-9084-8

Mande Worlds
edited by Jan Jansen, Mohamed Saidou N'Daou, Dorothea Schulz, and Stephen Wooten

Stephen Wooten (ed.)
Meanings and Modalities of Money in West Africa
Ethnographic Explorations of Commercialization in the Mande World
Bd. 1, Herbst 2005, ca. 304 S., ca. 29,90 €, br., ISBN 3-8258-9045-7

Religionswissenschaft: Forschung und Wissenschaft

Jamal Malik (Ed.)
Muslims in Europe
From the Margin to the Centre
This volume embodies an uptodate and sensitive set of studies exploring the ongoing negotiation of European Muslim identities in Europe. The Editor argues there has been hitherto a three-fold response on the part of Muslims in Europe (some of whom are now 3rd generation Europeans) – integrationism, isolationism, and escapism. Today the latter two responses are giving way, it is argued, to an active shaping of Muslim European identities. The central issue remains: what degree of freedom and what potential for cultural and religious diversity can minorities have in an outwardly secular and plural European society?
Bd. 1, 2004, 272 S., 39,90 €, br., ISBN 3-8258-7638-1

IUAES-Series
edited for the International Union of Anthropological and Ethnological Sciences by Brunetto Chiarelli (Florence) and Peter J. M. Nas (Leiden)

Brigitta Benzing; Bernd Herrmann (Eds.)
Exploitation and Overexploitation in Societies Past and Present
IUAES-Intercongress 2001 Goettingen
Bd. 1, 2003, 392 S., 45,90 €, br., ISBN 3-8258-5654-2

Soheila Shashahani
Body as Medium of Meaning
Bd. 2, 2004, 160 S., 25,90 €, br., ISBN 3-8258-7154-1

TRANS
anthropologische texte/anthropological texts
hrsg. von /edited by Ina-Maria Greverus and George Marcus

Alexei Elfimov
Russian Intellectual Culture in Transition
The Future in the Past
Bd. 2, 2004, 216 S., 24,90 €, br., ISBN 3-8258-6820-6

LIT Verlag Münster – Berlin – Hamburg – London – Wien
Grevener Str./Fresnostr. 2 48159 Münster
Tel.: 0251 – 62 03 22 – Fax: 0251 – 23 19 72
e-Mail: vertrieb@lit-verlag.de – http://www.lit-verlag.de

Wiener Zentralasien Studien – Vienna Central Asian Studies
hrsg. von Ass. Prof. Mag. Dr. Gabriele Rasuly-Paleczek (Universität Wien)

Gabriele Rasuly-Paleczek; Julia Katschnig (eds.)
Central Asia on Display
Proceedings of the VII. Conference of the European Society for Central Asian Studies
Bd. 1, 2005, 480 S., 49,90 €, br., ISBN 3-8258-8309-4

Gabriele Rasuly-Paleczek; Julia Katschnig (eds.)
Central Asia on Display
Proceedings of the VII. Conference of the European Society for Central Asian Studies. Volume 2
Bd. 2, 2005, 240 S., 49,90 €, br., ISBN 3-8258-8586-0

Schweizerische Afrikastudien – Études africaines suisses
hrsg. von der Schweizerischen Gesellschaft für Afrikastudien (SGAS)/édité par la Société suisse d'études africaines (SSEA)

Willemijn de Jong; Claudia Roth; Fatoumata Badini-Kinda; Seema Bhagyanath
Ageing in Insecurity. Vieillir dans l'insécurité
Case Studies on Social Security and Gender in India and Burkina Faso. Sécurité sociale et genre en Inde et au Burkina Faso – Etudes de cas
Bd. 5, 2005, 400 S., 29,90 €, br., ISBN 3-8258-7846-5

Sandra Bott; Thomas David; Claude Lützelschwab; Janick Marina Schaufelbuehl (Ed.)
Suisse – Afrique (18e – 20e siècles): De la traite des Noirs à la fin du régime de l'apartheid
Schweiz – Afrika (18. – 20. Jahrhundert): Vom Sklavenhandel zum Ende des Apartheid-Regimes
Bd. 6, Herbst 2005, ca. 288 S., ca. 39,90 €, br., ISBN 3-8258-7794-9

Anne Mayor; Claudia Roth; Yvan Droz (éds./Hg.)
Sécurité sociale et developpement – Soziale Sicherheit und Entwicklung
Le forum suisse des africanistes 5/Werkschau Afrikastudien 5
Bd. 7, Herbst 2005, ca. 288 S., ca. 29,90 €, br., ISBN 3-8258-9031-7

Gesellschaftliche Transformationen/Societal Transformations
hrsg. von /edited by Eckhard Dittrich, Nikolai Genov, Raj Kollmorgen, Ingrid Oswald, Heiko Schrader, Melanie Tatur

Nikolai Genov (Ed.)
Ethnic Relations in South Eastern Europe
Problems of Social Inclusion and Exclusion
Bd. 4, 2004, 152 S., 19,90 €, br., ISBN 3-8258-7869-4

Nikolai Genov (Hg.)
Ethnicity and Educational Policies in South Eastern Europe
Bd. 7, 2005, 216 S., 24,90 €, br., ISBN 3-8258-8594-1

LIT Verlag Münster – Berlin – Hamburg – London – Wien
Grevener Str./Fresnostr. 2 48159 Münster
Tel.: 0251 – 62 032 22 – Fax: 0251 – 23 19 72
e-Mail: vertrieb@lit-verlag.de – http://www.lit-verlag.de

Market, Culture and Society
edited by Hans-Dieter Evers, Rüdiger Korff, Gudrun Lachenmann, Joanna Pfaff-Czarnecka, Günther Schlee, and Heiko Schrader

Günther Schlee (ed.)
Imagined Differences
Hatred and the construction of identity
Bd. 5, 2. Aufl. 2004, 296 S., 25,90 €, br.,
ISBN 3-8258-3956-7

Nursyirwan Effendi
Minangkabau Rural Markets
Trade and Traders in West Sumatra, Indonesia
Bd. 9, 2005, 168 S., 20,90 €, br.,
ISBN 3-8258-4387-4

Maximilian Martin
Globalization, Macroeconomic Stabilization, and the Construction of Social Reality
An Essay in Interpretive Political Economy
Bd. 13, 2004, 488 S., 39,90 €, br.,
ISBN 3-8258-7526-1

ZEF Development Studies
edited by Prof. Dr. Hans-Dieter Evers (Center for Development Research (ZEF), University of Bonn)

Shahjahan H. Bhuiyan
Benefits of Social Capital
Urban Solid Waste Management in Bangladesh
Bd. 1, 2005, 288 S., 19,90 €, br.,
ISBN 3-8258-8382-5

Literatur: Forschung und Wissenschaft

Susanne Gehrmann;
János Riesz (Éd.)
Le Blanc du Noir
Représentations de l'Europe et des Européens dans les littératures africaines
Bd. 2, 2004, 264 S., 25,90 €, br.,
ISBN 3-8258-6744-7

Jan Jansen; Henk M. J. Maier (eds.)
Epic Adventures
Heroic Narrative in the Oral Performance Traditions of Four Continents
Bd. 3, 2004, 200 S., 20,90 €, br.,
ISBN 3-8258-6758-7

Christopher F. Laferl
"Record it, and let it be known"
Song Lyrics, Gender, and Ethnicity in Brazil, Cuba, Martinique, and Trinidad and Tobago from 1920 to 1960
Popular music from Brazil and the Caribbean belongs to those cultural practices that are considered, both inside and outside of their countries of origin, to bear the indelible marks of ethnicity. On the basis of a corpus made up of over one thousand songs recorded between 1920 and 1960 in Brazil, Cuba, Martinique, and Trinidad and Tobago, *"Record it, and let it be known"* offers an exemplary textual analysis of the ways in which these countries' main musical genres staged the encounters of the identity categories of ethnicity and gender in song lyrics during the decades preceding the emergence of more ideologically conscious musical currents. Special attention is paid to the following topics: the relations between ethnicity and national identity; the presence of Africa and slavery; the pre-

LIT Verlag Münster – Berlin – Hamburg – London – Wien
Grevener Str./Fresnostr. 2 48159 Münster
Tel.: 0251 – 62 032 22 – Fax: 0251 – 23 19 72
e-Mail: vertrieb@lit-verlag.de – http://www.lit-verlag.de

sentation of the gendered and ethnically marked body; and, finally, the description of cultural blackness.
Bd. 6, 2005, 384 S., 19,90 €, br.,
ISBN 3-8258-7636-5

Anthropological Abstracts
Cultural/Social Anthropology from German-speaking countries
edited by Ulrich Oberdiek

Anthropological Abstracts
Bd. 2, 2005, 336 S., 39,90 €, br.,
ISBN 3-8258-8010-9, ISSN 0173-2986

African Connections in Post-Colonial Theory and Literatures
edited by David Attwell, Ulrike Auga, Ulrike Kistner, Rita Schäfer

Rita Schäfer
Im Schatten der Apartheid
Frauen-Rechtsorganisationen und geschlechtsspezifische Gewalt in Südafrika
Bd. 3, 2005, 496 S., 29,90 €, br.,
ISBN 3-8258-8676-x

Forum Europäische Ethnologie
hrsg. von Dorle Dracklé, Thomas Hauschild, Wolfgang Kaschuba, Orvar Löfgren, Bernd Jürgen Warneken und Gisela Welz

Thomas Hauschild;
Bernd Jürgen Warneken (Hg.)
Inspecting Germany
Internationale Deutschland-Ethnographie der Gegenwart
Bd. 1, 2003, 568 S., 30,90 €, br.,
ISBN 3-8258-6123-6

Ethnologie

Mongameli Mabona
Diviners and Prophets among the Xhosa (1593 – 1856)
A study in Xhosa cultural history
The South African anthropologist, Dr M. Mabona, uses the main title of this book as a convenient platform to launch an investigation into the roots of Xhosa culture and history. Many of the findings break new ground in Southern African anthropology and history such as: the original stock of the Bantu peoples arose from a cradle-land between the Orange and Vaal rivers in South Africa; the word 'Guinea' is identical with the Xhosa 'ebu Nguni' (Nguniland); Xhosa as well as Bantu history stretches back 50'000 years ago into the Middle Stone Ages (MSA) and into the Acheulian Age - the age of hominisation; the basic paradigmatic structure of Bantu speech; Xhosa thought structures; the fundamental relationship between the Xhosa language and mythology.
Bd. 12, 2005, 464 S., 35,90 €, br.,
ISBN 3-8258-6700-5

LIT Verlag Münster – Berlin – Hamburg – London – Wien
Grevener Str./Fresnostr. 2 48159 Münster
Tel.: 0251 – 62 032 22 – Fax: 0251 – 23 19 72
e-Mail: vertrieb@lit-verlag.de – http://www.lit-verlag.de